wxPython 2.8
Application Development Cookbook

Quickly create robust, reliable, and reusable
wxPython applications

Cody Precord

BIRMINGHAM - MUMBAI

wxPython 2.8
Application Development Cookbook

First published: December 2010

Production Reference: 1031210

Published by Packt Publishing Ltd.
32 Lincoln Road
Olton
Birmingham, B27 6PA, UK.

ISBN 978-1-849511-78-0

www.packtpub.com

Cover Image by Vinayak Chittar (vinayak.chittar@gmail.com)

Credits

Author
Cody Precord

Reviewers
Maurice HT Ling
Steve McMahon
Jeff McNeil
Chukwudi Nwachukwu

Acquisition Editor
Steven Wilding

Development Editor
Maitreya Bhakal

Technical Editor
Conrad Sardinha

Indexers
Tejal Daruwale
Rekha Nair

Editorial Team Leader
Akshara Aware

Project Team Leader
Lata Basantani

Project Coordinator
Vincila Colaco

Proofreader
Dirk Manuel

Graphics
Nilesh Mohite

Production Coordinator
Aparna Bhagat

Cover Work
Aparna Bhagat

About the Author

Cody Precord is a Software Engineer based in Minneapolis, MN, USA. He has been designing and writing systems and application software for AIX, Linux, Windows, and Macintosh OS X for the last ten years using primarily C, C++, Perl, Bash, Korn Shell, and Python. The constant need of working on multiple platforms naturally led Cody to the wxPython toolkit, which he has been using intensely for that last five years. Cody has been primarily using wxPython for his open source project, Editra, which is a cross-platform development tool. He is interested in promoting cross-platform development practices and improving usability in software.

About the Reviewers

Maurice HT Ling completed his Ph.D. in Bioinformatics and B.Sc.(Hons.) in Molecular and Cell Biology from The University of Melbourne where he worked on microarray analysis and text mining for protein-protein interactions. He is currently an Honorary Fellow of The University of Melbourne, Australia. Maurice holds several Chief Editorships including The Python Papers, iConcept Journal of Computational and Mathematical Biology, and Methods and Cases in Computational, Mathematical, and Statistical Biology. In his free time, Maurice likes to train in the gym, read, and enjoy a good cup of coffee. He is also a Senior Fellow of the International Fitness Association, USA.

Steve McMahon is a Python and Plone developer located in Davis, California. His company, Reid-McMahon, LLC specializes in developing Content Management Systems for non-profit organizations. He's been involved in many aspects of the Plone project, including training and core, installer, and add-on development.

Jeff McNeil cut his teeth during the Internet boom, being one of the first employees at one of the larger web-hosting shops. He's done just about everything from server installs to platform development and software architecture. Technical interests include systems management and doing things Pythonically. Jeff recently joined Google.

Chukwudi Nwachukwu, aka Chux, studied Computer Science at Olabisi Onabanjo University, Nigeria. He has, over the years, worked on both Windows and Linux operating systems. Programming is fun. He had to join the programming wagon because programmers are known to solve problems by making computers do things that they visualize in their minds. He programs in over a dozen languages such as Processing, D, Python, and so on. He loves to travel, discover new places, meet interesting people, and learn new human languages too. You can reach him on chux@users.berlios.de. He has worked on Java CourseWare, an in-house Java textbook for teaching students.

I acknowledge the following people, who have stood by me through thick and thin, and without whom I wouldn't have gotten to this point in my life. Chinonye, Chigbonkpa, and Chimenka, my siblings. My mom and dad, Mr. and Mrs. Richard Nwachukwu, for their support. Olugbenga Owolabi, you lead me through the land of programming by helping me know what algorithms are all about. Bertrand Ogu, who has always been there for me, thank you. Tola Johnny Odule, a lecturer in Olabisi Onabanjo University, Nigeria, and the elder brother of Dele Odule, the Nollywood actor. Wale Adewoyin and Shirley Otukpa, by God's grace I expect you guys to walk down the aisle soon. Kenneth Oraegbunam of IITA, Nigeria. Olugbenga Siyanbola and Bukola Ibironke of Lintak Enterprises, Lagos, Nigeria. The Adenekans in NNPC, Abuja: Beatrice, Olukayode, Damilola and Tobilola. Adedayo Adenekan in Lagos and other members of the family. Pastor Femi Adeboye of Prodigy Ventures, Ikorodu, Lagos. Dr. Shola Olalude of Shola Medical Centre, Ikorodu, Lagos: thank you for believing in me. Tobi Ojo in Ibadan. Bro. Williams Anthony, you've acted like a father for me, God bless you. Olowooribi Kolawole Taofeek, you are a friend. Yakubu Friday Kelvin, you are lovely. Olaleye Peace, I love you.

www.PacktPub.com

Support files, eBooks, discount offers and more

You might want to visit www.PacktPub.com for support files and downloads related to your book.

Did you know that Packt offers eBook versions of every book published, with PDF and ePub files available? You can upgrade to the eBook version at www.PacktPub.com and as a print book customer, you are entitled to a discount on the eBook copy. Get in touch with us at service@packtpub.com for more details.

At www.PacktPub.com, you can also read a collection of free technical articles, sign up for a range of free newsletters and receive exclusive discounts and offers on Packt books and eBooks.

 PACKTLiB®

http://PacktLib.PacktPub.com

Do you need instant solutions to your IT questions? PacktLib is Packt's online digital book library. Here, you can access, read and search across Packt's entire library of books.

Why Subscribe?

- ▸ Fully searchable across every book published by Packt
- ▸ Copy and paste, print and bookmark content
- ▸ On demand and accessible via web browser

Free Access for Packt account holders

If you have an account with Packt at www.PacktPub.com, you can use this to access PacktLib today and view nine entirely free books. Simply use your login credentials for immediate access.

Table of Contents

Preface	**1**
Chapter 1: Getting Started with wxPython	**7**
Introduction	7
The application object	8
The main frame	9
Understanding the window hierarchy	12
Referencing controls	13
Using Bitmaps	15
Adding icons to Windows	17
Utilizing Stock IDs	18
Accessing the clipboard	20
Supporting drag and drop	22
Two-stage widget creation	24
Understanding inheritance limitations	25
Chapter 2: Responding to Events	**29**
Introduction	29
Handling events	30
Understanding event propagation	32
Handling Key events	34
Using UpdateUI events	37
Playing with the mouse	39
Creating custom event classes	41
Managing event handlers with EventStack	43
Validating input with validators	45
Handling Apple events	48

Chapter 3: Basic Building Blocks of a User Interface   51

Introduction   51
Creating Stock Buttons   52
Buttons, buttons, and more buttons   53
Offering options with CheckBoxes   57
Using the TextCtrl   59
Providing choices with the Choice control   62
Adding Menus and MenuBars   63
Working with ToolBars   66
How to use PopupMenus   69
Grouping controls with a StaticBox   71

Chapter 4: Advanced Building Blocks of a User Interface   73

Introduction   73
Listing data with a ListCtrl   74
Browsing files with the CustomTreeCtrl   77
Creating a VListBox   81
StyledTextCtrl using lexers   84
Working with tray icons   89
Adding tabs to a Notebook   90
Using the FlatNotebook   93
Scrolling with a ScrolledPanel   96
Simplifying the FoldPanelBar   97

Chapter 5: Providing Information and Alerting Users   99

Introduction   99
Showing a MessageBox   100
Providing help with ToolTips   102
Using SuperToolTips   104
Displaying a BalloonTip   107
Creating a custom SplashScreen   109
Showing task progress with the Progress dialog   111
Creating an AboutBox   115

Chapter 6: Retrieving Information from Users   121

Introduction   121
Selecting files with a FileDialog   122
Searching text with a FindReplaceDialog   127
Getting images with ImageDialog   132
Using the Print dialogs   135

Chapter 7: Window Layout and Design — 143

Introduction — 143
Using a BoxSizer — 144
Understanding proportions, flags, and borders — 148
Laying out controls with the GridBagSizer — 152
Standard dialog button layout — 154
Using XML resources — 157
Making a custom resource handler — 160
Using the AuiFrameManager — 163

Chapter 8: Drawing to the Screen — 167

Introduction — 167
Screen drawing — 168
Drawing shapes — 171
Utilizing SystemSettings — 174
Using a GraphicsContext — 177
Drawing with RendererNative — 180
Reducing flicker in drawing routines — 184

Chapter 9: Design Approaches and Techniques — 187

Introduction — 187
Creating Singletons — 188
Implementing an observer pattern — 190
Strategy pattern — 194
Model View Controller — 197
Using mixin classes — 203
Using decorators — 206

Chapter 10: Creating Components and Extending Functionality — 209

Introduction — 209
Customizing the ArtProvider — 210
Adding controls to a StatusBar — 212
Making a tool window — 215
Creating a SearchBar — 217
Working with ListCtrl mixins — 220
StyledTextCtrl custom highlighting — 222
Creating a custom control — 225

Chapter 11: Using Threads and Timers to Create Responsive Interfaces — 231

Introduction — 231
Non-Blocking GUI — 232
Understanding thread safety — 236

Threading tools   **241**
Using Timers   **246**
Capturing output   **249**

Chapter 12: Building and Managing Applications for Distribution   **255**
Introduction   **255**
Working with StandardPaths   **256**
Persisting the state of the UI   **258**
Using the SingleInstanceChecker   **260**
Exception handling   **265**
Optimizing for OS X   **266**
Supporting internationalization   **269**
Distributing an application   **273**

Index   **279**

Preface

In today's world of desktop applications, there is a great amount of incentive to be able to develop applications that can run in more than one environment. Currently, there are a handful of options available for cross-platform frameworks to develop desktop applications in Python. wxPython is one such cross-platform GUI toolkit for the Python programming language. It allows Python programmers to create programs with a complete, highly-functional graphical user interface, simply and easily. wxPython code style has changed quite a bit over the years, and has become much more Pythonic. The examples that you will find in this book are fully up-to-date and reflect this change in style. This cookbook provides you with the latest recipes to quickly create robust, reliable, and reusable wxPython applications. These recipes will guide you from writing simple, basic wxPython scripts all the way through complex concepts, and also feature various design approaches and techniques in wxPython.

This book starts off by covering a variety of topics, from the most basic requirements of a wxPython application, to some of the more in-depth details of the inner workings of the framework, laying the foundation for any wxPython application. It then explains event handling, basic and advanced user interface controls, interface design and layout, creating dialogs, components, extending functionality, and so on. We conclude by learning how to build and manage applications for distribution.

For each of the recipes, there is an introductory example, then more advanced examples, along with plenty of example code that shows how to develop and manage user-friendly applications. For more experienced developers, most recipes also include an additional discussion of the solution, allowing you to further customize and enhance the component.

What this book covers

Chapter 1, *Getting Started with wxPython,* introduces you to the basics of creating a wxPython application. The topics covered in this chapter will provide you with the information needed to start building your own applications, as well as some insight into the inner workings and structure of the framework.

Chapter 2, Responding to Events, shows how to make use of events to drive an application and allow the user to interact with it through the user interface. This chapter starts with an overview of what events are and how they work, and then continues on to cover how to interact with a number of common events.

Chapter 3, Basic Building Blocks of a User Interface, discusses a number of the basic widgets that are critical to the creation of nearly all user interfaces. You will be introduced to the usage of widgets such as Buttons, Menus, and ToolBars in this chapter.

Chapter 4, Advanced Building Blocks of a User Interface, introduces you to some of the more advanced widgets available in the wxPython control library. These widgets will allow you to create tabbed interfaces and display more complex types of data in your user interface.

Chapter 5, Providing Information and Alerting Users, shows multiple techniques for keeping the users of an application informed about what is going on and to provide them with help on interacting with the various controls in the applications interface. This chapter will show you how to use various tooltip controls, message boxes, and splash screens.

Chapter 6, Retrieving Information from Users, covers the use of common dialogs to retrieve information from users in order to perform tasks such as opening files, searching text, and even printing. As a part of the recipes for the usage of `FileDialog` and `FindDialogs` you will create a simple Notepad-like application.

Chapter 7, Window Layout and Design, is where you will be introduced to a number of concepts and techniques for designing your user interfaces in wxPython. The majority of this chapter will explain the use of Sizers to allow you to quickly implement cross-platform user interfaces.

Chapter 8, Drawing to the Screen, gives an introduction to the basics of how a user interface works, by showing you how to use some of the primitive tools to implement your own custom user interface objects. This chapter will show you how to use Device Contexts to perform custom drawing routines by creating a number of custom display controls.

Chapter 9, Design Approaches and Techniques, introduces you to a number of common programming patterns, and explain how to apply them to wxPython applications. The information in this chapter will provide you with an understanding of some strong approaches and techniques to software design that will not only serve you in writing wxPython applications but can also be generally applied to other frameworks as well, to expand your programming toolbox.

Chapter 10, Creating Components and Extending Functionality, shows you how to extend the functionality of existing user interface components, as well as how to create your own controls. The recipes in this chapter combine much of the information presented in Chapters 2, 7, 8, and 9 together to create new controls and to enhance the capabilities of some of the more basic ones provided by wxPython.

Chapter 11, Using Threads and Timers to Create Responsive Interfaces, dives into the world of concurrent programming. This chapter shows you how to create multi-threaded applications, and covers the special care that is needed when interacting with the user interface from worker threads in order to create stable and responsive interfaces.

Chapter 12, Building and Managing Applications for Distribution, concludes the tour of the wxPython framework by introducing you to some useful recipes for bolstering the infrastructure of any application that will be distributed to end users. This includes how to store configuration information, exception handling, internationalization, and how to create and distribute stand-alone binaries of your application.

What you need for this book

All that you will need to get started with wxPython is a good text editor for editing Python source code. There are a number of choices available, but I will provide a shameless plug for my own application, Editra, here since it is included in the wxPython Docs and Demo package, as well as at `http://editra.org`. It is written in wxPython and provides good syntax highlighting and auto-completion support for Python that will help you in learning the wxPython API.

This book is primarily written for Python 2.5/2.6 and wxPython 2.8, although the content of the book also directly applies to later versions of wxPython as well. The suggested software to install is as follows:

1. Latest version of Python 2.6 (`http://www.python.org/download/releases/2.6/`).

2. Latest version of wxPython 2.8 (`http://www.wxpython.org/download.php`).

Who this book is for

This book is written for Python programmers wanting to develop GUI applications. A basic knowledge of Python and object oriented programming concepts is required.

Conventions

In this book, you will find a number of styles of text that distinguish between different kinds of information. Here are some examples of these styles, and an explanation of their meaning.

Code words in text are shown as follows: "The `App` object also maintains the `MainLoop`, which is used to drive a wxPython application".

A block of code is set as follows:

```
import wx

class MyApp(wx.App):
    def OnInit(self):
        wx.MessageBox("Hello wxPython", "wxApp")
        return True
```

When we wish to draw your attention to a particular part of a code block, the relevant lines or items are set in bold:

```
class MyPanel(wx.Panel):
    __metaclass__ = ClassSynchronizer
    def __init__(self, parent, *args, **kwargs)
```

Any command-line input or output is written as follows:

python setup.py py2exe

New terms and **important words** are shown in bold. Words that you see on the screen, in menus or dialog boxes for example, appear in the text like this: "Click on **OK** to close it and exit the application".

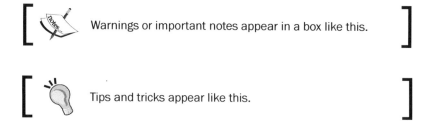

Warnings or important notes appear in a box like this.

Tips and tricks appear like this.

Reader feedback

Feedback from our readers is always welcome. Let us know what you think about this book—what you liked or may have disliked. Reader feedback is important for us to develop titles that you really get the most out of.

To send us general feedback, simply send an e-mail to feedback@packtpub.com, and mention the book title via the subject of your message.

If there is a book that you need and would like to see us publish, please send us a note in the **SUGGEST A TITLE** form on www.packtpub.com or e-mail suggest@packtpub.com.

If there is a topic that you have expertise in and you are interested in either writing or contributing to a book, see our author guide on www.packtpub.com/authors.

Customer support

Now that you are the proud owner of a Packt book, we have a number of things to help you to get the most from your purchase.

Downloading the example code for this book

You can download the example code files for all Packt books you have purchased from your account at http://www.PacktPub.com. If you purchased this book elsewhere, you can visit http://www.PacktPub.com/support and register to have the files e-mailed directly to you.

Errata

Although we have taken every care to ensure the accuracy of our content, mistakes do happen. If you find a mistake in one of our books—maybe a mistake in the text or the code—we would be grateful if you would report this to us. By doing so, you can save other readers from frustration and help us improve subsequent versions of this book. If you find any errata, please report them by visiting http://www.packtpub.com/support, selecting your book, clicking on the **errata submission form** link, and entering the details of your errata. Once your errata are verified, your submission will be accepted and the errata will be uploaded on our website, or added to any list of existing errata, under the Errata section of that title. Any existing errata can be viewed by selecting your title from http://www.packtpub.com/support.

Piracy

Piracy of copyright material on the Internet is an ongoing problem across all media. At Packt, we take the protection of our copyright and licenses very seriously. If you come across any illegal copies of our works, in any form, on the Internet, please provide us with the location address or website name immediately so that we can pursue a remedy.

Please contact us at copyright@packtpub.com with a link to the suspected pirated material.

We appreciate your help in protecting our authors, and our ability to bring you valuable content.

Questions

You can contact us at questions@packtpub.com if you are having a problem with any aspect of the book, and we will do our best to address it.

1
Getting Started with wxPython

In this chapter, we will cover the components that are at the foundation of nearly all wxPython applications, such as:

- ▶ The application object
- ▶ The main frame
- ▶ Understanding the window hierarchy
- ▶ Referencing controls
- ▶ Using Bitmaps
- ▶ Adding icons to Windows
- ▶ Utilizing Stock IDs
- ▶ Accessing the clipboard
- ▶ Supporting drag and drop
- ▶ Two-stage widget creation
- ▶ Understanding inheritance limitations

Introduction

In today's world of desktop applications there is a great amount of incentive to be able to develop applications that can run on multiple operating systems and desktop platforms. Currently there are a handful of cross-platform Python frameworks that can be used to develop desktop applications. The wxPython Library is a set of Python bindings to the wxWidgets Library, which is a powerful cross-platform C++ application framework that can be used to create user interfaces. What sets wxPython apart is that, unlike other UI toolkits that draw their own controls, wxPython uses the platform's own native UI toolkit for creating and displaying UI components. This means that a wxPython application will have the same look and feel as other applications on the system since it is using the same controls and themes as the rest of the system.

Developing an application in wxPython provides great flexibility for writing applications that will run on Windows, Macintosh OS X, Linux, and other UNIX like environments. Applications can rapidly be developed on one platform and often deployed to another with little or no changes necessary.

The application object

The App object bootstraps the library and initializes the underlying toolkit. All wxPython applications must create an App object. This should be instantiated before trying to create any other GUI objects to ensure that all the dependant parts of the library have been properly initialized. The App object also maintains the MainLoop, which is used to drive a wxPython application.

This recipe will demonstrate the basic pattern that all wxPython applications can be built from.

How to do it...

Here we will create a "Hello World" like application to show the basic structure of a wxPython application:

```python
import wx

class MyApp(wx.App):
    def OnInit(self):
        wx.MessageBox("Hello wxPython", "wxApp")
        return True

if __name__ == "__main__":
    app = MyApp(False)
    app.MainLoop()
```

Running the previous script will result in the following pop-up dialog shown on the screen. Click on **OK** to close it and exit the application.

How it works...

The application object calls its `OnInit` method when it is created. This method is overridden and used as the main entry point for initializing this application. By returning `True`, the method informs the framework that it is good to go. `OnInit` is where most applications will do their initialization and create their main window(s).

In this example, we created the `App` object by passing `False` as the first argument. This argument is used to tell wxPython whether to redirect output or not. When developing an application, it is advised to always set this to `False`, and to run scripts from the command line so that you can see any error output that might be missed when running the script by double clicking on it.

After creating the application object and once all initializations are complete, the last thing that you need to do is to call the `App` objects `MainLoop` method in order to start the event loop. This method will not return until the last top-level window is destroyed or until the `App` object is told to exit. wxPython is an event-driven system and the `MainLoop` is the heart of the whole system. During each iteration of the loop, events are dispatched to perform all of the tasks in the GUI, such as handling mouse clicks, moving the window, and redrawing the screen.

There's more...

The `wx.App` class constructor has four optional keyword arguments:

```
wx.App(redirect=True, filename=None,
       useBestVisual=False, clearSigInt=True)
```

The four optional keyword arguments are as follows:

- ▶ `redirect`: Redirect `stdout`.
- ▶ `filename`: If redirect is `True` this can be used to specify an output file to redirect to.
- ▶ `useBestVisual`: Specifies whether the application should try to use the best visuals provided by the underlying toolkit. (It does not have an affect on most systems.)
- ▶ `clearSigInt`: Should `SIGINT` be cleared? Setting this to `True` will allow the application to be terminated by pressing *Ctrl + C*, like most other applications.

The main frame

For most applications, you will want to display a window for its users to interact with. In wxPython, the most typical window object is known as a `Frame`. This recipe will show you how to sublass a `Frame` and display it in an application.

How to do it...

This example extends upon the previous recipe to add a minimal empty application window:

```python
import wx

class MyApp(wx.App):
    def OnInit(self):
        self.frame = MyFrame(None, title="The Main Frame")
        self.SetTopWindow(self.frame)
        self.frame.Show()

        return True

class MyFrame(wx.Frame):
    def __init__(self, parent, id=wx.ID_ANY, title="",
                 pos=wx.DefaultPosition, size=wx.DefaultSize,
                 style=wx.DEFAULT_FRAME_STYLE,
                 name="MyFrame"):
        super(MyFrame, self).__init__(parent, id, title,
                                      pos, size, style, name)

        # Attributes
        self.panel = wx.Panel(self)

if __name__ == "__main__":
    app = MyApp(False)
    app.MainLoop()
```

Running the previous code will result in a window like the following being shown:

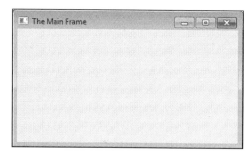

How it works...

The `Frame` is the main top-level window and container for most applications. Let's start by examining our `MyFrame` class. In this class there is one important thing to note. We created a `Panel` object as a child window of the `Frame`. You can think of a `Panel` as a box for containing other controls. Also, in order for a `Frame` to operate and look correct on all platforms, it is important that it has a `Panel` as its main child.

Firstly, in the `OnInit` method of our `App`, we create an instance of `MyFrame`, passing `None` as its first parameter. This parameter is used to specify the parent window of the `Frame`. Because this is our main window, we pass in `None` to indicate that it has no parent. Secondly, we call the `SetTopWindow` method of our `App` in order to set our newly-created `MyFrame` instance as the application's top window. Thirdly and finally, we call `Show` on our `Frame`; this simply does what its name suggests, and shows the `Frame` so that a user can see it, though the `Frame` will not actually be visible on the screen until the `MainLoop` is started.

There's more...

The `Frame` class has a number of style flags that can be set in its constructor to modify the behavior and appearance of the window. These style flags can be combined as a bitmask and are supplied as the value to the constructors' style parameter. The following table outlines some of the common ones. A full list of all available styles can be found in the wxPython online documentation, at `http://wxpython.org/onlinedocs.php`.

Style flags	Description
`wx.DEFAULT_FRAME_STYLE`	This is a bitwise OR of the following flags: ▶ `wx.MINIMIZE_BOX` ▶ `wx.MAXIMIZE_BOX` ▶ `wx.RESIZE_BORDER` ▶ `wx.SYSTEM_MENU` ▶ `wx.CAPTION` ▶ `wx.CLOSE_BOX` ▶ `wx.CLIP_CHILDREN`
`wx.MINIMIZE_BOX`	Display a title bar button that minimizes the Frame
`wx.MAXIMIZE_BOX`	Display a title bar button that maximizes the Frame
`wx.CLOSE_BOX`	Display a title bar button that allows the Frame to be closed. (the "X" button)
`wx.RESIZE_BORDER`	Allow the Frame to be resized by the user when they drag the border
`wx.CAPTION`	Displays a caption on the Frame
`wx.SYSTEM_MENU`	Display a system menu (that is, the menu that is shown when clicking in the frames icon on Windows)
`wx.CLIP_CHILDREN`	Eliminates flicker caused by the background being repainted (Windows only)

Understanding the window hierarchy

All of the different windows and controls in wxPython have a hierarchy of containment. Some controls can be containers for other controls and some cannot. This recipe is geared towards giving an understanding of this hierarchy.

Getting ready

We will be making just a minor change to the `Frame` from the previous recipe, so let's open the code from that recipe to get ready for the new changes.

How to do it...

Here is the new code that will replace our existing Frame class.

```
class MyFrame(wx.Frame):
    def __init__(self, parent, id=wx.ID_ANY, title="",
                    pos=wx.DefaultPosition, size=wx.DefaultSize,
                    style=wx.DEFAULT_FRAME_STYLE,
                    name="MyFrame"):
        super(MyFrame, self).__init__(parent, id, title,
                                        pos, size, style, name)

        # Attributes
        self.panel = wx.Panel(self)
        self.panel.SetBackgroundColour(wx.BLACK)
        self.button = wx.Button(self.panel,
                        label="Push Me",
                        pos=(50, 50))
```

How it works...

Basically, there are three general categories of window objects that are tiered, in the following containment order:

- ▶ Top-Level Windows (Frames and Dialogs)
- ▶ General Containers (Panels and Notebooks, ...)
- ▶ Controls (Buttons, CheckBoxes, ComboBoxes, ...)

The Top-Level Window is at the top of the hierarchy and it can contain any kind of window except another Top-Level Window. General Containers come next, and they can arbitrarily hold any other General Container or Control. Finally, at the bottom of the Hierarchy are the Controls. These are the functional part of a UI that the user will interact with. They can, in some cases, be used to hold other controls, but typically will not. The containment hierarchy is connected to the parental hierarchy of controls. A parent will be the container for its children.

When running the previous sample, this hierarchy becomes apparent. The `Frame`, as we have previously seen, is the outer-most container object; next you can see the `Panel`, which we turned black to make it more visible; finally you can see the `Button`, which was added as a child of the `Panel`.

See also

▶ The *Referencing controls* recipe in this chapter offers further explanation as to how the window hierarchy is connected together.

Referencing controls

All `Window` objects in an application are connected in various ways. Quite often it is useful to get a reference to an instance of a control so that you can perform some operation on the control or retrieve some data from it. This recipe will show some of the facilities that are available for finding and getting references to controls.

How to do it...

Here we extend the `MyFrame` class from the previous recipe to have an event handler for when its Button is clicked. In the event handler we can see some ways to access different controls in our UI during runtime:

```python
class MyFrame(wx.Frame):
    def __init__(self, parent, id=wx.ID_ANY, title="",
                 pos=wx.DefaultPosition, size=wx.DefaultSize,
                 style=wx.DEFAULT_FRAME_STYLE,
                 name="MyFrame"):
        super(MyFrame, self).__init__(parent, id, title,
                                      pos, size, style, name)


        # Attributes
        self.panel = wx.Panel(self)
        self.panel.SetBackgroundColour(wx.BLACK)
        button = wx.Button(self.panel,
                           label="Get Children",
                           pos=(50, 50))
        self.btnId = button.GetId()
```

```
                    # Event Handlers
                    self.Bind(wx.EVT_BUTTON, self.OnButton, button)

            def OnButton(self, event):
                """Called when the Button is clicked"""
                print "\nFrame GetChildren:"
                for child in self.GetChildren():
                    print "%s" % repr(child)

                print "\nPanel FindWindowById:"
                button = self.panel.FindWindowById(self.btnId)
                print "%s" % repr(button)
                # Change the Button's label
                button.SetLabel("Changed Label")

                print "\nButton GetParent:"
                panel = button.GetParent()
                print "%s" % repr(panel)

                print "\nGet the Application Object:"
                app = wx.GetApp()
                print "%s" % repr(app)

                print "\nGet the Frame from the App:"
                frame = app.GetTopWindow()
                print "%s" % repr(frame)
```

How it works...

Each window in the framework keeps a reference to its parent and to its children. Running our program now will print out the results of using the accessor functions that all windows have for finding and retrieving references to their children and other related controls.

- ▶ GetChildren: This method will return a list of all of the children that the given control has

- ▶ FindWindowById: This can be used to find a specific child window by using its ID

- ▶ GetParent: This method will retrieve the window's parent window

- ▶ wx.GetApp: This is a global function for getting access to the one and only application object

- ▶ App.GetTopWindow: This gets the main Top-Level Window in the application

Clicking on the `Button` will cause the `OnButton` method to be called. In `OnButton`, there are examples that show how to use each of the above methods. Each of them will return a reference to a GUI object. In our example, calling `GetChildren` on the `Panel` will return a list of its children controls. Iterating over this list, we print out each of the children, which will just be the Button in this case. `FindWindowById` can be used to find a specific child control; again, we called this on our `Panel` to find the `Button` control. Just to show that we found the `Button`, we used its `SetLabel` method to change its label. Next, calling `GetParent` on the `Button` will return the `Button`'s parent, which is the `Panel`. Finally, by using the global `GetApp` function, we can get a reference to the application object. The `App` object's `GetTopWindow` will return a reference to our Frame.

There's more...

Here are a few more useful methods available for getting references to controls.

Function Name	Description
`wx.FindWindowByLabel(label)`	Finds a child window by looking for it by Label
`wx.FindWindowByName(name)`	Finds a child window by looking for it by Name
`wx.GetTopLevelParent()`	Gets the Top-Level Window, which is at the top of the given control's parental hierarchy

See also

▶ The *Understanding the window hierarchy* recipe in this chapter outlines the structure of how windows are contained within and are related to each other.

Using Bitmaps

It's likely that, at some point, you will want to be able to display an image in your application. A `Bitmap` is the basic data type that is used to display images in an application. This recipe will show how to load an image file into a `Bitmap` and then display it in a `Frame`.

How to do it...

To see how to use Bitmaps, we will create a little application that loads an image from the hard disk and displays it in a Frame:

```
import os
import wx

class MyApp(wx.App):
    def OnInit(self):
        self.frame = MyFrame(None, title="Bitmaps")
```

```python
        self.SetTopWindow(self.frame)
        self.frame.Show()

        return True

class MyFrame(wx.Frame):
    def __init__(self, parent, id=wx.ID_ANY, title="",
                    pos=wx.DefaultPosition, size=wx.DefaultSize,
                    style=wx.DEFAULT_FRAME_STYLE,
                    name="MyFrame"):
        super(MyFrame, self).__init__(parent, id, title,
                                        pos, size, style, name)

        # Attributes
        self.panel = wx.Panel(self)

        img_path = os.path.abspath("./face-grin.png")
        bitmap = wx.Bitmap(img_path, type=wx.BITMAP_TYPE_PNG)
        self.bitmap = wx.StaticBitmap(self.panel,
                                        bitmap=bitmap)

if __name__ == "__main__":
    app = MyApp(False)
    app.MainLoop()
```

How it works...

The `StaticBitmap` control is the simplest method of displaying a Bitmap in an application. In the example code that accompanies this recipe, we have an image in the same directory as our script, called `face-grin.png`, that we want to display. In order to display the image we first use the `Bitmap` constructor to load the image into memory, and then pass it to the `StaticBitmap` control in order to display the image on the screen. The constructor takes a path to the file, and a type argument that specifies the image format.

There's more...

There is built-in support for the most common image formats. The following list shows the supported image file formats:

► `wx.BITMAP_TYPE_ANY`

► `wx.BITMAP_TYPE_BMP`

► `wx.BITMAP_TYPE_ICO`

► `wx.BITMAP_TYPE_CUR`

► `wx.BITMAP_TYPE_XBM`

► `wx.BITMAP_TYPE_XPM`

- wx.BITMAP_TYPE_TIF
- wx.BITMAP_TYPE_GIF
- wx.BITMAP_TYPE_PNG
- wx.BITMAP_TYPE_JPEG
- wx.BITMAP_TYPE_PNM
- wx.BITMAP_TYPE_PCX
- wx.BITMAP_TYPE_PICT
- wx.BITMAP_TYPE_ICON
- wx.BITMAP_TYPE_ANI
- wx.BITMAP_TYPE_IFF

See also

- The *Working with ToolBars* recipe in *Chapter 3, Basic Building Blocks of a User Interface* contains some more Bitmap usage examples.
- The *Customizing the ArtProvider* recipe in *Chapter 10, Creating Components and Extending Functionality* provides more on information how to create Bitmaps.

Adding icons to Windows

Adding an icon to your application's title bar as a way of branding the application that will help to set it apart and distinguish it from the other applications running on the desktop. This recipe will show how easy it is to add an icon to a Frame.

 Support for adding an Icon to the title bar on OS X is currently not supported by wxPython 2.8.

How to do it...

Here we will create a `Frame` subclass that loads an image file from the hard disk and displays it on its title bar:

```
class MyFrame(wx.Frame):
    def __init__(self, parent, id=wx.ID_ANY, title="",
                 pos=wx.DefaultPosition, size=wx.DefaultSize,
                 style=wx.DEFAULT_FRAME_STYLE,
                 name="MyFrame"):
        super(MyFrame, self).__init__(parent, id, title, pos,
                                      size, style, name)
```

```
# Attributes
self.panel = wx.Panel(self)

# Setup
path = os.path.abspath("./face-monkey.png")
icon = wx.Icon(path, wx.BITMAP_TYPE_PNG)
self.SetIcon(icon)
```

Displaying this Frame subclass will result in a window like the following. Comparing this to the one in the Main Frame recipe, you can see the new icon to the left of the title:

How it works...

In this recipe we have a small (16x16) image of a monkey that we want to show in the title bar of the `Frame`. For simplicity, this image is located in the same directory as our script and we load it using a relative path. The `Frame` requires an icon instead of a `Bitmap`, so we have to use an `Icon` to load our image into memory. After loading the image, all that is left is to call the Frame's `SetIcon` method in order to set the Icon for the `Frame`.

See also

▶ The *Using Bitmaps* recipe in this chapter discusses the more commonly-used Bitmap image type.

Utilizing Stock IDs

All controls, and many other user-interface elements, such as menus, take an ID as an argument in their constructor that can be used to identify the control or object inside event handlers. Typically, the value of `wx.ID_ANY` is used to let the system automatically generate an ID for the item, or the `wx.NewId` function is used to create a new ID. However, there are also a number of predefined IDs available in the `wx` module that have special meaning for certain common items that many applications tend to have, such as Copy/Paste menu items or Ok/Cancel buttons. The expected behavior and appearance of some of these items can vary from platform to platform. By using the stock ID, wxPython will take care of the differences for you. This recipe will show a few of the places in which these IDs can come in handy.

How to do it...

This code snippet shows how to make use of some of the predefined IDs to simplify the creation of some common UI elements:

```
class MyFrame(wx.Frame):
    def __init__(self, parent, id=wx.ID_ANY, title="",
                 pos=wx.DefaultPosition, size=wx.DefaultSize,
                 style=wx.DEFAULT_FRAME_STYLE,
                 name="MyFrame"):
        super(MyFrame, self).__init__(parent, id, title,
                                      pos, size, style, name)

        # Attributes
        self.panel = wx.Panel(self)

        # Setup
        ok_btn = wx.Button(self.panel, wx.ID_OK)
        cancel_btn = wx.Button(self.panel, wx.ID_CANCEL,
                               pos=(100, 0))

        menu_bar = wx.MenuBar()
        edit_menu = wx.Menu()
        edit_menu.Append(wx.NewId(), "Test")
        edit_menu.Append(wx.ID_PREFERENCES)
        menu_bar.Append(edit_menu, "Edit")
        self.SetMenuBar(menu_bar)
```

The previous class will create the following window:

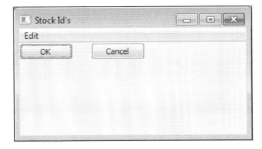

How it works...

The first thing to notice in this recipe is that no labels were specified for the two buttons that we created. By using the Stock IDs for OK and Cancel as their IDs, the framework will automatically put the proper label on the control.

This also applies to menu items, as can be seen in our Edit menu for the Preferences item. Another important thing to note is that if this sample is run on Macintosh OS X, the framework will also automatically move the Preferences menu item to its expected location in the Application menu.

There's more...

Using buttons with Stock IDs in a Modal Dialog will also allow the dialog to be dismissed, and return the appropriate value, such as wx.OK or wx.CANCEL, without the need to connect event handlers to the buttons for performing this standard action. Automatically getting the correct button layout for a dialog can also be achieved by using Stock IDs with StdDialogButtonSizer.

See also

- ▶ The *Creating Stock Buttons* recipe in *Chapter 3, Basic Building Blocks of a User Interface* shows how Stock IDs can be used to construct standard buttons.

- ▶ The *Standard dialog button layout* recipe in *Chapter 7, Window Layout and Design* shows how to easily add common buttons to dialogs by using Stock IDs.

- ▶ The *Optimizing for OS X* recipe in *Chapter 12, Building and Managing Applications for Distribution* shows more uses for Stock IDs.

Accessing the clipboard

The Clipboard is a system-wide, accessible way of getting data to and from one application to another. This recipe will show how to get text from the clipboard, as well as how to put text in the clipboard for other applications to access.

How to do it...

The following two functions can be used to get text from and put text on the clipboard:

```python
def SetClipboardText(text):
    """Put text in the clipboard
    @param text: string
    """
    data_o = wx.TextDataObject()
    data_o.SetText(text)
    if wx.TheClipboard.IsOpened() or wx.TheClipboard.Open():
        wx.TheClipboard.SetData(data_o)
        wx.TheClipboard.Close()
```

```
def GetClipboardText():
    """Get text from the clipboard
    @return: string
    """
    text_obj = wx.TextDataObject()
    rtext = ""
    if wx.TheClipboard.IsOpened() or wx.TheClipboard.Open():
        if wx.TheClipboard.GetData(text_obj):
            rtext = text_obj.GetText()
        wx.TheClipboard.Close()
    return rtext
```

How it works...

wxPython provides a singleton clipboard object that can be used to interact with the systems clipboard. This class works with data objects that are used to represent the underlying system data types. The use of the clipboard is a three-step process:

- ▶ Open the Clipboard
- ▶ Set/Get the DataObject
- ▶ Close the Clipboard

There's more...

The clipboard supports many other data types besides just text. wxPython provides built-in support for some additional types, as well as classes for defining your own custom types. The usage of these different data types follows the same general pattern as the `TextDataObject`.

Data types	Description
`wx.BitmapDataObject`	Used to get Bitmaps from and put Bitmaps on the Clipboard
`wx.CustomDataObject`	Can hold any Python picklable data type
`wx.DataObjectComposite`	Can contain any arbitrary number of simple data types and make them all available at once
`wx.FileDataObject`	Used for holding filenames
`wx.URLDataObject`	Used for holding URLs

See also

- ▶ The *Supporting drag and drop* recipe in this chapter is related to the clipboard in that it allows for the transfer of data between applications.

Supporting drag and drop

In order to improve usability, it is good to support drag and drop in an application so that the user can simply drop files or other objects into your application. This recipe will show how to support accepting a `CompositeDataObject` that supports both files and text.

How to do it...

First we will define a custom drop target class:

```python
class FileAndTextDropTarget(wx.PyDropTarget):
    """Drop target capable of accepting dropped
    files and text
    """
    def __init__(self, file_callback, text_callback):
        assert callable(file_callback)
        assert callable(text_callback)
        super(FileAndTextDropTarget, self).__init__()
        # Attributes
        self.fcallback = file_callback # Drop File Callback
        self.tcallback = text_callback # Drop Text Callback
        self._data = None
        self.txtdo = None
        self.filedo = None

        # Setup
        self.InitObjects()

    def InitObjects(self):
        """Initializes the text and file data objects"""
        self._data = wx.DataObjectComposite()
        self.txtdo = wx.TextDataObject()
        self.filedo = wx.FileDataObject()
        self._data.Add(self.txtdo, False)
        self._data.Add(self.filedo, True)
        self.SetDataObject(self._data)

    def OnData(self, x_cord, y_cord, drag_result):
        """Called by the framework when data is dropped
        on the target
        """
```

```
        if self.GetData():
            data_format = self._data.GetReceivedFormat()
            if data_format.GetType() == wx.DF_FILENAME:
                self.fcallback(self.filedo.GetFilenames())
            else:
                self.tcallback(self.txtdo.GetText())

        return drag_result
```

Then to make use of the `FileAndTextDropTarget`, we assign it to a window using the window object's `SetDropTarget` method.

```
class DropTargetFrame(wx.Frame):
    def __init__(self, parent, id=wx.ID_ANY, title="",
                 pos=wx.DefaultPosition, size=wx.DefaultSize,
                 style=wx.DEFAULT_FRAME_STYLE,
                 name="DropTargetFrame"):
        super(DropTargetFrame, self).__init__(parent, id,
                                              title, pos,
                                              size, style,
                                              name)

        # Attributes
        choices = ["Drag and Drop Text or Files here",]
        self.list = wx.ListBox(self,
                               choices=choices)
        self.dt = FileAndTextDropTarget(self.OnFileDrop,
                                        self.OnTextDrop)
        self.list.SetDropTarget(self.dt)

        # Setup
        self.CreateStatusBar()

    def OnFileDrop(self, files):
        self.PushStatusText("Files Dropped")
        for f in files:
            self.list.Append(f)

    def OnTextDrop(self, text):
        self.PushStatusText("Text Dropped")
        self.list.Append(text)
```

How it works...

The framework will call the `OnData` method of our `DropTarget` when the window has received the drop data. When `OnData` is called, we simply get the data from our `DataObject` and pass it to the appropriate callback function to let our window decide how to handle the data.

All window objects have a `SetDropTarget` method that can be used to assign a `DropTarget`, so this class can be reused for almost any type of control. In the previous example, we assigned it to a `ListBox` and then appended the dropped data to the list in each of our callbacks.

There's more...

The `PyDropTarget` class provides a few more methods that can be called at different times during the drag operation. These methods can also be overridden in order to do things such as change the mouse cursor, show a custom drag image, or reject the drag object.

Methods	When the methods are called
`OnEnter(x, y, drag_result)`	Called when a drag object enters the window. Returns a drag result value (that is, `wx.DragNone`, `wx.DragCopy`, ...)
`OnDragOver(x, y, drag_result)`	Called while the mouse is dragging the object over the target
`OnLeave()`	Called when the mouse leaves the drop target
`OnDrop(x, y)`	Called when the user drops the object. Return `True` to accept the object or `False` to reject it
`OnData(x, y, drag_result)`	Called after `OnDrop`, when the data object was accepted

See also

▶ *The Accessing the clipboard* recipe in this chapter shows another way to perform data transfer between applications.

Two-stage widget creation

Two-stage widget creation is a way of initialzing a widget and then its UI part, in two steps. This method of object creation is used by class factories such as XRC (XML Resource) and to set extra style flags that cannot be set by using the constructor's regular style parameter. This recipe will show how to use two-stage creations to create a frame that has a special button that can be used to put it into a context-sensitive help mode.

This is a Windows-specific example; other platforms do not support having a `ContextButton` in their title bar.

How to do it...

Here we will create a `Frame` subclass that uses two stage creation in order to set an extra style flag:

```
class MyFrame(wx.Frame):
    def __init__(self, parent, *args, **kwargs):
        pre = wx.PreFrame()
        pre.SetExtraStyle(wx.FRAME_EX_CONTEXTHELP)
        pre.Create(parent, *args, **kwargs)
        self.PostCreate(pre)
```

How it works...

In wxPython, two-stage widget creation is actually a three-step process. First, each class that supports it has its own `PreClass` that is used as a factory constructor that pre-creates the object. At this point, the pre object can be used to set the extra style flag. The next step is to call `Create`. `Create` acts like the regular constructor and creates the UI portion of the control. The final step is to call `PostCreate`, `PostCreate` does the work of translating the pre object into `self` so that the object will appear just as if the class's `__init__` method had been called normally.

See also

▸ The *Using XRC* recipe in *Chapter 7, Window Layout and Design* discusses XRC.

Understanding inheritance limitations

wxPython is a wrapper around the wxWidgets C++ framework. This relationship means that inside most wxPython objects there is a C++ object. Because of this, methods that belong to wxPython classes cannot always be overridden in the same way as they can with a normal Python object.

To demonstrate this behavior, this recipe will show how to create a class that will automatically add its children windows to its `Sizer` layout. This will be contrasted to a class that does not expose its virtual methods to the Python layer of the class.

How to do it...

To demonstrate the difference in overriding methods, we will create two similar classes first starting with one that derives from the standard `Panel` class:

```python
import wx

class MyPanel(wx.Panel):
    def __init__(self, parent):
        super(MyPanel, self).__init__(parent)

        sizer = wx.BoxSizer()
        self.SetSizer(sizer)

    def AddChild(self, child):
        sizer = self.GetSizer()
        sizer.Add(child, 0, wx.ALIGN_LEFT|wx.ALL, 8)
        return super(MyPanel, self).AddChild(child)
```

Now we will create a class that is exactly the same except that it derives from the `Py` version of the class:

```python
class MyVirtualPanel(wx.PyPanel):
    """Class that automatically adds children
    controls to sizer layout.
    """
    def __init__(self, parent):
        super(MyVirtualPanel, self).__init__(parent)

        sizer = wx.BoxSizer()
        self.SetSizer(sizer)

    def AddChild(self, child):
        sizer = self.GetSizer()
        sizer.Add(child, 0, wx.ALIGN_LEFT|wx.ALL, 8)
        return super(MyVirtualPanel, self).AddChild(child)
```

Now below we have a little sample application that uses the above two classes:

```python
class MyFrame(wx.Frame):
    def __init__(self, parent, *args, **kwargs):
        super(MyFrame, self).__init__(parent,
                                      *args, **kwargs)

        # Attributes
        self.mypanel = MyPanel(self)
        self.mypanel.SetBackgroundColour(wx.BLACK)
        self.virtpanel = MyVirtualPanel(self)
```

```
            self.virtpanel.SetBackgroundColour(wx.WHITE)

            # Setup
            self.__DoLayout()

    def __DoLayout(self):
        """Layout the window"""
        # Layout the controls using a sizer
        sizer = wx.BoxSizer(wx.VERTICAL)
        sizer.Add(self.mypanel, 1, wx.EXPAND)
        sizer.Add(self.virtpanel, 1, wx.EXPAND)
        self.SetSizer(sizer)

        # Create 3 children for the top panel
        for x in range(3):
            wx.Button(self.mypanel,
                        label="MyPanel %d" % x)
        # Create 3 children for the bottom panel
        for x in range(3):
            wx.Button(self.virtpanel,
                        label="VirtPanel %d" % x)

        self.SetInitialSize(size=(300, 200))

class MyApp(wx.App):
    def OnInit(self):
        self.frame = MyFrame(None,
                                title="Virtualized Methods")
        self.SetTopWindow(self.frame)
        self.frame.Show()

        return True

if __name__ == "__main__":
    app = MyApp(False)
    app.MainLoop()
```

Running this code will result in a window like the following one being displayed:

How it works...

In each version of our `Panel` class we override the `AddChild` method, which is called every time that a window has a new child window created. `AddChild` is called inside the C++ part of the class when this happens, so in order to be able to override the method in our Python version of the class, we need to use the special version that provides access to overriding the virtualized method from the C++ class.

The classes in wxPython that have a version of the class prefixed with `Py` have the virtualized versions of many of the methods exposed, so that when they are overridden in a Python subclass they get bound to the method in the C++ layer of the object and will be called by the framework instead of the base class's implementation.

This can be seen in the screenshot of our recipe application that was shown above. The top version of the class that does not derive from `PyPanel` has all three of its `Button`s stacked on top of each other in the top left-hand corner of the window, because its overridden `AddChild` method is never called. On the other hand, the version of the class that does derive from `PyPanel` has its `AddChild` method called and is able to lay out the `Button`s in its `Sizer`.

There's more...

It is not well documented as to which methods are exposed as virtual methods and which ones are not. Here is a little trick that can help you to identify which virtual methods are available in a given class. Just run the following code inside the Python interpreter:

```
import wx
for method in dir(wx.PyPanel):
    if method.startswith('base_'):
        print method
```

The argument in the `dir()` call can be changed to whatever class you want to inspect. Running this will print out a list of all of the methods in the class that are virtualized. The `base_` methods are generated by SWIG as a part of the wxPython bindings to wxWidgets, and should not be used directly in your code. Instead, the methods without the `base_` prefix should be used.

See also

- ▶ The *Creating a custom control* recipe in *Chapter 10, Creating Components and Extending Functionality*, shows more usage examples of overriding virtual methods.
- ▶ The *Using a BoxSizer* recipe in *Chapter 7, Window Design and Layout*, explains how the BoxSizer class can be used to perform the layout of controls in a window.

2
Responding to Events

In this chapter, we will cover:

- ▸ Handling events
- ▸ Understanding event propagation
- ▸ Handling Key events
- ▸ Using UpdateUI events
- ▸ Playing with the mouse
- ▸ Creating custom event classes
- ▸ Managing event handlers with EventStack
- ▸ Validating input with validators
- ▸ Handling Apple events

Introduction

In an event-driven system, events are used to connect actions within the framework to callback functions that are linked to those events. Applications that are built upon an event-driven framework make use of these events in order to know when to respond to actions that are initiated by the user or the system. In a user interface, events are the way to know when a button is clicked, when a menu has been selected, or any other one of a wide variety of actions that a user could take while interacting with the applications interface.

As you can see, knowing how to respond to events that occur during the life of an application is a crucial part of creating a functional application. So let's dive into the event-driven world of wxPython.

Handling events

wxPython is an event-driven system. The usage of this system is pretty straightforward and regular across the framework. The basic patterns of working with events are the same regardless of the type of control or event that your application will interact with. This recipe will introduce the basics of working in wxPython's event system.

How to do it...

Let's create a simple `Frame` with two buttons in it to show how to work with events:

```python
class MyFrame(wx.Frame):
    def __init__(self, parent, id=wx.ID_ANY, title="",
                 pos=wx.DefaultPosition, size=wx.DefaultSize,
                 style=wx.DEFAULT_FRAME_STYLE,
                 name="MyFrame"):
        super(MyFrame, self).__init__(parent, id, title,
                                      pos, size, style, name)

        # Attributes
        self.panel = wx.Panel(self)

        self.btn1 = wx.Button(self.panel, label="Push Me")
        self.btn2 = wx.Button(self.panel, label="push me too")

        sizer = wx.BoxSizer(wx.HORIZONTAL)
        sizer.Add(self.btn1, 0, wx.ALL, 10)
        sizer.Add(self.btn2, 0, wx.ALL, 10)
        self.panel.SetSizer(sizer)

        self.Bind(wx.EVT_BUTTON, self.OnButton, self.btn1)
        self.Bind(wx.EVT_BUTTON,
                  lambda event:
                  self.btn1.Enable(not self.btn1.Enabled),
                  self.btn2)

    def OnButton(self, event):
        """Called when self.btn1 is clicked"""
        event_id = event.GetId()
        event_obj = event.GetEventObject()
        print "Button 1 Clicked:"
        print "ID=%d" % event_id
        print "object=%s" % event_obj.GetLabel()
```

How it works...

The lines of code to take notice of in this recipe are the two `Bind` calls. The `Bind` method is used to associate an event handler function with an event that may be sent to a control. Events always propagate up the window hierarchy and never down. In this example, we bound the button event to the `Frame`, but the events will originate from the `Button` objects that are children of the `Panel`. The `Frame` object is at the top of the hierarchy containing the `Panel`, which in turn contains the two `Buttons`. Because of this, since the event callback is not handled by the `Button` or the `Panel`, it will propagate to the `Frame` where our `OnButton` handler will be called.

The `Bind` method takes two required parameters:

- ▶ The event binder object (`EVT_FOO`)
- ▶ A callable object that takes an event object as its first parameter. This is the event handler function that will be called when the event occurs.

The optional parameters are for specifying the originating control to bind the event handler to. We bound one handler for each of our buttons in this example by specifying the `Button` objects as the third parameter to `Bind`.

`EVT_BUTTON` is the event binder for when a `Button` is clicked by the user of the application. When the first button is clicked, the event handler `OnButton` will be called to notify our program that this action occurred. The event object will be passed to the handler function as its first parameter. The event object has a number of methods that can be used to get information about the event and what control it came from. Each event may have different data available, depending on the type of event that is related to the type of control it originated from.

For our second `Button`, we used a `lambda` function as a shorthand way of creating an event-handler function without needing to define a new function. This is a handy way of handling events that only need to perform simple actions.

See also

- ▶ The *Application object* recipe in *Chapter 1, Getting Started with wxPython* talks about the MainLoop, which is at the core of the event system.
- ▶ The *Understanding the window hierarchy* recipe in *Chapter 1, Getting Started with wxPython* describes the window containment hierarchy.
- ▶ The *Creating Stock Buttons* recipe in *Chapter 3, Basic Building Blocks of a User Interface* explains Buttons in detail.
- ▶ The *Using a BoxSizer* recipe in *Chapter 7, Window Layout and Design* explains how to use the `BoxSizer` class to lay out controls.

Understanding event propagation

There are two main types of Event Objects in wxPython, each with its own distinct behavior:

- ▸ Events
- ▸ Command Events

Basic `Events` are events that do not propagate upwards in the window hierarchy. Instead, they stay local to the window that they were sent to or originated in. The second type, `CommandEvents`, are the more common type of events, and differ from regular events in that they propagate up the window parental hierarchy until they are handled or reach the end of the line at the application object. This recipe will explore how to work with, understand, and control the propagation of events.

How to do it...

To explore how events propagate, lets create another simple application:

```python
import wx

ID_BUTTON1 = wx.NewId()
ID_BUTTON2 = wx.NewId()

class MyApp(wx.App):
    def OnInit(self):
        self.frame = MyFrame(None, title="Event Propagation")
        self.SetTopWindow(self.frame)
        self.frame.Show()

        self.Bind(wx.EVT_BUTTON, self.OnButtonApp)

        return True

    def OnButtonApp(self, event):
        event_id = event.GetId()
        if event_id == ID_BUTTON1:
            print "BUTTON ONE Event reached the App Object"

class MyFrame(wx.Frame):
    def __init__(self, parent, id=wx.ID_ANY, title="",
                 pos=wx.DefaultPosition, size=wx.DefaultSize,
                 style=wx.DEFAULT_FRAME_STYLE,
                 name="MyFrame"):
        super(MyFrame, self).__init__(parent, id, title,
                                      pos, size, style, name)
```

```
        # Attributes
        self.panel = MyPanel(self)

        self.btn1 = wx.Button(self.panel, ID_BUTTON1,
                              "Propagates")
        self.btn2 = wx.Button(self.panel, ID_BUTTON2,
                              "Doesn't Propagate")

        sizer = wx.BoxSizer(wx.HORIZONTAL)
        sizer.Add(self.btn1, 0, wx.ALL, 10)
        sizer.Add(self.btn2, 0, wx.ALL, 10)
        self.panel.SetSizer(sizer)

        self.Bind(wx.EVT_BUTTON, self.OnButtonFrame)

    def OnButtonFrame(self, event):
        event_id = event.GetId()
        if event_id == ID_BUTTON1:
            print "BUTTON ONE event reached the Frame"
            event.Skip()
        elif event_id == ID_BUTTON2:
            print "BUTTON TWO event reached the Frame"

class MyPanel(wx.Panel):
    def __init__(self, parent):
        super(MyPanel, self).__init__(parent)

        self.Bind(wx.EVT_BUTTON, self.OnPanelButton)

    def OnPanelButton(self, event):
        event_id = event.GetId()
        if event_id == ID_BUTTON1:
            print "BUTTON ONE event reached the Panel"
            event.Skip()
        elif event_id == ID_BUTTON2:
            print "BUTTON TWO event reached the Panel"
            # Not skipping the event will cause its
            # propagation to end here

if __name__ == "__main__":
    app = MyApp(False)
    app.MainLoop()
```

Running this will create an application with two buttons on it. Click each of the buttons to see how the events propagate differently.

How it works...

The chain of event handlers that will be called starts at the object that the event originates from. In this case, it will be one of our two buttons. Each level in the window hierarchy of this application has a general event handler bound to it, that will receive any button events.

Clicking the first button will show that all of the event handlers get called. This is because for the first button we called the event's `Skip` method. Calling `Skip` on an event will tell it to continue propagating to the next level of event handlers in the hierarchy. This will be apparent, as three statements will be printed to the console. On the other hand, clicking the second button will result in only one event handler being called, because `Skip` is not called.

See also

▸ The *Handling events* recipe in this chapter explains how event handlers work.

▸ The *Understanding the window hierarchy* recipe in *Chapter 1, Getting Started with wxPython* describes the window hierarchy that events propagate through.

Handling Key events

`KeyEvents` are events that are associated with keyboard actions. Many controls can accept keyboard events. Each time that a key is pressed on the keyboard, there will be two or three events sent to the control that has the keyboard focus, depending on what key was pressed. This recipe will create a simple text editor window, in order to demonstrate how to use `KeyEvents` to filter text that is added to a `TextCtrl`.

How to do it...

To see some `KeyEvents` in action, let's make a simple window that has a `TextCtrl` on it:

```
class MyFrame(wx.Frame):
    def __init__(self, parent, *args, **kwargs):
        super(MyFrame, self).__init__(parent, *args, **kwargs)

        # Attributes
        self.panel = wx.Panel(self)
        self.txtctrl = wx.TextCtrl(self.panel,
                                   style=wx.TE_MULTILINE)

        # Layout
        sizer = wx.BoxSizer(wx.HORIZONTAL)
        sizer.Add(self.txtctrl, 1, wx.EXPAND)
        self.panel.SetSizer(sizer)
        self.CreateStatusBar() # For output display
```

```
        # Event Handlers
        self.txtctrl.Bind(wx.EVT_KEY_DOWN, self.OnKeyDown)
        self.txtctrl.Bind(wx.EVT_CHAR, self.OnChar)
        self.txtctrl.Bind(wx.EVT_KEY_UP, self.OnKeyUp)

    def OnKeyDown(self, event):
        """KeyDown event is sent first"""
        print "OnKeyDown Called"
        # Get information about the event and log it to
        # the StatusBar for display.
        key_code = event.GetKeyCode()
        raw_code = event.GetRawKeyCode()
        modifiers = event.GetModifiers()
        msg = "key:%d,raw:%d,modifers:%d" % \
              (key_code, raw_code, modifiers)
        self.PushStatusText("KeyDown: " + msg)

        # Must Skip the event to allow OnChar to be called
        event.Skip()

    def OnChar(self, event):
        """The Char event comes second and is
        where the character associated with the
        key is put into the control.
        """
        print "OnChar Called"
        modifiers = event.GetModifiers()
        key_code = event.GetKeyCode()
        # Beep at the user if the Shift key is down
        # and disallow input.
        if modifiers & wx.MOD_SHIFT:
            wx.Bell()
        elif chr(key_code) in "aeiou":
            # When a vowel is pressed append a
            # question mark to the end.
            self.txtctrl.AppendText("?")
        else:
            # Let the text go in to the buffer
            event.Skip()

    def OnKeyUp(self, event):
        """KeyUp comes last"""
        print "OnKeyUp Called"
        event.Skip()
```

When typing in this window, it will not allow text to be entered when the *Shift* key is pressed and it will turn all vowels into question marks.

How it works...

The `KeyEvents` are sent by the system in the following order:

- ▶ `EVT_KEY_DOWN`
- ▶ `EVT_CHAR` (only for keys that have a character associated with them)
- ▶ `EVT_KEY_UP`

It's important to notice that we called `Bind` on our `TextCtrl` and not the `Frame`. This is necessary because the `KeyEvents` will only be sent to the control that has the keyboard focus, which in this window will be `TextCtrl`.

Each `KeyEvent` has a number of attributes attached to it in order to specify what key was pressed and what other modifier keys were held down during the event, such as the *Shift*, *Alt*, and *Ctrl* keys.

Calling `Skip` on the event allows the control to process it and for the next handler in the chain to be called. For example, not skipping the event in the `EVT_KEY_DOWN` handler will block the `EVT_CHAR` and `EVT_KEY_UP` handlers from being called.

In this sample, when a key on the keyboard is pressed, our `OnKeyDown` handler will be called first. All we do there is `print` a message to `stdout` and display some information about the event in the `StatusBar`, before calling `Skip`. Then, in our `OnChar` handler, we do some simple filtering of uppercase letters by checking to see if the *Shift* key is in the event's modifiers mask. If it is, we beep at the user and don't call `Skip` on the event, in order to prevent the character from appearing in the `TextCtrl`. Also, as an example of modifying what the event does, we perform a check for vowels by converting the raw key code into a character string and if the key was for a vowel, we simply insert a question mark into the `TextCtrl` instead. Finally, if the event was skipped in the `OnChar` handler, our `OnKeyUp` handler will be called, where we simply print a message to `stdout` to show it was called.

There's more...

Some controls require the `wx.WANTS_CHARS` style flag to be specified in their constructor in order to receive character events. The `Panel` class is the most common example that requires this special style flag in order to receive `EVT_CHAR` events. Often, this is used to perform special processing when creating a new custom control type that is derived from a `Panel`.

See also

- ▶ The *Validating input with validators* recipe in this chapter uses `KeyEvents` to perform input validation.

Using UpdateUI events

`UpdateUIEvents` are events that are sent by the framework on a regular basis in order to allow an application to update the state of its controls. These are useful for performing tasks such as changing when a control is enabled or disabled, based on the application's business logic. This recipe will show how to use `UpdateUIEvents` to update the state of menu items, depending on the current context of the UI.

How to do it...

In this example, we create a simple window with an `Edit` Menu and a `TextCtrl`. The `Edit` Menu has three items in it that will be enabled or disabled based on the current selection status in the `TextCtrl` by using `UpdateUIEvents`.

```python
class TextFrame(wx.Frame):
    def __init__(self, parent, *args, **kwargs):
        super(TextFrame, self).__init__(parent,
                                        *args,
                                        **kwargs)

        # Attributes
        self.panel = wx.Panel(self)
        self.txtctrl = wx.TextCtrl(self.panel,
                                   value="Hello World",
                                   style=wx.TE_MULTILINE)

        # Layout
        sizer = wx.BoxSizer(wx.HORIZONTAL)
        sizer.Add(self.txtctrl, 1, wx.EXPAND)
        self.panel.SetSizer(sizer)
        self.CreateStatusBar() # For output display

        # Menu
        menub = wx.MenuBar()
        editm = wx.Menu()
        editm.Append(wx.ID_COPY, "Copy\tCtrl+C")
        editm.Append(wx.ID_CUT, "Cut\tCtrl+X")
        editm.Append(ID_CHECK_ITEM, "Selection Made?",
                     kind=wx.ITEM_CHECK)
        menub.Append(editm, "Edit")
        self.SetMenuBar(menub)
```

```
# Event Handlers
self.Bind(wx.EVT_UPDATE_UI, self.OnUpdateEditMenu)

def OnUpdateEditMenu(self, event):
    event_id = event.GetId()
    sel = self.txtctrl.GetSelection()
    has_sel = sel[0] != sel[1]
    if event_id in (wx.ID_COPY, wx.ID_CUT):
        event.Enable(has_sel)
    elif event_id == ID_CHECK_ITEM:
        event.Check(has_sel)
    else:
        event.Skip()
```

How it works...

UpdateUIEvents are sent periodically by the framework during idle time to allow the application to check if the state of a control needs to be updated. Our TextFrame class has three menu items in its Edit Menu that will be managed by our OnUpdateUI event handler. In OnUpdateUI, we check the event's ID to see which object the event is being sent for, and then call the appropriate UpdateUIEvent method on the event to change the state of the control. The states of each of our menu items are dependent upon whether there is a selection in the TextCtrl or not. Calling the GetSelection method of TextCtrl will return a tuple with the start and end positions of the selection. When the two positions differ, there is a selection in the control and we will Enable the Copy and Cut items, or in the case of our Selection Made item we will set the check mark. If there is no selection, then the items will become disabled or un-checked.

It's important to call the method on the event object to update the control and not the method on the control itself, as it will allow for it to be updated far more efficiently. See the wxPython API documentation for UpdateUIEvent to see the full listing of what methods are available.

There's more...

There are some static methods available in the UpdateUIEvent class that allow applications to change the behavior of how the events are delivered. Most notable are the following two methods:

1. wx.UpdateUIEvent.SetUpdateInterval
2. wx.UpdateUIEvent.SetMode

SetUpdateInterval can be used to configure how often the UpdateUIEvents are sent. It takes a number of milliseconds as an argument. This is useful if you find that there is a noticeable amount of overhead in handling UpdateUIEvents in your application. You can use this to slow down the rate at which these events are sent.

`SetMode` can be used configure the behavior of what windows will receive the events, by setting one of the following modes:

Mode	Description
`wx.UPDATE_UI_PROCESS_ALL`	Process `UpdateUI` events for all windows
`wx.UPDATE_UI_PROCESS_SPECIFIED`	Only process `UpdateUI` events for the windows that have the `WS_EX_PROCESS_UI_UPDATES` extra style flag set.

See also

> ▶ The *Managing event handlers with EventStack* recipe in this chapter shows a way to manage `UpdateUI` events in a centralized way.

Playing with the mouse

`MouseEvents` can be used to interact with the mouse-position changes and mouse-button clicks that a user makes within a window. This recipe will provide a quick crash course on some of the common mouse events that are available for use in a program.

How to do it...

Here as an example, we will create a simple Frame class that has a `Panel` and a Button to see how to interact with `MouseEvents`.

```
class MouseFrame(wx.Frame):
    def __init__(self, parent, *args, **kwargs):
        super(MouseFrame, self).__init__(parent,
                                         *args,
                                         **kwargs)

        # Attributes
        self.panel = wx.Panel(self)
        self.btn = wx.Button(self.panel)

        # Event Handlers
        self.panel.Bind(wx.EVT_ENTER_WINDOW, self.OnEnter)
        self.panel.Bind(wx.EVT_LEAVE_WINDOW, self.OnLeave)
        self.panel.Bind(wx.EVT_LEFT_UP, self.OnLeftUp)
        self.panel.Bind(wx.EVT_LEFT_DOWN, self.OnLeftDown)

    def OnEnter(self, event):
        """Called when the mouse enters the panel"""
        self.btn.SetForegroundColour(wx.BLACK)
```

```
        self.btn.SetLabel("EVT_ENTER_WINDOW")
        self.btn.SetInitialSize()

    def OnLeave(self, event):
        """Called when the mouse leaves the panel"""
        self.btn.SetLabel("EVT_LEAVE_WINDOW")
        self.btn.SetForegroundColour(wx.RED)

    def OnLeftDown(self, event):
        """Called for left down clicks on the Panel"""
        self.btn.SetLabel("EVT_LEFT_DOWN")

    def OnLeftUp(self, event):
        """Called for left clicks on the Panel"""
        position = event.GetPosition()
        self.btn.SetLabel("EVT_LEFT_UP")
        # Move the button
        self.btn.SetPosition(position - (25, 25))
```

How it works...

In this recipe, we made use of the events for when the mouse cursor enters the `Panel` and for when the left mouse button is clicked on the `Panel`, to modify our `Button`. When the mouse cursor enters a window's area, an `EVT_ENTER_WINDOW` event will be sent to it; conversely, it will receive an `EVT_LEAVE_WINDOW` event when the cursor leaves the window. When the mouse enters or leaves the Panel's area, we update the Button's label to show what happened. When our `Panel` receives a left click event, we move the `Button` to where the click took place.

The important thing to notice is that we called `Bind` on the `Panel` directly and not on the `Frame`. This is important because `MouseEvents` are not `CommandEvents` so they will only be sent to the window they originated from, and will not propagate up the containment hierarchy.

There's more...

There are a large number of `MouseEvents` that can be used to interact with other mouse actions. The following table contains a quick reference to each of them:

MouseEvents	Description
wx.EVT_MOUSEWHEEL	Sent for mouse wheel scroll events. See the `GetWheelRotation` and `GetWheelDelta` methods that belong to the `MouseEvent` class for working with this event.
wx.EVT_LEFT_DCLICK	Sent for left mouse button double-clicks.
wx.EVT_RIGHT_DOWN	Sent when the right mouse button is pressed down.

MouseEvents	Description
wx.EVT_RIGHT_UP	Sent when the right mouse button is released.
wx.EVT_RIGHT_DCLICK	Sent for right mouse button double-clicks.
wx.EVT_MIDDLE_DOWN	Sent when the middle mouse button is pressed down.
wx.EVT_MIDDLE_UP	Sent when the middle mouse button is released.
wx.EVT_MIDDLE_DCLICK	Sent for middle mouse button double-clicks.
wx.EVT_MOTION	Sent every time the mouse cursor moves within the window.
wx.EVT_MOUSE_EVENTS	This event binder can be used to get notifications for all mouse related events.

See also

▸ The *Understanding event propagation* recipe in this chapter discusses how different types of events propagate.

Creating custom event classes

Sometimes it is necessary to define your own event types to signal custom actions and/or transport data from one place in the application to another. This recipe will show two ways of creating your own custom event class.

How to do it...

In this little snippet, we define two new event types using two different methods:

```
import wx
import wx.lib.newevent

# Our first custom event
MyEvent, EVT_MY_EVENT = wx.lib.newevent.NewCommandEvent()

# Our second custom event
myEVT_TIME_EVENT = wx.NewEventType()
EVT_MY_TIME_EVENT = wx.PyEventBinder(myEVT_TIME_EVENT, 1)
class MyTimeEvent(wx.PyCommandEvent):
    def __init__(self, id=0, time="12:00:00"):
        evttype = myEVT_TIME_EVENT
        super(MyTimeEvent, self).__init__(evttype, id)

        # Attributes
        self.time = time

    def GetTime(self):
        return self.time
```

How it works...

The first example shows the easiest way to create a custom event class. The `NewCommandEvent` function from the wx.lib.newevent module will return a tuple that contains a new event class and an event binder for that class. The class definition that is returned can be used to construct an event object. This method of creating a new event type is of most use when you just want a new event type and don't need to send any custom data with the event.

In order to make use of an event object, the object needs to be sent for processing by the event loop. There are two ways to do this, one of which is the `PostEvent` function. `PostEvent` takes two arguments: the first is the window that should receive the event, and the second is the event itself. For example, the following two lines of code could be used to create and send an instance of our custom `MyEvent` to a `Frame`:

```
event = MyEvent(eventID)
wx.PostEvent(myFrame, event)
```

The second way to send an event for processing is to use a window's `ProcessEvent` method:

```
event = MyEvent(eventID)
myFrame.GetEventHandler().ProcessEvent(event)
```

The difference between the two is that `PostEvent` will put the event into the application's event queue to have it processed on the next iteration of the `MainLoop`, whereas `ProcessEvent` will cause the event to be processed right then.

The second approach shows how to derive a new event type from the `PyCommandEvent` base class. In order to create an event in this way, there are three things that need to be done.

1. Define a new event type using the `NewEventType` function.
2. Create the event binder object for binding event handlers with the `PyEventBinder` class. This object takes the event type as its first argument.
3. Define the event class that is used for creating the event object.

This `MyTimeEvent` class can hold a custom value that we are using to send a formatted time string. It is necessary to derive this from `PyCommandEvent` so that the custom Python data and methods that we are attaching to this object will pass through the event system.

These events can now be sent to any event handler object, by using the `PostEvent` function or the windows `ProcessEvent` method. Either of these methods will cause the event to be dispatched to the event handler(s) that has been associated with the event by calling `Bind`.

See also

▸ The *Understanding inheritance limitations* recipe in *Chapter 1, Getting Started with wxPython* explains the need for the Py versions of some classes.

▸ The *Handling events* recipe in this chapter discusses the use of event handlers.

Managing event handlers with EventStack

EventStack is a module in wx.lib that provides a mix in class for the wx application object that can be used to help manage event handlers for Menu and UpdateUI events. It can be useful in programs that have multiple top-level windows or that need to switch the context of which handlers are called depending on the control that has the focus. This recipe will present a simple framework for managing events in Frame-based applications that make use of the AppEventHandlerMixin class. A full working example, showing how to use this recipe's classes, is included in the example code that accompanies this recipe.

How to do it...

With this code, we define two classes that work together. First we define an App base class that uses the AppEventHandlerMixin.

```python
import wx
import wx.lib.eventStack as eventStack

class EventMgrApp(wx.App, eventStack.AppEventHandlerMixin):
    """Application object base class that
    event handler managment.
    """
    def __init__(self, *args, **kwargs):
        eventStack.AppEventHandlerMixin.__init__(self)
        wx.App.__init__(self, *args, **kwargs)

class EventMgrFrame(wx.Frame):
    """Frame base class that provides event
    handler managment.
    """
    def __init__(self, parent, *args, **kwargs):
        super(EventMgrFrame, self).__init__(parent,
                                            *args,
                                            **kwargs)

        # Attributes
        self._menu_handlers = []
        self._ui_handlers = []
```

```
        # Event Handlers
        self.Bind(wx.EVT_ACTIVATE, self._OnActivate)

    def _OnActivate(self, event):
        """Pushes/Pops event handlers"""
        app = wx.GetApp()
        active = event.GetActive()
        if active:

            mode = wx.UPDATE_UI_PROCESS_SPECIFIED
            wx.UpdateUIEvent.SetMode(mode)
            self.SetExtraStyle(wx.WS_EX_PROCESS_UI_UPDATES)

            # Push this instances handlers
            for handler in self._menu_handlers:
                app.AddHandlerForID(*handler)

            for handler in self._ui_handlers:
                app.AddUIHandlerForID(*handler)
        else:
            self.SetExtraStyle(0)
            wx.UpdateUIEvent.SetMode(wx.UPDATE_UI_PROCESS_ALL)
            # Pop this instances handlers
            for handler in self._menu_handlers:
                app.RemoveHandlerForID(handler[0])

            for handler in self._ui_handlers:
                app.RemoveUIHandlerForID(handler[0])

    def RegisterMenuHandler(self, event_id, handler):
        """Register a MenuEventHandler
        @param event_id: MenuItem ID
        @param handler: Event handler function
        """
        self._menu_handlers.append((event_id, handler))

    def RegisterUpdateUIHandler(self, event_id, handler):
        """Register a controls UpdateUI handler
        @param event_id: Control ID
        @param handler: Event handler function
        """
        self._ui_handlers.append((event_id, handler))
```

How it works...

The `EventMgrApp` class is just a base class for creating an application object that uses `AppEventHandlerMixin`. This `mixin` provides methods for adding and removing event handlers for the `MenuEvent` and `UpdateUIEvent` handlers.

The `EventMgrFrame` class is a base class for frames to derive from. This class will handle adding, removing, and binding event handlers that are registered using either its `RegisterMenuHandler` or `RegisterUpdateUIHandler` methods. These methods take care of adding the event handlers to the stack that will be pushed or popped as the `Frame` is activated or deactivated. The `AppEventHandlerMixin` will internally manage Binding and Unbinding of these handlers.

See also

▶   The *Using UpdateUI events* recipe in this chapter discusses `UpdateUI` events in detail.

Validating input with validators

`Validators` are a general type of helper class for validating data and filtering events that are input to a control. Most controls that accept user input can dynamically have a `Validator` associated with them. This recipe will show how to create a `Validator` that checks if the data that has been entered into a window is an integer that is within a given range of values.

How to do it...

Here we will define a Validator for a `TextCtrl` that can be used to validate that the value input is an integer and between a given range.

```
import wx
import sys

class IntRangeValidator(wx.PyValidator):
    """An integer range validator for a TextCtrl"""
    def __init__(self, min_=0, max_=sys.maxint):
        """Initialize the validator
        @keyword min: min value to accept
        @keyword max: max value to accept

        """
        super(IntRangeValidator, self).__init__()
        assert min_ >= 0, "Minimum Value must be >= 0"
        self._min = min_
        self._max = max_
```

```
            # Event managment
            self.Bind(wx.EVT_CHAR, self.OnChar)

    def Clone(self):
        """Required override"""
        return IntRangeValidator(self._min, self._max)

    def Validate(self, win):
        """Override called to validate the window's value.
        @return: bool
        """
        txtCtrl = self.GetWindow()
        val = txtCtrl.GetValue()
        isValid = False
        if val.isdigit():
            digit = int(val)
            if digit >= self._min and digit <= self._max:
                isValid = True

        if not isValid:
            # Notify the user of the invalid value
            msg = "Value must be between %d and %d" % \
                    (self._min, self._max)
            wx.MessageBox(msg,
                          "Invalid Value",
                          style=wx.OK|wx.ICON_ERROR)

        return isValid

    def OnChar(self, event):
        txtCtrl = self.GetWindow()
        key = event.GetKeyCode()
        isDigit = False
        if key < 256:
            isDigit = chr(key).isdigit()

        if key in (wx.WXK_RETURN,
                   wx.WXK_DELETE,
                   wx.WXK_BACK) or \
           key > 255 or isDigit:
            if isDigit:
                # Check if in range
                val = txtCtrl.GetValue()
                digit = chr(key)
```

```
                        pos = txtCtrl.GetInsertionPoint()
                        if pos == len(val):
                            val += digit
                        else:
                            val = val[:pos] + digit + val[pos:]

                        val = int(val)
                        if val < self._min or val > self._max:
                            if not wx.Validator_IsSilent():
                                wx.Bell()
                            return

                    event.Skip()
                    return

                if not wx.Validator_IsSilent():
                    # Beep to warn about invalid input
                    wx.Bell()

                return

    def TransferToWindow(self):
        """Overridden to skip data transfer"""
        return True

    def TransferFromWindow(self):
        """Overridden to skip data transfer"""
        return True
```

How it works...

`Validator` classes have a number of virtual methods that need to be overridden in order for them to function properly. Hence, it is important to derive a subclass from the `PyValidator` class, instead of `Validator`, in order to get access to the virtual method aware version of the class.

All `Validator` subclasses must override the `Clone` method. This method simply needs to return a copy of the `Validator`.

The `Validate` method is called to check if the value is valid or not. This method will be called if the control is the child of a modal dialog, prior to calling `EndModal` for an `Ok` button. This is a good time to notify the user of any issues with the input.

`Validator`s can also bind to any events that their window may bind to and can be used to filter the events. The events will be sent to the `OnChar` method of the `Validator` before they are sent to the window, allowing the `Validator` to filter which events are allowed to get to the control.

The `TransferToWindow` and `TransferFromWindow` methods can be overridden if you wish to only do the validation in a `Dialog` at the time when the `Dialog` is being shown or closed. `TransferToWindow` will be called when a `Dialog` is shown, and `TransferFromWIndow` will be called when the `Dialog` is closed. Returning `True` from either of the methods indicates that the data is valid, and returning `False` will indicate that there is invalid data.

See also

▸ The *Understanding inheritance limitations* recipe in *Chapter 1, Getting Started with wxPython* discusses the use of the Py versions of classes and overriding virtual methods.

▸ The *Handling Key events* recipe in this chapter discusses `KeyEvents` in detail.

Handling Apple events

AppleEvents are high-level system events used by the Macintosh operating system to pass information between processes. For an application to handle things such as opening files that are dropped on the application icon, it is necessary to handle these events. The wxPython application object has some built-in support for some of the most common events, by way of virtual overrides in the application object. This recipe will show how to create an application object that can make use of the built-in and somewhat hidden-event callback functions.

 This is an OS X specific recipe, and will have will have no effect on other platforms.

How to do it...

This little sample application shows all of the built-in callback methods available in the `App` for handling some of the commonly needed `AppleEvents`.

```
import wx

class MyApp(wx.App):
    def OnInit(self):
        self.frame = MyFrame(None, title="AppleEvents")
        self.SetTopWindow(self.frame)
        self.frame.Show()
        return True
```

```
def MacNewFile(self):
    """Called for an open-application event"""
    self.frame.PushStatusText("MacNewFile Called")

def MacOpenFile(self, filename):
    """Called for an open-document event"""
    self.frame.PushStatusText("MacOpenFile: %s" % \
                                    filename)

def MacOpenURL(self, url):
    """Called for a get-url event"""
    self.frame.PushStatusText("MacOpenURL: %s" % url)

def MacPrintFile(self, filename):
    """Called for a print-document event"""
    self.frame.PushStatusText("MacPrintFile: %s" % \
                                    filename)

def MacReopenApp(self):
    """Called for a reopen-application event"""
    self.frame.PushStatusText("MacReopenApp")
    # Raise the application from the Dock
    if self.frame.IsIconized():
        self.frame.Iconize(False)
    self.frame.Raise()
```

How it works...

There are five built-in handler methods for some of the common `AppleEvents`. All that needs to be done to use them in your application is to override them in your application object, as previously shown. Since what an application does in response to these events is highly application-specific, this recipe does not do much, other than report to the frame's status bar when the method is called.

The two most-common events that should be implemented are the `MacOpenFile` and `MacReopenApp` methods, as these are necessary to get standard expected behavior in an application on OS X. `MacOpenFile` is called when a user drops a file on an application's Dock icon. When this happens, it will be passed the path of the file as an argument. `MacReopenApp` is called when a user left-clicks on the Dock icon of a running application. As shown in the recipe, this is used to bring an application to the front and/or raise it from a minimized state in the Dock.

There's more...

It is possible to add support for more `AppleEvents` to a wxPython application, although it is not a particularly easy task as it requires writing a native extension module to catch the event, block the wx `EventLoop`, and then restore the Python interpreter's state back to wx after handling the event. There is a pretty good example that can be used as a starting point in the wxPython Wiki (see `http://wiki.wxpython.org/Catching%20AppleEvents%20 in%20wxMAC`), if you find yourself needing to venture down this route.

See also

▶ The *Understanding inheritance limitations* recipe in *Chapter 1, Getting Started with wxPython* includes more information on overriding virtual methods.

▶ The *Optimizing for OS X* recipe in *Chapter 12, Application Infrastructure* includes more information on making wxPython applications work well on OS X.

3
Basic Building Blocks of a User Interface

In this chapter, we will cover:

- ▸ Creating Stock Buttons
- ▸ Buttons, buttons, and more buttons
- ▸ Offering options with CheckBoxes
- ▸ Using the TextCtrl
- ▸ Providing choices with the Choice control
- ▸ Adding Menus and MenuBars
- ▸ Working with ToolBars
- ▸ How to use PopupMenus
- ▸ Grouping controls with a StaticBox

Introduction

Even the most complex objects are typically created from many smaller, simpler objects or parts. The task of the application developer is to utilize these smaller parts and link them together in a way that is meaningful, in order to achieve the desired function of the application. In order to be able to build the application, it is necessary to know what parts are available to you.

wxPython provides a large collection of classes and utilities. In fact, the basic collection is so rich that it is very much possible to construct a fully-functional application without inventing any of your own parts. So lets jump in and take a look at some of the most common and basic parts that can be found in nearly any desktop application.

Creating Stock Buttons

Nearly all applications have buttons in them and among the buttons there are many common ones such as Ok and Cancel that appear over and over again. In wxPython, these common buttons are known as Stock Buttons, because they are constructed by passing a Stock ID to the constructor of a `Button`.

How to do it...

Let's make a simple `Panel` that has four `Button`s on it, to see how Stock Buttons can be created:

```python
class MyPanel(wx.Panel):
    def __init__(self, parent):
        super(MyPanel, self).__init__(parent)

        # Make some buttons
        sizer = wx.BoxSizer(wx.HORIZONTAL)
        for bid in (wx.ID_OK, wx.ID_CANCEL,
                    wx.ID_APPLY, wx.ID_HELP):
            button = wx.Button(self, bid)
            sizer.Add(button, 0, wx.ALL, 5)
        self.SetSizer(sizer)
```

How it works...

Common buttons are created by using a standard `Button` with a Stock ID and no label. The framework will then create the correct type of button with the proper label for the current platform. Each platform has slightly different standards for these common buttons. By using Stock Buttons, these cross-platform differences can be handled by the framework. For example, take a look at the following two screenshots of the previous sample code being run on Windows 7 and OS X respectively.

Screenshot of Windows 7:

Screenshot of OS X:

Platform Notice: On Linux, depending upon the version of GTK, Stock Buttons will also have the proper theme provided icon displayed on them as well.

There's more...

Stock buttons can be created from nearly all of the Stock IDs. If your text editor does not provide completion hints, here is a quick way to see all of the available Stock IDs: Just run the following code in your Python interpreter to introspect the wx namespace for all of the ID constants.

```
import wx
for x in dir(wx):
    if x.startswith('ID_'):
        print x
```

See also

▸ The *Utilizing Stock IDs* recipe in *Chapter 1, Getting Started with wxPython* contains a detailed discussion about the IDs used to construct Stock Buttons.

▸ The *Buttons, buttons, and more buttons* recipe in this chapter shows how to use the other button classes available in wxPython.

▸ The *Standard dialog button layout* recipe in Chapter 7, *Window Layout and Design* shows how Stock Buttons are used to achieve easy control layout in dialogs.

Buttons, buttons, and more buttons

The regular Button class only allows for displaying a label on the button. If this is a little too plain for the needs of your application, you're in luck. wxPython also provides a wide variety of other types of buttons that provide a different look and feel, as well as extended functionality. This recipe will introduce a number of the other button controls that are available in wxPython.

 Version Notice: The agw package and GradientButton class used in the following code are only available in wxPython 2.8.9.2 and later.

How to do it...

To see what these different `Buttons` look like and what they can do, we will make a simple `Panel` with some different examples of these additional button classes:

```python
import wx
import wx.lib.platebtn as pbtn
import wx.lib.agw.gradientbutton as gbtn

class ButtonTestPanel(wx.Panel):
    def __init__(self, parent):
        super(ButtonTestPanel, self).__init__(parent)

        # Attributes
        # Make a ToggleButton
        self.toggle = wx.ToggleButton(self,
                                      label="Toggle Button")

        # Make a BitmapButton
        bmp = wx.Bitmap("./face-monkey.png",
                        wx.BITMAP_TYPE_PNG)
        self.bmpbtn = wx.BitmapButton(self, bitmap=bmp)

        # Make a few PlateButton variants
        self.pbtn1 = pbtn.PlateButton(self,
                                      label="PlateButton")
        self.pbtn2 = pbtn.PlateButton(self,
                                      label="PlateBmp",
                                      bmp=bmp)
        style = pbtn.PB_STYLE_SQUARE
        self.pbtn3 = pbtn.PlateButton(self,
                                      label="Square Plate",
                                      bmp=bmp,
                                      style=style)
        self.pbtn4 = pbtn.PlateButton(self,
                                      label="PlateMenu")
        menu = wx.Menu()
        menu.Append(wx.NewId(), text="Hello World")
        self.pbtn4.SetMenu(menu)

        # Gradient Buttons
        self.gbtn1 = gbtn.GradientButton(self,
                                         label="GradientBtn")
```

```
self.gbtn2 = gbtn.GradientButton(self,
                                 label="GradientBmp",
                                 bitmap=bmp)

# Layout
vsizer = wx.BoxSizer(wx.VERTICAL)
vsizer.Add(self.toggle, 0, wx.ALL, 12)
vsizer.Add(self.bmpbtn, 0, wx.ALL, 12)
hsizer1 = wx.BoxSizer(wx.HORIZONTAL)
hsizer1.AddMany(([(self.pbtn1, 0, wx.ALL, 5),
                  (self.pbtn2, 0, wx.ALL, 5),
                  (self.pbtn3, 0, wx.ALL, 5),
                  (self.pbtn4, 0, wx.ALL, 5)]))
vsizer.Add(hsizer1, 0, wx.ALL, 12)
hsizer2 = wx.BoxSizer(wx.HORIZONTAL)
hsizer2.AddMany(([(self.gbtn1, 0, wx.ALL, 5),
                  (self.gbtn2, 0, wx.ALL, 5)]))
vsizer.Add(hsizer2, 0, wx.ALL, 12)
self.SetSizer(vsizer)
```

This code generates the following window:

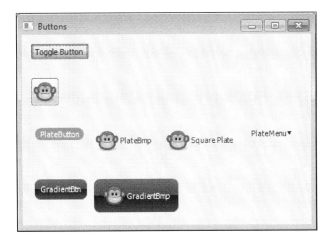

How it works...

This recipe shows the basic use of four different button classes, so let's take a look at each of them one by one to see what they can do.

ToggleButton

The `ToggleButton` is another native button provided by wxPython. It is just like the standard `Button`, but provides two states. The button will be toggled from its regular state to a pressed state when clicked on. A second click will toggle it back to its regular state once again.

BitmapButton

The `BitmapButton` is a native platform button used for showing an image instead of label text. The usage of this button is just like the standard `Button` except that it takes a `Bitmap` as an argument instead of a label string. The `Bitmap` for each state of when the button is being pressed or interacted with by the mouse can also be customized with the following methods:

Method	Description
`SetBitmapDisabled`	Sets the Bitmap to show when the button is disabled.
`SetBitmapFocus`	Sets the Bitmap to show when the button has the keyboard focus.
`SetBitmapHover`	Sets the Bitmap to show when the mouse cursor is hovering over the button.
`SetBitmapLabel`	Sets the default button (same as what is provided to the constructor). In the absence of other bitmaps, this one will be used for all states.
`SetBitmapSelected`	Sets the Bitmap to use when the button is pressed.

PlateButton

The `PlateButton` is an owner-drawn button class provided by the `platebtn` module in `wx.lib`. `PlateButtons` are a type of flat button control that will change its background colour when the mouse hovers over it or when it is clicked on. A `PlateButton` can be displayed with just a label, with just a `Bitmap`, with both a label and a `Bitmap`, or any of the previous combinations plus as a drop-down `Menu`.

The look and feel of the button can also be customized to control the color of the highlighting, the text label color, the button shape, and how the highlight is drawn. The `PB_STYLE_SQUARE` style flag will make the button take up a square shape instead of using its default rounded edges and the `PB_STYLE_GRADIENT` style flag will cause the background to be drawn as a gradient based on the highlighting colour. In addition to this customizability, the `PlateButton` also fully implements the `BitmapButton` API so it can be used as a drop-in replacement for a `BitmapButton` in existing applications.

GradientButton

The `GradientButton` is very similar to the `PlateButton`. The only difference is that it is not a flat button, it doesn't support a drop-down menu, and it is more flexible in what it allows for configuring the gradient colors.

There are still quite a few more button implementations out there that you may find useful in your application.

GenericButtons

GenericButtons are a collection of classes in wx.lib.buttons that provide some basic owner-drawn buttons as well as owner-drawn implementations of the native buttons that maintain the look of the native buttons but work around some limitations. For example, there is GenBitmapTextButton which provides a bitmap button that also supports displaying a label, and GenBitmapToggleButton which allows for a toggle button that shows a Bitmap.

AquaButton

AquaButtons are an owner-drawn button class with a glassy appearance that approximates the look and feel of native Macintosh Aqua Buttons. Because the class is owner drawn, it will provide the same look and feel on all platforms. This class can be found in wx.lib.agw.aquabutton.

> ▶ The *Creating Stock Buttons* recipe in this chapter shows how to create standard buttons.

Offering options with CheckBoxes

A CheckBox is a common, basic control that allows for a user to select one of two or three states, depending on the style of CheckBox, though it is typically associated with just a True or False state. In this recipe, we will take a look at how to use the CheckBox control.

To see how CheckBoxes work, we will create a little window with two different kinds of CheckBoxes in it:

```
class CheckBoxFrame(wx.Frame):
    def __init__(self, *args, **kwargs):
        super(CheckBoxFrame, self).__init__(*args, **kwargs)

        # Attributes
        self.panel = wx.Panel(self)
        self.checkbox1 = wx.CheckBox(self.panel,
                                     label="2 State CheckBox")
```

```
        style = wx.CHK_3STATE|wx.CHK_ALLOW_3RD_STATE_FOR_USER
        self.checkbox2 = wx.CheckBox(self.panel,
                                     label="3 State CheckBox",
                                     style=style)

        # Layout
        sizer = wx.BoxSizer(wx.VERTICAL)
        sizer.Add(self.checkbox1, 0, wx.ALL, 15)
        sizer.Add(self.checkbox2, 0, wx.ALL, 15)
        self.panel.SetSizer(sizer)
        self.CreateStatusBar()

        # Event Handlers
        self.Bind(wx.EVT_CHECKBOX, self.OnCheck)

    def OnCheck(self, event):
        e_obj = event.GetEventObject()
        if e_obj == self.checkbox1:
            checked = self.checkbox1.GetValue()
            msg = "Two State Clicked: %s" % checked
            self.PushStatusText(msg)
        elif e_obj == self.checkbox2:
            state = self.checkbox2.Get3StateValue()
            msg = "Three State Clicked: %d" % state
            self.PushStatusText(msg)
        else:
            event.Skip()
```

How it works...

We created two CheckBoxes; the first is the standard two-state CheckBox and the second is a three-state CheckBox. The state of a two state CheckBox can be programmatically controlled through its GetValue and SetValue methods.

The three-state checkbox is created by specifying the two style flags CHK_3STATE and CHK_ALLOW_3RD_STATE_FOR_USER. The second style flag can be omitted if you want to limit users from being able to set the undetermined state, so that it can only be done programmatically. Three-state checkboxes use the Get3StateValue and Set3StateValue methods with the following values to programmatically control the CheckBox state:

► wx.CHK_CHECKED

► wx.CHK_UNCHECKED

► wx.CHK_UNDETERMINED

> ▶ The *Using a BoxSizer* recipe in *Chapter 7, Window Layout and Design* shows how to use the `BoxSizer` class to control layout.

Using the TextCtrl

The `TextCtrl` is the basic means of allowing users to input textual data into an application. This control has many possible uses and modes of operation. This recipe will show how to create a simple login dialog that uses two `TextCtrls` to provide input fields for the login name and password.

How to do it...

First, lets create the `Dialog` class that will hold the other controls:

```
class LoginDialog(wx.Dialog):
    def __init__(self, *args, **kwargs):
        super(LoginDialog, self).__init__(*args, **kwargs)

        # Attributes
        self.panel = LoginPanel(self)

        # Layout
        sizer = wx.BoxSizer(wx.VERTICAL)
        sizer.Add(self.panel, 1, wx.EXPAND)
        self.SetSizer(sizer)
        self.SetInitialSize()

    def GetUsername(self):
        return self.panel.GetUsername()

    def GetPassword(self):
        return self.panel.GetPassword()
```

Next let's make the `Panel` that will hold the `TextCtlr` controls for the users to enter their login information into:

```
class LoginPanel(wx.Panel):
    def __init__(self, parent):
        super(LoginPanel, self).__init__(parent)

        # Attributes
```

```
self._username = wx.TextCtrl(self)
self._passwd = wx.TextCtrl(self, style=wx.TE_PASSWORD)

# Layout
sizer = wx.FlexGridSizer(2, 2, 8, 8)
sizer.Add(wx.StaticText(self, label="Username:"),
          0, wx.ALIGN_CENTER_VERTICAL)
sizer.Add(self._username, 0, wx.EXPAND)
sizer.Add(wx.StaticText(self, label="Password:"),
          0, wx.ALIGN_CENTER_VERTICAL)
sizer.Add(self._passwd, 0, wx.EXPAND)
msizer = wx.BoxSizer(wx.VERTICAL)
msizer.Add(sizer, 1, wx.EXPAND|wx.ALL, 20)
btnszr = wx.StdDialogButtonSizer()
button = wx.Button(self, wx.ID_OK)
button.SetDefault()
btnszr.AddButton(button)
msizer.Add(btnszr, 0, wx.ALIGN_CENTER|wx.ALL, 12)
btnszr.Realize()

self.SetSizer(msizer)

def GetUsername(self):
    return self._username.GetValue()

def GetPassword(self):
    return self._passwd.GetValue()
```

How it works...

We did a number of things in the previous code, but since the focus of this recipe is on the TextCtrl object, let's start by taking a look at the two TextCtrl object that we created.

The first text control for the username is just a default `TextCtrl` created with all of the default arguments. By default, a `TextCtrl` object is created as a single line control. This creates just a simple text box that the user can type any arbitrary number of characters into.

The second text control uses the special `TE_PASSWORD` style flag. This creates a `TextCtrl` that will disguise its input with asterisk characters, just like you see in any password entry field in most applications or websites. As a user types in this control, each character that is typed in will be displayed as an asterisk, but the actual character values are stored internally by the control and can be accessed via `GetValue`.

This dialog should be shown with `ShowModal`, and when `ShowModal` returns you can just retrieve the values by using the accessor methods `GetUsername` and `GetPassword` in order to perform the login validation.

There's more...

The `TextCtrl` class has a fairly large collection of style flags that can be supplied to its constructor to modify its behavior for different use cases. Included below is a list of most-commonly-used style flags and a description of what each one does. The rest can be found in wxPython's online API documentation (`http://wxpython.org/docs/api/`).

Style flags	Description
`wx.TE_PROCESS_ENTER`	Will cause the control to generate a `wx.EVT_COMMAND_TEXT_ENTER` event when the *Enter* key is pressed.
`wx.TE_PROCESS_TAB`	Allows a `wx.EVT_CHAR` event to be issued when the *Tab* key is pressed. Without this style set, the *Tab* key will allow the user to tab into the next control in the window.
`wx.TE_MULTILINE`	Allows the `TextCtrl` to have multiple lines.
`wx.TE_READONLY`	Makes the control read only, so that the user cannot enter text into it.
`wx.TE_RICH2`	Use the `RichText` version of the control. (only applicable on Windows).
`wx.TE_LEFT`	Aligns all text to the left-hand side of the control.
`wx.TE_CENTER`	Aligns all text to the center of the control
`wx.TE_RIGHT`	Aligns all text to the right-hand side of the control.

See also

▶ The *Validating Input with validators* recipe in *Chapter 2, Responding to Events* shows how to use a Validator to validate user input.

▶ The *Using a BoxSizer* recipe in *Chapter 7, Window Layout and Design* shows how to use the BoxSizer class to control layout

Providing choices with the Choice control

The Choice control is a means to allow the user to make a single selection from a list of possible selections. It does this by displaying the currently-selected choice and offering the list of other possible choices in a pop-up when the control is clicked on by the user. This makes it very efficient in its use of screen space.

How to do it...

To see how the Choice control works, we will make a simple Panel that has a Choice control with three choices in it:

```python
class ChoicePanel(wx.Panel):
    def __init__(self, parent):
        super(ChoicePanel, self).__init__(parent)

        # Attributes
        items = ["item 1", "item 2", "item 3"]
        self.choice = wx.Choice(self, choices=items)
        self.choice.SetSelection(0)

        # Layout
        sizer = wx.BoxSizer()
        sizer.Add(self.choice, 1,
                  wx.EXPAND|wx.ALL, 20)
        self.SetSizer(sizer)

        # Event Handlers
        self.Bind(wx.EVT_CHOICE, self.OnChoice)

    def OnChoice(self, event):
        selection = self.choice.GetStringSelection()
        index = self.choice.GetSelection()
        print "Selected Item: %d '%s'" % (index, selection)
```

How it works...

The Choice control manages a list of strings. The list of strings that the control contains can be specified either in the constructor or by calling the SetItems method with a list of strings to put in the control. When clicked on, the control will display a pop-up list of all of the strings. After the user makes a selection, an EVT_CHOICE event will be fired.

Platform Notice: The `Choice` control in Windows does not automatically select its first item when created. Due to this inconsistency, it is sometimes desirable to explicitly set the selection after creating the control, as we have done in this example, in order to ensure consistent behavior across platforms.

There's more...

The items in the control can be manipulated or changed after the control has been created by using the following methods:

Method	Description
Append	Append a string to the end of the list managed by the control
AppendItems	Append a list of strings to the list managed by the control
Insert	Insert a string into the list managed by the control
SetItems	Set the list of strings that the control displays

Adding Menus and MenuBars

Most applications have menus. Menus are a means to providing the users of the application with a way to execute actions either by clicking on them or by using keyboard shortcuts that can be associated with each menu item. An application's menus consist of three components: a `MenuBar`, `Menus`, and `MenuItems`. The `MenuBar` contains the `Menus` and the `Menus` contain the `MenuItems`. This recipe will show how to add a `MenuBar` with some `Menus` to a `Frame`.

How to do it...

Here we will make a `Frame` that has some `Menu` options for controlling actions in a `TextCtrl`:

```
ID_READ_ONLY = wx.NewId()

class MenuFrame(wx.Frame):
    def __init__(self, *args, **kwargs):
        super(MenuFrame, self).__init__(*args, **kwargs)

        # Attributes
        self.panel = wx.Panel(self)
        self.txtctrl = wx.TextCtrl(self.panel,
                                   style=wx.TE_MULTILINE)
```

```python
        # Layout
        sizer = wx.BoxSizer(wx.HORIZONTAL)
        sizer.Add(self.txtctrl, 1, wx.EXPAND)
        self.panel.SetSizer(sizer)
        self.CreateStatusBar() # For output display

        # Setup the Menu
        menub = wx.MenuBar()

        # File Menu
        filem = wx.Menu()
        filem.Append(wx.ID_OPEN, "Open\tCtrl+O")
        menub.Append(filem, "&File")

        # Edit Menu
        editm = wx.Menu()
        editm.Append(wx.ID_COPY, "Copy\tCtrl+C")
        editm.Append(wx.ID_CUT, "Cut\tCtrl+X")
        editm.Append(wx.ID_PASTE, "Paste\tCtrl+V")
        editm.AppendSeparator()
        editm.Append(ID_READ_ONLY, "Read Only",
                        kind=wx.ITEM_CHECK)
        menub.Append(editm, "E&dit")
        self.SetMenuBar(menub)

        # Event Handlers
        self.Bind(wx.EVT_MENU, self.OnMenu)

    def OnMenu(self, event):
        """Handle menu clicks"""
        evt_id = event.GetId()
        actions = { wx.ID_COPY  : self.txtctrl.Copy,
                    wx.ID_CUT   : self.txtctrl.Cut,
                    wx.ID_PASTE : self.txtctrl.Paste }
        action = actions.get(evt_id, None)
        if action:
            action()
        elif evt_id == ID_READ_ONLY:
            # Toggle enabled state
            self.txtctrl.Enable(not self.txtctrl.Enabled)
        elif evt_id == wx.ID_OPEN:
            dlg = wx.FileDialog(self, "Open File",
                                style=wx.FD_OPEN)
```

```
        if dlg.ShowModal() == wx.ID_OK:
            fname = dlg.GetPath()
            handle = open(fname, 'r')
            self.txtctrl.SetValue(handle.read())
            handle.close()
    else:
        event.Skip()
```

How it works...

The first thing to look at is where we created the `MenuBar` object. The `MenuBar` is what we need to attach all of our `Menus` to, and it will ultimately become responsible for managing them. Next we start to make our `Menus`, which is a rather straightforward process. All that needs to be done is to call `Append` for each new item that we wish to add to the `Menu`.

`Append` accepts a few arguments, but the important one to notice is the one for the label. The string that we pass can have some special formatting options in it to setup keyboard shortcuts for the `MenuItem`. Placing an '`&`' before a letter in the label will setup a keyboard mnemonic that will allow for keyboard navigation to the item. More importantly, though, is that placing a *Tab* character (`\t`) followed by a shortcut option *Ctrl + C* will setup a keyboard shortcut to select the menu option and cause an `EVT_MENU` event to be generated.

Platform Notice: On OS X, the *Ctrl* keyword will be automatically translated to the Apple/Command key.

Finally, we just need to call `Append` on our `MenuBar` in order to add each of the `Menus` that we created to it, and then finally call `SetMenuBar` on the `Frame` to add the `MenuBar` to our `Frame`.

There's more...

Menus have some additional functionality that we did not cover above. Following below are some references to a few more things that you can do with `Menus`.

SubMenus

`Menus` can have submenus appended to them, via the `AppendMenu` function.

Customizing MenuItems

`MenuItems` are created when calling `Append` on a `Menu`. The `Append` method takes a "kind" keyword parameter that can accept any of the following values:

Value	Description
`wx.ITEM_NORMAL`	Default value
`wx.ITEM_SEPARATOR`	Creates a separator item. It's easier to just call `AppendSeparator` than do this.
`wx.ITEM_CHECK`	Adds a `CheckBox` to the `Menu`.
`wx.ITEM_RADIO`	Adds a `RadioButton` to the `Menu`.

`MenuItems` can also have `Bitmaps` added to them by calling `SetBitmap` on the `MenuItem` object returned by calling `Append` on the `Menu`.

 Platform Notice: On Linux/GTK, `MenuItems` that use Stock IDs will automatically get system theme provided bitmaps associated with them.

See also

▸ The *Utilizing Stock IDs* recipe in *Chapter 1, Getting Started with wxPython* discusses the use of the built-in standard control IDs.

▸ The *Using UpdateUI events* recipe in *Chapter 2, Responding to Events* discusses how to use `UpdateUI` events to manage the UI's state.

Working with ToolBars

`ToolBars` are a lot like `Menus` in that they provide a means to link an action in the interface with an action in the application. They differ in that `ToolBars` use images to represent actions and must be clicked on directly in order to initiate the action. They make for an easy point and click interface for the user to interact with. This recipe will show a custom `ToolBar` class that automatically gets bitmaps from the system's `ArtProvider`.

How to do it...

Let's start by defining our custom `ToolBar` class, and then map some Stock IDs to art resource IDs:

```
ART_MAP = { wx.ID_CUT : wx.ART_CUT,
            wx.ID_COPY : wx.ART_COPY,
            wx.ID_PASTE : wx.ART_PASTE }
```

```
class EasyToolBar(wx.ToolBar):
    def AddEasyTool(self, id, shortHelp="", longHelp=""):
        """Simplifies adding a tool to the toolbar
        @param id: Stock ID

        """
        assert id in ART_MAP, "Unknown Stock ID"
        art_id = ART_MAP.get(id)
        bmp = wx.ArtProvider.GetBitmap(art_id, wx.ART_TOOLBAR)
        self.AddSimpleTool(id, bmp, shortHelp, longHelp)
```

Now we can make use of this custom `ToolBar` class anywhere that we want to have a `ToolBar`. The following code snippet is a minimal example of creating an `EasyToolBar` with three items:

```
class ToolBarFrame(wx.Frame):
    def __init__(self, *args, **kwargs):
        super(ToolBarFrame, self).__init__(*args, **kwargs)

        # Setup the ToolBar
        toolb = EasyToolBar(self)
        toolb.AddEasyTool(wx.ID_CUT)
        toolb.AddEasyTool(wx.ID_COPY)
        toolb.AddEasyTool(wx.ID_PASTE)
        toolb.Realize()
        self.SetToolBar(toolb)

        # Event Handlers
        self.Bind(wx.EVT_TOOL, self.OnToolBar)

    def OnToolBar(self, event):
        print "ToolBarItem Clicked", event.GetId()
```

How it works...

The `EasyToolBar` class makes use of a map of stock IDs to art resource IDs. When the `AddEasyTool` method is called, it will look up that art resource in the system's art provider. This simplifies the use of the `ToolBar` by quite a bit since we don't need to repeat the code for getting the appropriate bitmap each time we want to add a tool.

The `ToolBarFrame` class shows an example of the use of the `EasyToolBar`. Using a `ToolBar` can be summed up in a four-step process. First, create the `ToolBar`, second add the tools, third call `Realize` to tell the `ToolBar` that all of the tools have been added, and then fourth and finally call the `SetToolBar` method of the `Frame` in order to add the `ToolBar` to the `Frame`.

There's more...

ToolBar styles

There a number of style flags that can be passed to a `ToolBars` constructor to modify its appearance and behavior. Following is a list of some of the more useful ones:

Style flags	Description
wx.TB_DOCKABLE	Allows the `ToolBar` to be undocked from the `Frame` (GTK Only)
wx.TB_FLAT	Makes the `ToolBar` look flat (MSW and GTK ONLY)
wx.TB_HORIZONTAL	Horizontal tool layout
wx.TB_VERTICAL	Vertical tool layout
wx.TB_TEXT	Show labels below the tool icon
wx.TB_NO_TOOLTIPS	Don't show `ToolTips` when tools are hovered over
wx.TB_BOTTOM	Put the `ToolBar` at the bottom of the parent window
wx.TB_RIGHT	Put the `ToolBar` at the right-hand side of the parent window

Additional types of tools

It is possible to add different types of tools or controls to a `ToolBar` besides the standard icon tools. Here is a quick reference to some of these other `ToolBar` methods.

ToolBar methods	Description
AddControl	Allows for a control such as a `Button` to be added to the `ToolBar`.
AddCheckLabelTool	Adds a tool that can be toggled.
AddRadioLabelTool	Adds a tool that will work like a `RadioButton`.
AddSeparator	Adds a vertical line to the `ToolBar` to separate items.

Events

`ToolBar` tools will fire an `EVT_TOOL` event when clicked on. If you already have a `MenuItem` for the same ID that is bound to an `EVT_MENU` event handler, it is not necessary to create a separate event handler for the tool event. The system will automatically route the tool event to your menu handler.

▸ The *Adding Menus and MenuBars* recipe in this chapter discusses the use of menus and menu events, which are closely related to toolbars.

▸ The *Customizing the ArtProvider* recipe in *Chapter 10, Creating Components and Extending Functionality* includes further examples and information about retrieving bitmap resources.

How to use PopupMenus

Pop-up menus (a.k.a context menus) are a useful way of providing context-sensitive access to actions when a user right clicks on a control or on a part of a window. Pop-up menus work the same way as a regular menu but require some special handling since there is no `MenuBar` to manage them. This recipe will create a mixin class to help manage a pop-up menu.

How to do it...

Here we will define a mixin class to manage the creation and lifetime of a context menu:

```python
class PopupMenuMixin(object):
    def __init__(self):
        super(PopupMenuMixin, self).__init__()

        # Attributes
        self._menu = None

        # Event Handlers
        self.Bind(wx.EVT_CONTEXT_MENU, self.OnContextMenu)

    def OnContextMenu(self, event):
        """Creates and shows the Menu"""
        if self._menu is not None:
            self._menu.Destroy()

        self._menu = wx.Menu()
        self.CreateContextMenu(self._menu)
        self.PopupMenu(self._menu)

    def CreateContextMenu(self, menu):
        """Override in subclass to create the menu"""
        raise NotImplementedError
```

How it works...

This little mixin class is very generic and can be used with any type of window subclass to add custom context menu support. The subclass that uses this mixin must override the `CreateContextMenu` method to make its own `Menu`, and then the mixin will take care of the rest. Following is a minimal example of using the `PopupMenuMixin` class. It will create a `Panel` that has a context menu with three items on it; a more complete example is included in the example code that accompanies this topic.

```python
class PanelWithMenu(wx.Panel, PopupMenuMixin):
    def __init__(self, parent):
        wx.Panel.__init__(self, parent)
        PopupMenuMixin.__init__(self)

    def CreateContextMenu(self, menu):
        """PopupMenuMixin Implementation"""
        menu.Append(wx.ID_CUT)
        menu.Append(wx.ID_COPY)
        menu.Append(wx.ID_PASTE)
```

The `EVT_CONTEXT_MENU` is fired when a user right-clicks, or initiates a context menu from the keyboard. Because context menus can be shown in multiple ways, it is important to use `EVT_CONTEXT_MENU` instead of using the mouse right-click event. Our mixin class will catch this event and first clean up any existing `Menu`. Since pop-up menus do not have a `MenuBar` to manage them, it is necessary to clean them up ourselves, otherwise, if they are not destroyed, they can cause memory leaks. Next, the subclass's `CreateContextMenu` method will be called to add the items to the `Menu`. Finally, we display the `Menu` by calling the `PopupMenu` method.

When a user clicks on an item in the `Menu`, an `EVT_MENU` event will be sent to the window that the pop-up menu belongs to. Hence, it is necessary to `Bind` your own menu handlers to handle the `MenuEvents`.

See also

- ▶ The *Adding Menus and MenuBars* recipe in this chapter shows how to create menu objects.
- ▶ The *Using mixin classes* recipe in *Chapter 9, Design Approaches and Techniques* discusses how to use mixin classes.

Grouping controls with a StaticBox

The `StaticBox` is a fairly simple control used to group other related controls together, by drawing a border around them that optionally includes a label. The usage of the `StaticBox` control is a little different than other controls though, due to its relationship with the controls it contains. Hence, this recipe will show how to use a `StaticBox`, and will give an explanation of some of its quirks.

How to do it...

To see how to add controls to a `StaticBox`, let's make a `Panel` class that has a `StaticBox`, and add a few controls to it:

```
class MyPanel(wx.Panel):
    def __init__(self, parent):
        super(MyPanel, self).__init__(parent)

        # Layout
        sbox = wx.StaticBox(self, label="Box Label")
        sboxsz = wx.StaticBoxSizer(sbox, wx.VERTICAL)

        # Add some controls to the box
        cb = wx.CheckBox(self, label="Enable")
        sboxsz.Add(cb, 0, wx.ALL, 8)
        sizer = wx.BoxSizer(wx.HORIZONTAL)
        sizer.Add(wx.StaticText(self, label="Value:"))
        sizer.Add((5, 5))
        sizer.Add(wx.TextCtrl(self))
        sboxsz.Add(sizer, 0, wx.ALL, 8)

        msizer = wx.BoxSizer(wx.VERTICAL)
        msizer.Add(sboxsz, 0, wx.EXPAND|wx.ALL, 20)
        self.SetSizer(msizer)
```

How it works...

Even though a `StaticBox` is a container for other controls, it is actually a sibling of the controls that it contains, instead of being a parent window. The most important thing to remember when working with a `StaticBox` is that it must be created before any of the controls that it will contain. If it is not created before its siblings, then they will have issues processing mouse events.

The StaticBox uses a StaticBoxSizer to add the controls to the box, as well as to manage its size and to position the controls inside of it. The usage of a StaticBoxSizer is used just like a regular BoxSizer in all regards except that its constructor takes a StaticBox as the first argument. Calling the Add method of StaticBoxSizer is used to then add the controls to the StaticBox. Like with the BoxSizer, the Add method of StaticBoxSizer takes the object being added as the first parameter, and then optionally the proportion, the sizer flags, and border keyword parameters.

See also

▸ The *Using a BoxSizer* recipe in *Chapter 7, Window Layout and Design* contains more examples of sizer-based control layout.

4
Advanced Building Blocks of a User Interface

In this chapter, we will cover:

- ▸ Listing data with a `ListCtrl`
- ▸ Browsing files with the `CustomTreeCtrl`
- ▸ Creating a `VListBox`
- ▸ `StyledTextCtrl` using lexers
- ▸ Working with tray icons
- ▸ Adding tabs to a `Notebook`
- ▸ Using the `FlatNotebook`
- ▸ Scrolling with a `ScrolledPanel`
- ▸ Simplifying the `FoldPanelBar`

Introduction

Displaying collections of data and managing complex window layouts are a task that most UI developers will be faced with at some point. wxPython provides a number of components to help developers meet the requirements of these more demanding interfaces.

As the amount of controls and data that an application is required to display in its user interface increases, so does the task of efficiently managing available screen real estate. To fit this information into the available space requires the use of some more advanced controls and containers; so let's dive in and begin our exploration of some of the more advanced controls that wxPython has to offer.

Listing data with a ListCtrl

The `ListCtrl` is a versatile control for displaying collections of text and/or images. The control supports many different display formats, although typically its most often-used display mode is the report mode. Report mode has a visual representation that is very similar to a grid or spreadsheet in that it can have multiple rows and columns with column headings. This recipe shows how to populate and retrieve data from a `ListCtrl` that was created in report mode.

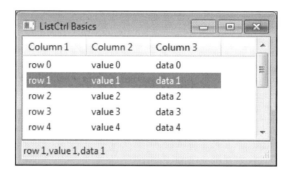

How to do it...

The `ListCtrl` takes a little more set up than most basic controls, so we will start by creating a subclass that sets up the columns that we wish to have in the control:

```python
class MyListCtrl(wx.ListCtrl):
    def __init__(self, parent):
        super(MyListCtrl, self).__init__(parent,
                                         style=wx.LC_REPORT)

        # Add three columns to the list
        self.InsertColumn(0, "Column 1")
        self.InsertColumn(1, "Column 2")
        self.InsertColumn(2, "Column 3")

    def PopulateList(self, data):
        """Populate the list with the set of data. Data
```

```
        should be a list of tuples that have a value for each
        column in the list.
        [('hello', 'list', 'control'),]
        """
        for item in data:
            self.Append(item)
```

Next we will create an instance of our `ListCtrl` and put it on a `Panel`, and then use our `PopulateList` method to put some sample data into the control:

```python
class MyPanel(wx.Panel):
    def __init__(self, parent):
        super(MyPanel, self).__init__(parent)

        # Attributes
        self.lst = MyListCtrl(self)

        # Setup
        data = [ ("row %d" % x,
                  "value %d" % x,
                  "data %d" % x) for x in range(10) ]
        self.lst.PopulateList(data)

        # Layout
        sizer = wx.BoxSizer(wx.VERTICAL)
        sizer.Add(self.lst, 1, wx.EXPAND)
        self.SetSizer(sizer)

        # Event Handlers
        self.Bind(wx.EVT_LIST_ITEM_SELECTED,
                  self.OnItemSelected)

    def OnItemSelected(self, event):
        selected_row = event.GetIndex()
        val = list()
        for column in range(3):
            item = self.lst.GetItem(selected_row, column)
            val.append(item.GetText())
        # Show what was selected in the frames status bar
        frame = self.GetTopLevelParent()
        frame.PushStatusText(",".join(val))
```

How it works...

Usually there tends to be a fair amount of set up with the `ListCtrl`, and due to this it is good to encapsulate the usage of the control in a specialized subclass instead of using it directly. We kept things pretty basic here in our `ListCtrl` class. We just used the `InsertColumn` method to set our list up with three columns. Then the `PopulateList` method was added for convenience, to allow the population of the `ListCtrl` from a Python list of data. It simply wraps the `Append` method of `ListCtrl`, which just takes an iterable that has a string for each column in the list.

The `MyPanel` class is there to show how to use the `ListCtrl` class that we created. First we populate it with some data by generating a list of tuples and calling our `PopulateList` method. To show how to retrieve data from the list, we created an event handler for `EVT_LIST_ITEM_SELECTED` which will be fired each time a new selection is made in the control. In order to retrieve a value from a `ListCtrl`, you need to know the row and column index of the cell that you wish to retrieve the data from, and then call `GetItem` with the row and column to get the `ListItem` object that represents that cell. Then the string value of the cell can be retrieved by calling the `GetText` method of `ListItem`.

There's more...

Depending on the style flags that are used to create a `ListCtrl`, it will behave in many different possible ways. Because of this, it is important to know some of the different style flags that can be used to create a `ListCtr`.

Style flags	Description
LC_LIST	In List mode, the control will calculate the columns automatically, so there is no need to call `InsertColumn`. It can be used to display strings and, optionally, small icons
LC_REPORT	Single or multicolumn report view that can be shown with or without headers
LC_ICON	Large icon view that can optionally have labels
LC_SMALL_ICON	Small icon view that can optionally have labels
LC_EDIT_LABELS	Allow the item labels to be editable by users
LC_NO_HEADER	Hide the column headers (report mode)
LC_SORT_ASCENDING	Sort items in ascending order (must provide a `SortItems` callback method)
LC_SORT_DESCENDING	Sort items in descending order (must provide a `SortItems` callback method)
LC_HRULE	Draw a horizontal line between rows (report mode)
LC_VRULE	Draw a vertical line between columns (report mode)

Style flags	Description
LC_SINGLE_SEL	Only allow a single item to be selected at a time (Default is to allow for multiple selections)
LC_VIRTUAL	Fetch items to display in the list on demand (report mode)

Virtual Mode

When a `ListCtrl` is created in virtual mode (using the `LC_VIRTUAL` style flag), it does not store the data internally; instead it will instead ask for the data from a datasource when it needs to display it. This mode is useful when you have a very large set of data where preloading it in the control would present performance issues. To use a `ListCtrl` in virtual mode, you must call `SetItemCount` to tell the control how many rows of data there are, and override the `OnGetItemText` method to return the text for the `ListItem` when the control asks for it.

See also

▸   The *Creating a VListBox* recipe in this chapter is another example of a control for presenting data as a list.

Browsing files with the CustomTreeCtrl

A `TreeCtrl` is a way of displaying hierarchical data in a user interface. The `CustomTreeCtrl` is a fully owner-drawn `TreeCtrl` that looks and functions much the same way as the default `TreeCtrl`, but that offers a number of additional features and customizability that the default native control cannot. This recipe shows how to make a custom file browser class by using the `CustomTreeCtrl`.

How to do it...

To create this custom `FileBrowser` control, we will use its constructor to set up the images to use for the folders and files in the tree:

```
import os
import wx
import wx.lib.customtreectrl as customtree

class FileBrowser(customtree.CustomTreeCtrl):
    FOLDER, \
    ERROR, \
    FILE = range(3)
    def __init__(self, parent, rootdir, *args, **kwargs):
        super(FileBrowser, self).__init__(parent,
                                          *args,
```

```
                                              **kwargs)
        assert os.path.exists(rootdir), \
                "Invalid Root Directory!"
        assert os.path.isdir(rootdir), \
                "rootdir must be a Directory!"

        # Attributes
        self._il = wx.ImageList(16, 16)
        self._root = rootdir
        self._rnode = None

        # Setup
        for art in (wx.ART_FOLDER, wx.ART_ERROR,
                    wx.ART_NORMAL_FILE):
            bmp = wx.ArtProvider.GetBitmap(art, size=(16,16))
            self._il.Add(bmp)
        self.SetImageList(self._il)
        self._rnode = self.AddRoot(os.path.basename(rootdir),
                                    image=FileBrowser.FOLDER,
                                    data=self._root)
        self.SetItemHasChildren(self._rnode, True)
        # use Windows-Vista-style selections
        self.EnableSelectionVista(True)

        # Event Handlers
        self.Bind(wx.EVT_TREE_ITEM_EXPANDING,
                  self.OnExpanding)
        self.Bind(wx.EVT_TREE_ITEM_COLLAPSED,
                  self.OnCollapsed)

    def _GetFiles(self, path):
        try:
            files = [fname for fname in os.listdir(path)
                     if fname not in ('.', '..')]
        except OSError:
            files = None
        return files
```

The following two event handlers are used to update which files are displayed when a node is expanded or collapsed in the tree:

```
    def OnCollapsed(self, event):
        item = event.GetItem()
        self.DeleteChildren(item)
```

```
def OnExpanding(self, event):
    item = event.GetItem()
    path = self.GetPyData(item)
    files = self._GetFiles(path)

    # Handle Access Errors
    if files is None:
        self.SetItemImage(item, FileBrowser.ERROR)
        self.SetItemHasChildren(item, False)
        return

    for fname in files:
        fullpath = os.path.join(path, fname)
        if os.path.isdir(fullpath):
            self.AppendDir(item, fullpath)
        else:
            self.AppendFile(item, fullpath)
```

The following methods are added as an API for working with the control to add items and retrieve their on-disk paths:

```
def AppendDir(self, item, path):
    """Add a directory node"""
    assert os.path.isdir(path), "Not a valid directory!"
    name = os.path.basename(path)
    nitem = self.AppendItem(item, name,
                            image=FileBrowser.FOLDER,
                            data=path)
    self.SetItemHasChildren(nitem, True)

def AppendFile(self, item, path):
    """Add a file to a node"""
    assert os.path.isfile(path), "Not a valid file!"
    name = os.path.basename(path)
    self.AppendItem(item, name,
                    image=FileBrowser.FILE,
                    data=path)

def GetSelectedPath(self):
    """Get the selected path"""
    sel = self.GetSelection()
    path = self.GetItemPyData(sel)
    return path
```

```
def GetSelectedPaths(self):
    """Get a list of selected paths"""
    sels = self.GetSelections()
    paths = [self.GetItemPyData(sel)
             for sel in sels ]
    return paths
```

How it works...

With just a few lines of code here we have created a pretty useful little widget for displaying and working with the file system. Let's take a quick look at how it works.

In the classes constructor, we added a root node with the control's `AddRoot` method. A root node is a top-level node that has no other parent nodes above it. The first argument is the text that will be shown, the `image` argument specifies the default image for the `TreeItem`, and the `data` argument specifies any type of data associated with the item—in this case we are setting a string for the items path. We then called `SetItemHasChildren` for the item so that it will get a button next to it to allow it to be expanded. The last thing that we did in the constructor was to `Bind` the control to two events so that we can update the tree when one of its nodes is being expanded or collapsed.

Immediately before the node is going to be expanded our handler for `EVT_TREE_ITEM_EXPANDING` will be called. It is here where we find all the files and folders under a directory node, and then add them as children of that node by calling `AppendItem`, which works just like `AddRoot` but is used to add items to already-existing nodes in the tree.

Conversely when a node in the tree is going to be collapsed, our `EVT_TREE_ITEM_COLLAPED` event handler will be called. Here we simply call `DeleteChildren` in order to remove the children items from the node so that we can update them more easily the next time that the node is expanded. Otherwise, we would have to find what was different the next time it was expanded, and then remove the items that have been deleted and insert new items that may have been added to the directory.

The last two items in our class are for getting the file paths of the selected items, which—since we store the file path in each node—is simply just a matter of getting the data from each of the currently-selected `TreeItems` with a call to `GetPyData`.

There's more...

Most of what we did in this recipe could actually also be replicated with the standard `TreeCtrl`. The difference is in the amount of extra customizability that the `CustomTreeCtrl` provides. Since it is a fully owner-drawn control, nearly all of the visible attributes of it can be customized. Following is a list of some of the functions that can be used to customize its appearance:

Functions	Description
`EnableSelectionGradient(bool)`	Use a gradient to draw the tree item selection rectangle.
`EnableSelectionVista(bool)`	Use a nice rounded rectangle for the item selections similar to the native control seen in Windows Vista.
`SetButtonsImageList(ImageList)`	Changes the expand/collapse buttons. `ImageList` should have four bitmaps for the following states, in this order: `Normal`, `Selected`, `Expanded`, and `Expanded Selected`.
`SetConnectionPen(pen)`	Changes how the connection lines are drawn between items in the tree. Takes a `wx.Pen` object that will be used to draw the lines.
`SetBackgroundImage(bitmap)`	Allows for an image to be used as the control's background.
`SetBackgroundColour(colour)`	Used to change the color of the control's background.

Creating a VListBox

The `VListBox` control is much like a `ListBox` control, but it is virtual (it doesn't store the data internally) and allows for items to have variable row heights. It works by providing a number of virtual callback methods that you must override in a subclass in order to draw the items on demand. Because of this requirement to override pure virtual methods, the `VListBox` will always be subclassed. This recipe shows how to create a `VListBox` derived control that supports an icon and text in each of its items.

How to do it...

To create our user list control, we just need to subclass a `VListBox` and override some of its callback methods to perform the necessary actions:

```
class UserListBox(wx.VListBox):
    """Simple List Box control to show a list of users"""
    def __init__(self, parent, users):
        """@param users: list of user names"""
        super(UserListBox, self).__init__(parent)

        # Attributes
        # system-users.png is a sample image provided with
        # this chapters sample code.
        self.bmp = wx.Bitmap("system-users.png",
```

```
                            wx.BITMAP_TYPE_PNG)
        self.bh = self.bmp.GetHeight()
        self.users = users

        # Setup
        self.SetItemCount(len(self.users))

    def OnMeasureItem(self, index):
        """Called to get an items height"""
        # All our items are the same so index is ignored
        return self.bh + 4

    def OnDrawSeparator(self, dc, rect, index):
        """Called to draw the item separator"""
        oldpen = dc.GetPen()
        dc.SetPen(wx.Pen(wx.BLACK))
        dc.DrawLine(rect.x, rect.y,
                    rect.x + rect.width,
                    rect.y)
        rect.Deflate(0, 2)
        dc.SetPen(oldpen)

    def OnDrawItem(self, dc, rect, index):
        """Called to draw the item"""
        # Draw the bitmap
        dc.DrawBitmap(self.bmp, rect.x + 2,
                      ((rect.height - self.bh) / 2) + rect.y)
        # Draw the label to the right of the bitmap
        textx = rect.x + 2 + self.bh + 2
        lblrect = wx.Rect(textx, rect.y,
                          rect.width - textx,
                          rect.height)
        dc.DrawLabel(self.users[index], lblrect,
                     wx.ALIGN_LEFT|wx.ALIGN_CENTER_VERTICAL)
```

Here is a screenshot of what the UserListBox looks like with some sample data in it.

How it works...

Our custom `VListBox` control could be used in any kind of application that wants to display a list of users. The constructor takes a list of usernames and calls `SetItemCount` to tell the control how many items it needs to be able to display. We also loaded a bitmap to use in our list's items. This bitmap is available in the sample code that accompanies this topic.

The main thing to take from this recipe is the three virtual callback methods that we overrode in order to draw the items in our control:

1. The first required override is `OnMeasureItem`. This method will be called for each item in the list, and it needs to return the height of the item.

2. The next method is `OnDrawSeparator`. This method is optional and can be used to draw a separator between each item in the control. It can also modify the `Rect` if necessary, so that when `OnDrawItem` is called it will know not to draw over the separator.

3. The final method is `OnDrawItem`. This method is used to draw the actual item. For our control, we draw a bitmap and then position the users' name as a label to the right of it. That's all there is to it; pretty easy right.

There's more...

There are a couple more methods available that can be useful in implementing a `VListBox` subclass. The following list describes these methods.

Methods	Description
OnDrawItemBackground	This method can be overridden, as `DrawItem` can, in order to draw a custom background for an item. The default base class does the reasonable thing of drawing the background of the selected item with the system default selection color.
IsSelected	This method can be used to see if an item is selected or not, in case you want to change the way in which you draw the item in `OnDrawItem`, for example making the font bold.

See also

▶ The *Understanding inheritance limitations* recipe in *Chapter 1, Getting Started with wxPython* contains an explanation about virtual methods in the C++ objects.

▶ The *Listing data with a ListCtrl* recipe in this chapter is another example of a control for presenting data as a list.

▶ The *Screen drawing* recipe in *Chapter 8, Drawing to the Screen*, discusses the usage of PaintEvents and Device Contexts.

StyledTextCtrl using lexers

The `StyledTextCtrl` is an advanced text control class supplied by the `wx.stc` module. The class is a wrapping around the Scintilla source control editing component (see `http://www.scintilla.org`). The `StyledTextCtrl` is primarily intended for displaying and working with source code for various programming languages. It provides built-in syntax highlighting support for many different types of source code files, and is extendable to work with custom lexers. This recipe shows how to setup the control to perform source code highlighting using its built-in lexer for Python.

How to do it...

To get started, we will define a language-generic editor class that will manage all the common style settings so that we can easily create other classes that support different types of programming languages:

```python
import wx
import wx.stc as stc
import keyword

class CodeEditorBase(stc.StyledTextCtrl):
    def __init__(self, parent):
        super(CodeEditorBase, self).__init__(parent)

        # Attributes
        font = wx.Font(10, wx.FONTFAMILY_MODERN,
                           wx.FONTSTYLE_NORMAL,
                           wx.FONTWEIGHT_NORMAL)
        self.face = font.GetFaceName()
        self.size = font.GetPointSize()

        # Setup
        self.SetupBaseStyles()

    def EnableLineNumbers(self, enable=True):
        """Enable/Disable line number margin"""
        if enable:
            self.SetMarginType(1, stc.STC_MARGIN_NUMBER)
            self.SetMarginMask(1, 0)
            self.SetMarginWidth(1, 25)
        else:
            self.SetMarginWidth(1, 0)
```

```
    def GetFaces(self):
        """Get font style dictionary"""
        return dict(font=self.face,
                    size=self.size)

    def SetupBaseStyles(self):
        """Sets up the the basic non lexer specific
        styles.
        """
        faces = self.GetFaces()
        default = "face:%(font)s,size:%(size)d" % faces
        self.StyleSetSpec(stc.STC_STYLE_DEFAULT, default)
        line = "back:#C0C0C0," + default
        self.StyleSetSpec(stc.STC_STYLE_LINENUMBER, line)
        self.StyleSetSpec(stc.STC_STYLE_CONTROLCHAR,
                          "face:%(font)s" % faces)
```

Now here we will derive a new class from our `CodeEditorBase` class that specializes the control for Python files:

```
class PythonCodeEditor(CodeEditorBase):
    def __init__(self, parent):
        super(PythonCodeEditor, self).__init__(parent)

        # Setup
        self.SetLexer(wx.stc.STC_LEX_PYTHON)
        self.SetupKeywords()
        self.SetupStyles()
        self.EnableLineNumbers(True)

    def SetupKeywords(self):
        """Sets up the lexers keywords"""
        kwlist = u" ".join(keyword.kwlist)
        self.SetKeyWords(0, kwlist)

    def SetupStyles(self):
        """Sets up the lexers styles"""
        # Python styles
        faces = self.GetFaces()
        fonts = "face:%(font)s,size:%(size)d" % faces
        default = "fore:#000000," + fonts
```

```
# Default
self.StyleSetSpec(stc.STC_P_DEFAULT, default)
# Comments
self.StyleSetSpec(stc.STC_P_COMMENTLINE,
                  "fore:#007F00," + fonts)
# Number
self.StyleSetSpec(stc.STC_P_NUMBER,
                  "fore:#007F7F," + fonts)
# String
self.StyleSetSpec(stc.STC_P_STRING,
                  "fore:#7F007F," + fonts)
# Single quoted string
self.StyleSetSpec(stc.STC_P_CHARACTER,
                  "fore:#7F007F," + fonts)
# Keyword
self.StyleSetSpec(stc.STC_P_WORD,
                  "fore:#00007F,bold," + fonts)
# Triple quotes
self.StyleSetSpec(stc.STC_P_TRIPLE,
                  "fore:#7F0000," + fonts)
# Triple double quotes
self.StyleSetSpec(stc.STC_P_TRIPLEDOUBLE,
                  "fore:#7F0000," + fonts)
# Class name definition
self.StyleSetSpec(stc.STC_P_CLASSNAME,
                  "fore:#0000FF,bold," + fonts)
# Function or method name definition
self.StyleSetSpec(stc.STC_P_DEFNAME,
                  "fore:#007F7F,bold," + fonts)
# Operators
self.StyleSetSpec(stc.STC_P_OPERATOR, "bold," + fonts)
# Identifiers
self.StyleSetSpec(stc.STC_P_IDENTIFIER, default)
# Comment-blocks
self.StyleSetSpec(stc.STC_P_COMMENTBLOCK,
                  "fore:#7F7F7F," + fonts)
# End of line where string is not closed
eol_style = "fore:#000000,back:#E0C0E0,eol," + fonts
self.StyleSetSpec(stc.STC_P_STRINGEOL, eol_style)
```

How it works...

We created two classes: a base editor class and a specialized class for Python source files. Let's first start by taking a look at the `CodeEditorBase` class.

The `CodeEditorBase` sets up the basic functionality of the control, and is just there to encapsulate some of the common items, should we decide to add other specialized classes for different types of source files later on.

First and foremost, it initializes the basic window styles and provides font information. The `StyledTextCtrl` has a number of style specifications for styling different text in the buffer. These styles are specified using the `StyleSetSpec` method, which takes the style ID and style specification string as arguments. The style IDs that are generic to all lexers are identified with the `STC_STYLE_` prefix. The style specification string is formatted in the following way:

```
ATTRIBUTE:VALUE,ATTRIBUTE:VALUE,MODIFIER
```

Here, `ATTRIBUTE` and `VALUE` are replaced by any combination of the possible specifications in the following table:

Attributes	Possible values
fore	Foreground color; can either be a color name (`black`) or hex color string (for example, `#000000`)
back	Background color; can either be a color name (white) or hex color string (for example, `#FFFFFF`)
face	A font face name (for example, `Monaco`)
size	A point size for the font (for example, `10`)

There is also support from some additional `MODIFER` attributes that don't take a `VALUE` argument:

Modifier	Description
bold	Makes the text bold
italic	Italicizes the text
eol	Extends the background style to the end of the current line
underline	Underlines the text

The `StyledTextCtrl` also supports special margins on the left-hand side of the buffer for displaying things such as line numbers, breakpoints, and code folding buttons. Our `CodeEditorBase` shows how to enable line numbers in the left-most margin with its `EnableLineNumbers` method.

Our derived `PythonCodeEditor` class simply does the three basic things necessary to set up the proper lexer:

1. First, it calls `SetLexer` to set the lexer mode. This method simply takes one of the `STC_LEX_FOO` values that are found in the `stc` module.

2. Second, it sets up the keywords for the lexer. There is little documentation on what keyword sets are available for each lexer, so it is sometimes necessary to look at the Scintilla source code to see what keyword sets have been defined for each lexer. The Python lexer supports two keyword sets: one for language keywords and a second for user- defined keywords. The `SetKeywords` method takes two arguments: a keyword ID and a string of space-separated keywords to associate with that ID. Each keyword ID is associated with a Style ID for the given lexer. In this example, the keyword ID of zero is associated with the Style ID: `STC_P_WORD`.

3. Third and finally, it sets all of the styling specifications for the lexer. This is done just as we did in our base class by calling `StyleSetSpec` for each lexer style specification ID that the lexer defines. A quick reference for what styles relate to what lexers can be found in the wxPython wiki (`http://wiki.wxpython.org/StyledTextCtrl%20Lexer%20Quick%20Reference`).

There's more...

The `StyledTextCtrl` is a big class that comes with a very large API. It has many additional features that we did not discuss here, such as pop-up lists for implementing auto-completion, clickable hotspots, code folding, and custom highlighting. Following are links to some references and documentation about the `StyledTextCtrl`:

▸ `http://www.yellowbrain.com/stc/index.html`

▸ `http://www.wxpython.org/docs/api/wx.stc.StyledTextCtrl-class.html`

▸ `http://wiki.wxpython.org/StyledTextCtrl`

See also

▸ The *Using the TextCtrl* recipe in *Chapter 3, Basic Building Blocks of a User Interface* shows how to use the basic text control.

▸ The *StyledTextCtrl custom highlighting* recipe in *Chapter 10, Creating Components and Extending Functionality* shows how to extend the `StyledTextCtrl` in order to perform custom text styling.

Working with tray icons

Tray icons are UI components that integrate with the window manager's Task Bar (Windows / Linux) or Dock (OS X). They can be used for notifications and to provide a pop-up menu when the user clicks on the notification icon. This recipe shows how to create and use a tray icon through the use of the `TaskBarIcon` class.

How to do it...

To create the icon bar for this recipe's sample code, we create a subclass of `TaskBarIcon` that loads an image to use for its display, and that has handling for showing a `Menu` when it is clicked on:

```python
class CustomTaskBarIcon(wx.TaskBarIcon):
    ID_HELLO = wx.NewId()
    ID_HELLO2 = wx.NewId()
    def __init__(self):
        super(CustomTaskBarIcon, self).__init__()

        # Setup
        icon = wx.Icon("face-monkey.png", wx.BITMAP_TYPE_PNG)
        self.SetIcon(icon)

        # Event Handlers
        self.Bind(wx.EVT_MENU, self.OnMenu)

    def CreatePopupMenu(self):
        """Base class virtual method for creating the
        popup menu for the icon.
        """
        menu = wx.Menu()
        menu.Append(CustomTaskBarIcon.ID_HELLO, "HELLO")
        menu.Append(CustomTaskBarIcon.ID_HELLO2, "Hi!")
        menu.AppendSeparator()
        menu.Append(wx.ID_CLOSE, "Exit")
        return menu

    def OnMenu(self, event):
        evt_id = event.GetId()
        if evt_id == CustomTaskBarIcon.ID_HELLO:
            wx.MessageBox("Hello World!", "HELLO")
        elif evt_id == CustomTaskBarIcon.ID_HELLO2:
            wx.MessageBox("Hi Again!", "Hi!")
        elif evt_id == wx.ID_CLOSE:
            self.Destroy()
        else:
            event.Skip()
```

How it works...

The `TaskBarIcon` class is pretty easy and straightforward to use. All that needs to be done is to create an icon and call `SetIcon` to create the UI part of the object that will be shown in the system tray. Then we override the `CreatePopupMenu` method that the base class will call when the icon is clicked on, to create the menu. All that this method needs to do is create a `Menu` object and then return it; the `TaskBarIcon` class will take care of the rest. Finally, we added an event handler for `EVT_MENU` to handle the menu events from our pop-up menu.

There's more...

The `TaskBarIcon` class has a number of events associated with it, if you want to customize what different types of clicks do. Please see the following table for a list of available events and a description of when they are called.

Events	Description
EVT_TASKBAR_CLICK	Icon was clicked on by the mouse
EVT_TASKBAR_LEFT_DCLICK	Left mouse button double clicked on the icon
EVT_TASKBAR_LEFT_DOWN	Left mouse button clicked down on the icon
EVT_TASKBAR_LEFT_UP	Left mouse button released on the icon
EVT_TASKBAR_MOVE	The `TaskBarIcon` moved
EVT_TASKBAR_RIGHT_DCLICK	Right mouse button double clicked on the icon
EVT_TASKBAR_RIGHT_DOWN	Right mouse button clicked down on the icon
EVT_TASKBAR_RIGHT_UP	Right mouse button released on the icon

See also

▶   The *Adding Menus and MenuBars* recipe in *Chapter 3, Basic Building Blocks of a User Interface* contains more examples of using and creating menus.

▶   The *How to use PopupMenus* recipe in *Chapter 3, Basic Building Blocks of a User Interface* contains another example of creating a context menu.

Adding tabs to a Notebook

The `Notebook` class is a container control that is used to manage multiple panels through the use of tabs. When a tab is selected, the associated panel is shown and the previous one is hidden. This recipe shows how to use the default native `Notebook` class to create a tab-based user interface like the one shown in the following screenshot:

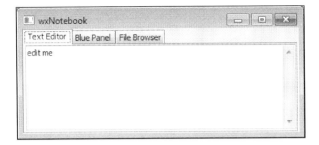

How to do it...

The following example code snippet defines a Notebook class that has three tabs in it:

```
class MyNotebook(wx.Notebook):
    def __init__(self, parent):
        super(MyNotebook, self).__init__(parent)

        # Attributes
        self.textctrl = wx.TextCtrl(self, value="edit me",
                                    style=wx.TE_MULTILINE)
        self.blue = wx.Panel(self)
        self.blue.SetBackgroundColour(wx.BLUE)
        self.fbrowser = wx.GenericDirCtrl(self)

        # Setup
        self.AddPage(self.textctrl, "Text Editor")
        self.AddPage(self.blue, "Blue Panel")
        self.AddPage(self.fbrowser, "File Browser")
```

How it works...

This recipe just shows the fundamental basics of how to use the Notebook control. We simply created some window objects that we wish to put in the Notebook. In this case, we created three different objects: a TextCtrl, a Panel, and a GenericDirCtrl. The important thing to note is that the items that we wish to put in the Notebook must be children of the Notebook.

The objects are then added to the Notebook by calling its AddPage method. This method takes a window object and a label to put on the tab as arguments.

There's more...

The basic `Notebook` class doesn't offer too many more features beyond what was shown above. However, there are a few additional styles, and some events related to when tabs are selected. Included below are some quick references to these additional items.

Styles

The following styles can be provided to the Notebook's constructor:

Style	Description
NB_BOTTOM	Put the tabs at the bottom of the control area
NB_FIXEDWIDTH	All tabs are the same size (Windows only)
NB_LEFT	Put the tabs on the left side of the control area
NB_MULTILINE	Allow for multiple rows of tabs (Windows only)
NB_NOPAGETHEME	Use a solid color for the tabs (Windows only)
NB_RIGHT	Put the tabs on the right-hand side of the control area
NB_TOP	Put the tabs at the top of the control area (Default)

Events

The Notebook emits the following events:

Event	Description
EVT_NOTEBOOK_PAGE_CHANGING	This event is fired when the Notebook is in the process of changing the page from one to another. Calling Veto on the event object will block the page from being changed.
EVT_NOTEBOOK_PAGE_CHANGED	This event is fired when the selected page has been changed.

See also

▶ The *Using the FlatNotebook* recipe in this chapter shows the usage of another type of tab control.

Using the FlatNotebook

The `FlatNotebook` class is a custom `Notebook` implementation that provides a large array of features over the default `Notebook`. The additional features include such things as being able to have a close button on each tab, drag and drop tabs to different positions, and a number of different tab styles to change the look and feel of the control. This recipe will explore some of the extended functionality that this control provides.

How to do it...

As an example of how to use the `FlatNotebook`, we will define a subclass that has some specializations for displaying multiple `TextCtrls`:

```python
import wx
import wx.lib
import wx.lib.flatnotebook as FNB

class MyFlatNotebook(FNB.FlatNotebook):
    def __init__(self, parent):
        mystyle = FNB.FNB_DROPDOWN_TABS_LIST|\
                  FNB.FNB_FF2|\
                  FNB.FNB_SMART_TABS|\
                  FNB.FNB_X_ON_TAB
        super(MyFlatNotebook, self).__init__(parent,
                                             style=mystyle)

        # Attributes
        self._imglst = wx.ImageList(16, 16)

        # Setup
        bmp = wx.Bitmap("text-x-generic.png")
        self._imglst.Add(bmp)
        bmp = wx.Bitmap("text-html.png")
        self._imglst.Add(bmp)
        self.SetImageList(self._imglst)

        # Event Handlers
        self.Bind(FNB.EVT_FLATNOTEBOOK_PAGE_CLOSING,
                  self.OnClosing)

    def OnClosing(self, event):
        """Called when a tab is closing"""
        page = self.GetCurrentPage()
        if page and hasattr(page, "IsModified"):
```

```
if page.IsModified():
    r = wx.MessageBox("Warning unsaved changes"
                      " will be lost",
                      "Close Warning",
                      wx.ICON_WARNING|\
                      wx.OK|wx.CANCEL)
if r == wx.CANCEL:
    event.Veto()
```

In the following screenshot, we can see the above subclass in action, in a simple file editor application. The full source code for the below application is available with the code that accompanies this recipe.

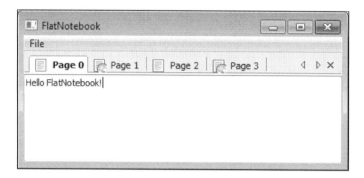

How it works...

This little recipe demonstrates quite a few of the features that the `FlatNotebook` offers over the standard `Notebook` class. So let's break it down, section by section, starting with the constructor.

In our subclass's constructor we specified four style flags. The first, `FNB_DROPDOWN_TAB_LIST`, specifies that we want to have a drop-down list that shows all the open tabs. The drop-down list is the small down-arrow button: clicking on it will show a pop-up menu that allows one of the currently open tabs to be selected from the list. The second style flag, `FNB_FF2`, specifies that we want tabs that use the Firefox 2 tab renderer, which will draw tabs that look and feel similar to the ones in Firefox 2. The third style flag, `FNB_SMART_TABS`, specifies that the *Ctrl + Tab* shortcut will pop up a dialog that shows the open tabs and allows them to be cycled through by pressing the *Tab* key. The fourth and final style flag that we used, `FNB_X_ON_TAB`, specifies that we want a close button to be shown on the active tab. This allows the user to dismiss a tab when this button is clicked on.

In order to be able to show icons on the tabs, we also created and assigned an `ImageList` to the control. An `ImageList` is simply a container for holding `Bitmap` objects, and the control will use it for retrieving the bitmap data when it draws the tabs. The important point to notice is that we keep a reference to the object by assigning it to `self._imglst`; it is important to keep a reference to it so that it doesn't get garbage collected.

The last thing that we did was `Bind` the control to the page closing event `EVT_FLATNOTEBOOK_PAGE_CLOSING`. In this example, we are expecting our pages to provide an `IsModified` method so that we can check for unsaved changes prior to closing the page, in order to give the user a chance to cancel closing the page.

There's more...

Because the `FlatNotebook` is a pure Python class, it is more customizable than the basic `Notebook` class. Included below is a listing of the style flags that can be used to customize the appearance and behavior of the control:

Style flags

Here is a list of the other style flags that are available that we didn't already cover:

Style flags	Description
FNB_ALLOW_FOREIGN_DND	Allow tabs to be dragged and moved to and accepted from other `FlatNotebook` instances
FNB_BACKGROUND_GRADIENT	Draw a gradient in the tabs background area
FNB_BOTTOM	Place the tabs at the bottom of the control area
FNB_COLORFUL_TABS	Use colorful tabs (VC8 style only)
FNB_DCLICK_CLOSES_TABS	Allow double-clicks to close the active tab
FNB_DEFAULT_STYLE	Combination of FNB_MOUSE_MIDDLE_CLOSES_TABS and FNB_HIDE_ON_SINGLE_TAB
FNB_FANCY_TABS	Use the `fancy` tab renderer for drawing the tabs
FNB_HIDE_ON_SINGLE_TAB	Hide the tab container area when there is only one tab open
FNB_MOUSE_MIDDLE_CLOSES_TABS	Allow middle mouse button clicks to close tabs
FNB_NODRAG	Don't allow tab drag and drop
FNB_NO_NAV_BUTTONS	Don't show the tab scroll buttons
FNB_NO_X_BUTTON	Don't show the **X** button on the right hand side of the tab container area
FNB_TABS_BORDER_SIMPLE	Draw a thin border around the page
FNB_VC71	Use Visual Studio 2003 style tabs
FNB_VC8	Use Visual Studio 2005 style tabs

See also

▶ The _Adding tabs to a Notebook_ recipe in this chapter shows how to use the basic tab control.

Scrolling with a ScrolledPanel

The `ScrolledPanel` class is a custom `Panel` class that has built in `ScrollBars`. This class is provided by the `scrolledpanel` module in `wx.lib`. By default, `Panels` do not have the ability to scroll when their contents overflow the windows given area. This recipe shows how to use the `ScrolledPanel`, by using it to create a custom image list widget.

How to do it...

To create our custom image viewer control that uses the `ScrolledPanel`, we will define this simple class that manages a list of `Bitmaps`:

```python
import wx
import wx.lib.scrolledpanel as scrolledpanel

class ImageListCtrl(scrolledpanel.ScrolledPanel):
    """Simple control to display a list of images"""
    def __init__(self, parent, bitmaps=list(),
                 style=wx.TAB_TRAVERSAL|wx.BORDER_SUNKEN):
        super(ImageListCtrl, self).__init__(parent,
                                            style=style)

        # Attributes
        self.images = list()
        self.sizer = wx.BoxSizer(wx.VERTICAL)

        # Setup
        for bmp in bitmaps:
            self.AppendBitmap(bmp)
        self.SetSizer(self.sizer)

    def AppendBitmap(self, bmp):
        """Add another bitmap to the control"""
        self.images.append(bmp)
        sbmp = wx.StaticBitmap(self, bitmap=bmp)
        self.sizer.Add(sbmp, 0, wx.EXPAND|wx.TOP, 5)
        self.SetupScrolling()
```

How it works...

The `ScrolledPanel` makes it pretty easy to work with `ScrollBars`, so let's take a quick look at how it works.

We created a simple class called `ImageListCtrl`. This control can be used for displaying a list of bitmaps. We derived our class from `ScrolledPanel` so that if it contains many images, the user will be able to scroll to see them all. The only special thing needed to use the `ScrolledPanel` is to call its `SetupScrolling` method when all of the panels' child controls have been added to its `Sizer`. Typically, this is done in the subclasses `__init__` method, but since our widget can add more `Bitmap` items at any time we need to call it after each `Bitmap` that is added in the `AppendBitmap` method.

The `SetupScrolling` method works by calculating the minimum size of the contents of the `Panel` and setting up the virtual size of the containment area for the `ScrollBar` objects to work with.

Simplifying the FoldPanelBar

The `FoldPanelBar` is a custom container class that allows multiple controls to be grouped together into `FoldPanelItem` controls that allow them to be expanded or contracted by clicking on its `CaptionBar`. The `FoldPanelBar` doesn't work with layouts based on a `Sizer` and as such its API can get a little cumbersome, because it requires you to add each control one by one and set its layout by using various flags. This recipe shows how to create a custom `FoldPanelBar` that works with `Panel` objects. This class will allow for you to modularize your code into `Panel` classes and then just add them to the `FoldPanelBar` instead of directly adding everything to the `FoldPanelBar` itself.

How to do it...

This custom `FoldPanelBar` class uses a factory approach to simplify and abstract the addition of a new `Panel` to the control:

```python
import wx
import wx.lib.foldpanelbar as foldpanel

class FoldPanelMgr(foldpanel.FoldPanelBar):
    """Fold panel that manages a collection of Panels"""
    def __init__(self, parent, *args, **kwargs):
        super(FoldPanelMgr, self).__init__(parent,
                                           *args,
                                           **kwargs)

    def AddPanel(self, pclass, title=u"", collapsed=False):
        """Add a panel to the manager
        @param pclass: Class constructor (callable)
        @keyword title: foldpanel title
        @keyword collapsed: start with it collapsed
        @return: pclass instance
```

```
"""
fpitem = self.AddFoldPanel(title, collapsed=collapsed)
wnd = pclass(fpitem)
best = wnd.GetBestSize()
wnd.SetSize(best)
self.AddFoldPanelWindow(fpitem, wnd)
return wnd
```

How it works...

Our subclass of `FoldPanelBar`, adds one new method to the class `AddPanel`. The `AddPanel` method is a simple wrapper around the `FoldPanelBar` control's `AddFoldPanel` and `AddFoldPanelWindow` methods. The `AddFoldPanel` method is used to create the `CaptionBar` and container for the controls and the `AddFoldPanelWindow` method is used to add a Window object to the `FoldPanel`.

Our `AddPanel` method takes a callable object as its first parameter. The callable must accept a "parent" argument and return a new window that is a child of that parent window when called. We do this because our panels need to be created as children of the `FoldPanelItem` that is returned by `AddFoldPanel`. This is an important point to remember when working with the `FoldPanelBar`. All of the controls that are added to it must be children of one of its `FoldPanelItems` and not children of the `FoldPanelBar` itself.

Since the `FoldPanelBar` internally works with a manual layout, we need to set an explicit size on each `Panel` as it is added. This is done by getting the best size from each Panel object's `GetBestSize` method.

There's more...

The `CaptionBar` of the `FoldPanelBar` can be customized by making a custom `CaptionBarStyle` object and passing it to the `AddFoldPanel` method. A `CaptionBarStyle` object has methods for changing the colors, fonts, and styles that the `CaptionBar` will use. The `AddFoldPanel` method also accepts an optional `foldIcons` argument, which accepts an `ImageList` object that must have two 16x16 pixel bitmaps in it. The first will be used for the button's expanded state and the second will be used for its collapsed state.

5
Providing Information and Alerting Users

In this chapter, we will cover:

- ▶ Showing a `MessageBox`
- ▶ Providing help with `ToolTips`
- ▶ Using `SuperToolTips`
- ▶ Displaying a `BalloonTip`
- ▶ Creating a custom `SplashScreen`
- ▶ Showing task progress with the Progress dialog
- ▶ Creating an `AboutBox`

Introduction

During an application's runtime, a wide variety of events can arise under a number of different circumstances. This gives rise to the need to be able to alert and inform users of these events in an equally wide variety of context-sensitive, intuitive, and effective ways.

Providing information in the right way at the right time is crucial to the usability of an application. wxPython includes many widgets to help meet the specific needs of any type of application. So let's take a look at some of these widgets and see how to use them to their fullest.

Showing a MessageBox

`MessageBoxes` are one of, if not, the most common and easy ways of alerting users and providing them with the ability to make simple choices. `MessageBoxes` come in a number of varying forms but all share two common points. They all have a (usually) short caption message and one or more buttons that allow the user to respond to the message. This recipe shows how to add a `MessageBox` that gives the user a chance to abort closing a `Frame`.

How to do it...

As an example of how to show a `MessageBox`, we will create a little Frame class that uses a `MessageBox` as a confirmation to the window close event:

```python
class MyFrame(wx.Frame):
    def __init__(self, parent, *args, **kwargs):
        super(MyFrame, self).__init__(parent, *args, **kwargs)

        # Layout
        self.CreateStatusBar()
        self.PushStatusText("Close this window")

        # Event Handlers
        self.Bind(wx.EVT_CLOSE, self.OnClose)

    def OnClose(self, event):
        result = wx.MessageBox("Are you sure you want "
                              "to close this window?",
                              style=wx.CENTER|\
                                    wx.ICON_QUESTION|\
                                    wx.YES_NO)
        if result == wx.NO:
            event.Veto()
        else:
            event.Skip()
```

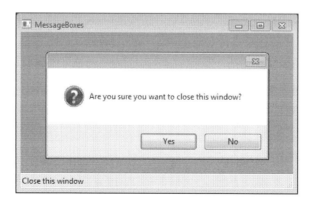

How it works...

`wx.MessageBox` is a function that will create, show, and clean up a modal dialog. It only requires the first parameter, which specifies the message that will be displayed:

```
wx.MessageBox(message, caption="", style=wx.OK|wx.CENTER,
              parent=None, x=-1, y=-1)
```

The other parameters are all optional keyword parameters. The second parameter is used to specify the dialog's title. The third parameter is the style parameter for specifying how the dialog will look and what buttons it will have on it. This parameter is just like any other widget constructor in that its value will be a bitmask of style flags. The fourth parameter can be used to specify the parent window of the dialog. The final two parameters can be used for explicitly setting the dialog's X and Y coordinates on the desktop.

In this recipe, we just used the message and the style parameters. In the style parameter, we specified the CENTER flag which indicates that the dialog should be centered on its parent, which in this case will be the desktop since we did not specify a parent window. The ICON_QUESTION flag specifies that we want to display the question mark icon on the dialog. The last flag, YES_NO, says that we want to have a Yes and a No button on the dialog, so that the user can reply to the yes/no question we asked in our message.

When the user clicks on one of the dialog's buttons, the dialog will end its modal loop and return the value of the button that was clicked, which in this case will be either YES or NO. Here we simply check the return value and either Veto the event to stop the Frame from closing, or Skip it to allow the Frame to be destroyed.

Platform Notice

On OS X, these dialogs will show the application icon. This is done to conform with Apple's Human Interface Guidelines. This means that unless you have built your script into an applet and given it its own icon, the dialog will show the Python.app icon.

There's more...

There are a number of style flags that the MessageBox function can accept. Here is a quick reference list, broken down by category.

Icons

The `MessageBox` can show only one icon, so only one of the following flags should be specified at a time:

Flags	Description
`wx.ICON_ERROR`	Display an icon on the dialog that signifies that an error has occurred.
`wx.ICON_INFORMATION`	Display an icon on the dialog that signifies that the dialog is only displaying information.
`wx.ICON_QUESTION`	Display an icon on the dialog that signifies that a question is being asked that the user needs to respond to.
`wx.ICON_WARNING`	Display an icon on the dialog that signifies a warning message to the user.

Buttons

The following flags are used to specify the buttons to show in the dialog. By default, the dialog will just show an OK button:

Flags	Description
`wx.CANCEL`	Add a Cancel button to the dialog.
`wx.OK`	Add an OK button to the dialog.
`wx.YES`	Add a Yes button to the dialog.
`wx.NO`	Add a No button to the dialog.
`wx.YES_NO`	Convenience for `wx.YES`/`wx.NO`.
`wx.YES_DEFAULT`	Set the Yes button as the default button.
`wx.NO_DEFAULT`	Set the No button as the default button.

Providing help with ToolTips

`ToolTips` are small pop-up help texts that are shown when the mouse cursor hovers over a window object for a few moments. When the mouse leaves the window's area they are automatically dismissed. They are very useful for places where it may be necessary to present extra information to your users about the function of a certain part of the interface. Nearly all window objects support having a `ToolTip` associated with them. This recipe shows how to add a `ToolTip` to a `Button`.

How to do it...

In order to see how to add a `ToolTip` to a control, let's just make a simple `Panel` class that has a single `Button` on it:

```python
class ToolTipTestPanel(wx.Panel):
    def __init__(self, parent):
        super(ToolTipTestPanel, self).__init__(parent)

        # Attributes
        self.button = wx.Button(self, label="Go")

        # Setup
        self.button.SetToolTipString("Launch the shuttle")
        self.timer = wx.Timer(self)
        self.count = 11

        # Layout
        sizer = wx.BoxSizer(wx.VERTICAL)
        sizer.Add(self.button, 0, wx.ALIGN_CENTER)
        msizer = wx.BoxSizer(wx.HORIZONTAL)
        msizer.Add(sizer, 1, wx.ALIGN_CENTER)
        self.SetSizer(msizer)

        # Event Handlers
        self.Bind(wx.EVT_BUTTON, self.OnGo, self.button)
        self.Bind(wx.EVT_TIMER, self.OnTimer, self.timer)

    def OnGo(self, event):
        self.button.Disable()
        print self.timer.Start(1000)
        tlw = self.GetTopLevelParent()
        tlw.PushStatusText("Launch initiated...")

    def OnTimer(self, event):
        tlw = self.GetTopLevelParent()
        self.count -= 1
        tlw.PushStatusText("%d" % self.count)
        if self.count == 0:
            self.timer.Stop()
            wx.MessageBox("Shuttle Launched!")
```

How it works...

Here, we just created a simple panel with a single button on it. The button just has a simple label that says Go. Since there is no other indication as to what this button may do, we then added a ToolTip to it by calling the SetToolTipString method. The SetToolTipString method belongs to the base wx.Window class so it can be used with any object that is visible on the screen. This method creates a ToolTip object and then calls the Window's SetToolTip method to associate ToolTip with the Window.

There's more...

▶   The *Using SuperToolTips* recipe in this chapter shows another way of providing context sensitive help to users.

▶   See the *Playing with the mouse* recipe in *Chapter 2, Responding to Events* for some insight into how the system shows the tips when the mouse cursor enters the window.

Using SuperToolTips

The SuperToolTip class is an advanced type of ToolTip provided by the wx.lib.agw. supertooltip module. Unlike the regular ToolTip, the SuperToolTip is a custom fully-owner-drawn control that supports a wide range of display options. It has the ability to show a header, a footer, a body section, and each section can also have an image shown in it. In addition to this, it also supports custom backgrounds, HTML rendering of the content, and hyperlinks. This recipe shows how to create and use a SuperToolTip.

 wx.lib.agw is available in wxPython 2.8.9.2 and higher.

How to do it...

Let's modify the sample from the *Providing help with ToolTips* recipe to show how a more verbose help message may be helpful in this case. This recipe uses two image files that are provided with the source code that accompanies this chapter:

```
import wx.lib.agw.supertooltip as supertooltip

class SuperToolTipTestPanel (wx.Panel):
    def __init__(self, parent):
        super(SuperToolTipTestPanel, self).__init__(parent)
```

```
# Attributes
self.button = wx.Button(self, label="Go")
msg = "Launches the shuttle"
self.stip = supertooltip.SuperToolTip(msg)

# Setup SuperToolTip
bodybmp = wx.Bitmap("earth.png", wx.BITMAP_TYPE_PNG)
self.stip.SetBodyImage(bodybmp)
self.stip.SetHeader("Launch Control")
footbmp = wx.Bitmap("warning.png", wx.BITMAP_TYPE_PNG)
self.stip.SetFooterBitmap(footbmp)
footer = "Warning: This is serious business"
self.stip.SetFooter(footer)
self.stip.ApplyStyle("XP Blue")
self.stip.SetTarget(self.button)
```

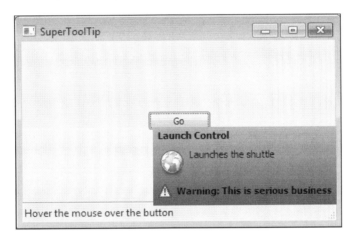

How it works...

Here, we took our previous recipe and changed it to use a `SuperToolTip` instead of the standard `ToolTip`.

First, we start by importing the extension module from the `wx.lib.agw` package so that we can access the `SuperToolTip` class. Then we proceed to create the `SuperToolTip` object for our button in the `SuperToolTipTestPanel` class. In our use case, this involves creating the tip with its body message, then setting a body image that will be shown to the left of our message. We then added some header text by calling the `SetHeader` method as well as a footer and footer image by using the `SetFooter` and `SetFooterBitmap` methods. The last setup step we make is to call `ApplyStyle`. This method allows for the use of one of the 30 or so built-in style themes for the background gradient.

The final step in using the `SuperToolTip` is the important difference between it and the standard `ToolTip`. We have to call `SetTarget` on the `SuperToolTip` object instead of calling `SetToolTip` on the `Window` object (in this case our `Button`). This is because the `SuperToolTip` manages when it is shown/hidden, and not the `Window` it belongs too.

There's more...

The `SuperToolTip` has a few more options not covered in this recipe. Included below are some additional references and information.

Styles

The `ApplyStyles` method takes one of the named built-in styles as a parameter. There are currently about 30 different built-in styles. They are all defined and can be found in the `supertooltip` module. They can also be found by looking at the return value of `supertooltip.GetStyleKeys()`, which will return a list of all the built-in styles.

Additional customization

There are a few more additional methods that can be used to customize the appearance of the `SuperToolTip`. The following table includes a quick reference for these methods:

Methods	Description
`SetDrawHeaderLine(bool)`	Draw a horizontal separator line between the header and the body.
`SetDrawFooterLine(bool)`	Draw a horizontal separator line between the footer and the body.
`SetDropShadow(bool)`	Use a drop shadow on the tip window. (Windows only)
`SetUseFade(bool)`	Fade in/out of view. (Windows only)
`SetEndDelay(int)`	Set the time for which the tip will be shown.
`SetTopGradientColour(colour)`	Sets the top gradient color.
`SetBottomGradientColour(colour)`	Sets the bottom gradient color.
`SetMiddleGradientColour(colour)`	Sets the middle gradient color.

See also

> ▶ The *Providing help with ToolTips* recipe in this chapter shows a way to provide simple help messages.

Displaying a BalloonTip

BalloonTips are yet another ToolTip implementation. They are fairly similar to the SuperToolTip but have a look and feel that imitates the Windows XP taskbar balloon notifications. When shown, the BalloonTip will create a tip window that has a point that extends towards the centre of its target window. This recipe shows how to add a BalloonTip to an application's TaskBarIcon.

 wx.lib.agw is available in wxPython 2.8.9.2 and higher.

How to do it...

Here, we will create a simple TaskBarIcon class that will show a BalloonTip when hovered over. In this example, we again use an external icon that is provided with the source code that accompanies this chapter:

```python
import wx.lib.agw.balloontip as btip

class TaskBarBalloon(wx.TaskBarIcon):
    def __init__(self):
        super(TaskBarBalloon, self).__init__()

        # Setup
        icon = wx.Icon("face-monkey.png", wx.BITMAP_TYPE_PNG)
        self.SetIcon(icon)

        # Setup BallooTip
        title="BalloonTip Recipe"
        msg = "Welcome to the Balloon Tip Recipe"
        bmp = wx.BitmapFromIcon(icon)
        self.tip = btip.BalloonTip(topicon=bmp,
                                   toptitle=title,
                                   message=msg,
                                   shape=btip.BT_ROUNDED,
                                   tipstyle=btip.BT_BUTTON)
        self.tip.SetStartDelay(1000)
        self.tip.SetTarget(self)

        # Event Handlers
        self.Bind(wx.EVT_MENU, self.OnMenu)
```

```
def CreatePopupMenu(self):
    menu = wx.Menu()
    menu.Append(wx.ID_CLOSE, "Exit")
    return menu

def OnMenu(self, event):
    self.RemoveIcon()
    self.tip.DestroyTimer()
    self.Destroy()
```

How it works...

The `BalloonTip` class is found in the `wx.lib.agw.balloontip` module. To make it easier to use, we imported it with the alias `btip`. The `BalloonTip` constructor takes up to five optional keyword arguments to specify the tip's contents and appearance:

Keyword arguments	Description
topicon	Accepts a `Bitmap` object that will be shown in the top left-hand corner of the `BalloonTip` window
toptitle	A string that specifies the title of the `BalloonTip` window
message	A string that specifies the main message for the `BalloonTip` window
shape	Either `BT_RECTANGLE` or `BT_ROUNDED` (default), which specify the shape of the `BalloonTip` window
tipstyle	One of the following values for specifying how the `BalloonTip` window will be dismissed: ▸ BT_LEAVE: The tip window will be dismissed when the mouse leaves the target window ▸ BT_CLICK: The tip window will be dismissed when a user clicks on the target window ▸ BT_BUTTON: The tip window will be dismissed by clicking on a close button on the tip window

After creating the `BalloonTip`, we modified its start delay by making a call to `SetStartDelay`, which sets the delay in milliseconds from which the tip window will be shown after the mouse is moved over the target window. Finally, we called `SetTarget` to set the `TaskBarIcon` as the target window for this `BalloonTip`. After this, the `BalloonTip` is all set up for use with our `TaskBarIcon`.

In the `TaskBarIcons` event handler for the exit menu event, we had to add a call to `DestroyTimer` on our `BalloonTip`. This is to ensure that the tip window is destroyed, otherwise if it is still open the applications main loop will not exit since there are still top-level windows in the application.

There's more...

As with most of the generic widgets available in `wx.lib`, the `BalloonTip` class offers a wide variety of methods to customize its appearance. The following table includes a quick reference to a number of these methods:

Method	Description
`SetBalloonColour(colour)`	Sets the `BalloonTips` background color. Pass `None` to revert back to the default.
`SetMessageColour(colour)`	Set the text `Colour` for the main message. Pass `None` to revert back to the default.
`SetMessageFont(font)`	Set the `Font` to use for the main message. Pass `None` to revert back to the default.
`SetTitleColour(colour)`	Set the text `Colour` for the title. Pass `None` to revert back to the default.
`SetTitleFont(font)`	Set the titles `Font`. Pass `None` to revert back to the default.

See also

▶ The *Using SuperToolTips* recipe in this chapter shows another way to provide context-sensitive information messages.

▶ The *Working with tray icons* recipe in *Chapter 4, Advanced Building Blocks of a User Interface* contains an explanation of using `TaskBarIcons` in an application.

Creating a custom SplashScreen

`SplashWindows` are commonly seen during the start up of an application. They are a means to show a software's logo and, more importantly, they are often used as a means to provide feedback to the user when an application takes a bit of time to start up so that the user knows that the application is in the process of loading up. This recipe shows how to create an advanced `SplashWindow` class that can show the incremental progress of where an application is during startup.

How to do it...

Here we will create our custom `SplashScreen` class. The source code that accompanies this chapter also includes a sample application showing how to use this class:

```
class ProgressSplashScreen(wx.SplashScreen):
    def __init__(self, *args, **kwargs):
        super(ProgressSplashScreen, self).__init__(*args,
                                                   **kwargs)
```

```
# Attributes
self.gauge = wx.Gauge(self, size=(-1, 16))

# Setup
rect = self.GetClientRect()
new_size = (rect.width, 16)
self.gauge.SetSize(new_size)
self.SetSize((rect.width, rect.height + 16))
self.gauge.SetPosition((0, rect.height))

def SetProgress(self, percent):
    """Set the indicator gauges progress"""
    self.gauge.SetValue(percent)

def GetProgress(self):
    """Get the current progress of the gauge"""
    return self.gauge.GetValue()
```

The screenshot is as follows:

How it works...

The basic `SplashScreen` uses the `Bitmap` that is passed into the constructor to set its size, and then the `Bitmap` is drawn to fill the background. In our subclass, we created a `Gauge` to allow for the program to give feedback to the user about the progress of the startup procedure.

To allow the `Gauge` to fit on the `SplashScreen`, we first changed the width of the `Gauge` to be the same width as the `SplashScreen`, by calling its `SetSize` method with the `Gauge`'s height and the `SplashScreen`'s width. Next, we changed the size of the `SplashScreen` to make it taller, so that we could position the `Gauge` at the bottom of it without overlapping the `SplashScreen` image. Then the final step was to manually position the `Gauge` into the extra space we added at the bottom, by calling its `SetPosition` method with the X and Y coordinates of where the top-left corner of the `Gauge` should be placed.

The last two things that we added to our class were just some simple access methods to allow the `Gauge` to be manipulated by the users of this class. For an example of this class in action, check out the sample code that accompanies this chapter.

There's more...

The `SplashScreen`'s constructor has two different style parameters. The first one, `splashStyle`, is a required bitmask of one or more of the following flags:

Flags	Description
wx.SPLASH_CENTRE_ON_PARENT	Center the SplashScreen on its parent window.
wx.SPLASH_CENTRE_ON_SCREEN	Center the SplashScreen on the desktop.
wx.SPLASH_NO_CENTRE	Don't center the SplashScreen.
wx.SPLASH_TIMEOUT	Allow the SplashScreen to be automatically destroyed when the timeout is reached.
wx.SPLASH_NO_TIMEOUT	Don't allow the SplashScreen to timeout (require explicit destruction of it).

The second style flag parameter is the typical optional one, and is for specifying `wx.Frame` style flags. The `SplashScreen` derives from `wx.Frame`, so these flags will be passed down to the base class. In most cases, the default flags are what you want to use here, otherwise it will end up behaving more like a `Frame` than a `SplashScreen`.

Showing task progress with the Progress dialog

The `ProgressDialog` is a dialog for showing the progress of a long-running task, such as downloading a file from the Internet, or exporting data from your program. The dialog shows a short message, a progress bar, and optionally Abort and/or Skip buttons. Additionally, it can also optionally show the estimated, elapsed, and remaining time. This recipe shows how to make a command-line script that can be used to download a file from the Internet and show the progress of the download using `ProgressDialog`.

How to do it...

We will create a full application here to allow downloading a file from a URL that is passed to the script on the command line. So first we will define the application object class:

```
import wx
import os
import sys
import urllib2

class DownloaderApp(wx.App):
    def OnInit(self):
```

```
                # Create a hidden frame so that the eventloop
                # does not automatically exit before we show
                # the download dialog.
                self.frame = wx.Frame(None)
                self.frame.Hide()
                return True

        def Cleanup(self):
                self.frame.Destroy()
```

Here, we define the method that will be used to show the `ProgressDialog`, and perform the actual downloading of the file by using the `urllib` module from the Python standard library:

```
        def DownloadFile(self, url):
                """Downloads the file
                @return: bool (success/fail)
                """
                dialog = None
                try:
                        # Open the url to read from and
                        # the local file to write the downloaded
                        # data to.
                        webfile = urllib2.urlopen(url)
                        size = int(webfile.info()['Content-Length'])
                        dlpath = os.path.abspath(os.getcwd())
                        dlfile = url.split('/')[-1]
                        dlpath = GetUniqueName(dlpath, dlfile)
                        localfile = open(dlpath, 'wb')

                        # Create the ProgressDialog
                        dlmsg = "Downloading: %s" % dlfile
                        style = (wx.PD_APP_MODAL
                                 |wx.PD_CAN_ABORT
                                 |wx.PD_ELAPSED_TIME
                                 |wx.PD_REMAINING_TIME)
                        dialog = wx.ProgressDialog("Download Dialog",
                                                   dlmsg,
                                                   maximum=size,
                                                   parent=self.frame,
                                                   style=style)

                        # Download the file
                        blk_sz = 4096
                        read = 0
                        keep_going = True
```

```
            while read < size and keep_going:
                data = webfile.read(blk_sz)
                localfile.write(data)
                read += len(data)
                keep_going, skip = dialog.Update(read)

            localfile.close()
            webfile.close()
        finally:
            # All done so cleanup top level windows
            # to cause the event loop to exit.
            if dialog:
                dialog.Destroy()
            self.Cleanup()
```

Here, we have an additional helper function that is used to get a unique path to write the downloaded data to:

```
#--- Utility Functions ----#

def GetUniqueName(path, name):
    """Make a file name that will be unique in case a file
    of the same name already exists at that path.
    @param path: Root path to folder of files destination
    @param name: desired file name base
    @return: string
    """
    tmpname = os.path.join(path, name)
    if os.path.exists(tmpname):
        if '.' not in name:
            ext = ''
            fbase = name
        else:
            ext = '.' + name.split('.')[-1]
            fbase = name[:-1 * len(ext)]

        inc = len([x for x in os.listdir(path)
                    if x.startswith(fbase)])
        newname = "%s-%d%s" % (fbase, inc, ext)
        tmpname = os.path.join(path, newname)
        while os.path.exists(tmpname):
            inc = inc + 1
            newname = "%s-%d%s" % (fbase, inc, ext)
            tmpname = os.path.join(path, newname)

    return tmpname
```

Finally, the main execution of the script that does the simple command-line argument handling for this application and starts the download is as follows:

```
#---- Main Execution ----#
if __name__ == "__main__":
    if len(sys.argv) > 1:
        url = sys.argv[1]
        app = DownloaderApp(False)
        # Start with a slight delay so the eventloop
        # can start running, to ensure our dialog gets
        # shown
        wx.CallLater(2000, app.DownloadFile, url)
        app.MainLoop()
    else:
        # Print some help text
        print(("wxPython Cookbook - ProgressDialog\n"
                "usage: downloader url\n"))
```

Here is an example of how to call this script from the command-line downloader:
`python downloader.py http://somewebsite.com/afile.zip`.

How it works...

The recipe above shows the code for the entire downloader application. Let's take a walk through how it works, starting at the top and working our way down.

First, we imported some modules from the standard Python library. We needed the `os` module for path manipulation, the `sys` module for getting the command-line arguments, and the `urllib2` module so that we can open remote URLs.

Next, we defined our `DownloaderApp`. This application object has two methods that are of interest to us. The first is the override of `wx.App.OnInit`. In our override, we created a Frame and hid it. We did this just to ensure that the event loop does not exit before we create and show our `ProgressDialog`, as the event loop will exit by default when there are no more top-level windows in the application. The second is the `DownloadFile` method. This is where the main action of this application takes place.

`DownloadFile` first opens the remote URL that was passed in using `urllib2`, and gets the size of the file that the URL points to. Next, it opens a file on the local file system to, write to as we read the data from the remote URL. We then create our `ProgressDialog`, giving it the style flags necessary to have an Abort button and show the elapsed and remaining time. Once the dialog has been created, we can start reading the data from the URL that we opened. We do this in a loop that checks how much we have read already and whether or not the Abort button was clicked. After reading a chunk from the URL, we call the `ProgressDialog`'s `Update` method, which will update the progress bar and return two Boolean flags that indicate if one of the two possible dialog buttons was clicked. Once the loop exits, we simply close the two files and `Destroy` our window objects, to cause the main loop to exit.

The final two things are the `GetUniqueName` function and the `__main__`. `GetUniqueName` is just a simple utility function to help generate the local filename, to make sure that we don't try to write over an already-existing file. The `__main__` execution makes just a simple check of the command-line arguments, and then creates the `DownloaderApp` and calls its `DownloadFile` method. We needed to use `wx.CallLater` to delay the call by a couple of seconds because `DownloadFile` will block when it is called. Without using `CallLater`, it would have blocked, performed the download, and returned before the `MainLoop` was started, which would have meant that our dialog would have never been displayed on the screen.

There's more...

Included below are some additional references and information to take into consideration when using the `ProgressDialog`.

Message parameter

There is some undesirable behavior that can be seen with the `ProgressDialog`'s message parameter in some cases. If the passed-in message string is very long, it will cause the dialog's width to be set very wide. So if you see that the dialog is showing up as being much wider than you would expect, try shortening your message.

Style flags

Here is a quick reference to the available style flags that the `ProgressDialog` can use:

Style flags	Description
`wx.PD_APP_MODAL`	The dialog should be application modal
`wx.PD_AUTO_HIDE`	Have the dialog automatically disappears when the progress bar reaches its maximum value
`wx.PD_SMOOTH`	Cause the progress bar to be updated smoothly
`wx.PD_CAN_ABORT`	Show the Abort button on the dialog
`wx.PD_CAN_SKIP`	Show the Skip button on the dialog
`wx.PD_ELAPSED_TIME`	Show the elapsed time status text
`wx.PD_ESTIMATED_TIME`	Show the estimated total time status text
`wx.PD_REMAININT_TIME`	Show the estimated remaining time status text

Creating an AboutBox

An About dialog is a simple dialog for displaying some information about an application to the user, such as the application's version number and license information. This dialog can be found in most applications on any operating system. It contains an icon and a small information section that usually contains at least the version information and credits. This recipe shows how to set up and show an About dialog in an application.

How to do it...

Here, we create a simple skeleton application that shows how to integrate an AboutBox into an application:

```python
import wx
import sys

class AboutRecipeFrame(wx.Frame):
    def __init__(self, *args, **kwargs):
        super(AboutRecipeFrame, self).__init__(*args,
                                               **kwargs)

        # Attributes
        self.panel = wx.Panel(self)

        # Setup Menus
        menubar = wx.MenuBar()
        helpmenu = wx.Menu()
        helpmenu.Append(wx.ID_ABOUT, "About")
        menubar.Append(helpmenu, "Help")
        self.SetMenuBar(menubar)

        # Setup StatusBar
        self.CreateStatusBar()
        self.PushStatusText("See About in the Menu")

        # Event Handlers
        self.Bind(wx.EVT_MENU, self.OnAbout, id=wx.ID_ABOUT)

    def OnAbout(self, event):
        """Show the about dialog"""
        info = wx.AboutDialogInfo()

        # Make a template for the description
        desc = ["\nwxPython Cookbook Chapter 5\n",
                "Platform Info: (%s,%s)",
                "License: Public Domain"]
        desc = "\n".join(desc)

        # Get the platform information
        py_version = [sys.platform,
                      ", python ",
```

```
                        sys.version.split()[0]]
        platform = list(wx.PlatformInfo[1:])
        platform[0] += (" " + wx.VERSION_STRING)
        wx_info = ", ".join(platform)

        # Populate with information
        info.SetName("AboutBox Recipe")
        info.SetVersion("1.0")
        info.SetCopyright("Copyright (C) Joe Programmer")
        info.SetDescription(desc % (py_version, wx_info))

        # Create and show the dialog
        wx.AboutBox(info)

class AboutRecipeApp(wx.App):
    def OnInit(self):
        self.frame = AboutRecipeFrame(None,
                                     title="AboutDialog",
                                     size=(300,200))

        self.SetTopWindow(self.frame)
        self.frame.Show()

        return True

if __name__ == "__main__":
    app = AboutRecipeApp(False)
    app.MainLoop()
```

How it works...

In this recipe, we created a very simple yet complete application for creating and displaying an About dialog. So let's go over the important parts of the code shown above.

Firstly, let's take a look a look at the part where we set up the menus in the AboutRecipeFrame class. Standard application About dialogs are shown from a menu item. On Windows and GTK Linux this menu entry is under the Help menu; on Macintosh OS X this menu entry is under the Application menu. wxPython will take care of these platform differences for us automatically since we assigned our About menu entry the wx.ID_ABOUT stock ID, which lets wx know that the menu entry is a standard about information menu entry.

The next and most important part of this recipe is the OnAbout menu event handler. This is the method that will get called when our About menu entry is activated and it is where we create and show the About dialog by calling the AboutBox function. The AboutBox function requires an AboutDialogInfo object that contains all of the information that we want to display in the dialog that it will create.

The `AboutDialogInfo` object has a number of methods for setting the different data fields that the dialog can support. These methods are all simple setter methods that take strings or lists of strings as arguments. We used four of these methods in this recipe:

1. `SetName` takes the application's name. This string will be shown in the dialog's title bar and as the first line in the main content area.

2. `SetVersion` is for setting and showing the application's version number. This is shown after the application name in the main content area.

3. `SetCopyright` sets the copyright information field. The special thing to note about this method is if the string contains a (C) in it, this will be automatically converted to the copyright symbol ©.

4. `SetDescription` is the main description field, which can contain any arbitrary information about the application.

The last thing that we did was to show the About dialog box. This is quite simple. All we needed to do was to call the `wx.AboutBox` function with the `AboutDialogInfo` that we created.

There's more...

The `AboutDialogInfo` object supports a number of additional fields for other special types of data and customization of the `AboutBox`. wxPython provides a native implementation of the About dialog on the three major platforms (MSW, GTK, OSX). However, only the GTK version of the `AboutBox` has native support for all the extra fields that the `AboutDialogInfo` supports. If the `AboutDialogInfo` contains any fields that the native dialog does not support, wxPython will automatically switch to the generic version of the dialog. This can be a problem if you want to maintain a native look and feel in your application. So following is a list of the other `AboutDialogInfo` fields that are available, and which ones will cause the generic dialog to be used on Windows and OS X:

Other `AboutDialogInfo` fields	Description
`SetArtists(list_of_strings)`	For crediting the application's graphic artists.
`SetDevelopers(list_of_strings)`	For crediting the application's developers.
`SetDocWriters(list_of_strings)`	For crediting the application's documentation writers.
`SetIcon(icon)`	Customize the dialog's icon. Default is the application icon (GTK only)
`SetLicense(license_string)`	For displaying the application's long license text (GTK only).
`SetTranslators(list_of_strings)`	For crediting the application's translators.
`SetWebSite(url_string)`	Creates a hyperlink to a website in the dialog (GTK only).

See also

▶ The *Utilizing Stock IDs* recipe in *Chapter 1, Getting Started with wxPython* explains the usage of the built-in IDs.

▶ The *Adding Menus and MenuBars* recipe in *Chapter 3, Basic Building Blocks of a User Interface* contains detailed information about creating menus and adding them to a Frame's `MenuBar`.

6
Retrieving Information from Users

In this chapter, we will cover:

▶ Selecting files with a `FileDialog`

▶ Searching text with a `FindReplaceDialog`

▶ Getting images with `ImageDialog`

▶ Using the Print dialogs

Introduction

Being able to retrieve information from users is an essential part of any application. Dialogs are one of the many ways of retrieving information from users; most desktop applications use a number of common dialogs for tasks such as opening, saving, and printing files.

There are two main types of dialogs: Modal and Modeless. Modal dialogs are dialogs that, when shown, block and disable interaction with their parent window or all other windows in an application (in the case of an application-modal dialog). Modal dialogs are used for cases where a program must retrieve data from a user before proceeding to its next task. Modeless dialogs, on the other hand, behave similarly to Frames. When modeless dialogs are shown, the other windows in the application remain accessible. When closed, modeless dialogs will usually post an event to their parent window to inform it that the dialog has closed.

wxPython supplies many built-in dialogs that can fill the needs of almost any common circumstance. So let's take a look at a handful of these common dialogs in action with the recipes in this chapter.

Selecting files with a FileDialog

Allowing users to open and save files is one of the most fundamental capabilities of many applications. To provide this functionality, it is often necessary to give the user the ability to select which files to open, what to name a file, and where to put it when saving a new file. The `FileDialog` can be used to fill this role in your application. This recipe creates a simple text editor application that can open and save text files to show how to use the `FileDialog`.

How to do it...

Here, we will create a complete text-editor application:

```
import wx

class FileEditorApp(wx.App):
    def OnInit(self):
        self.frame = FileEditorFrame(None,
                                     title="File Editor")
        self.frame.Show()
        return True
```

Our main application window is defined here, and consists of a Frame, TextCtrl, and MenuBar:

```
class FileEditorFrame(wx.Frame):
    def __init__(self, *args, **kwargs):
        super(FileEditorFrame, self).__init__(*args, **kwargs)

        # Attributes
        self.file = None
        style = style=wx.TE_MULTILINE|wx.TE_RICH2
        self.txtctrl = wx.TextCtrl(self, style=style)

        # Setup
        self._SetupMenus()

        # Layout
        sizer = wx.BoxSizer(wx.VERTICAL)
        sizer.Add(self.txtctrl, 1, wx.EXPAND)
        self.SetSizer(sizer)

        # Event Handlers
        self.Bind(wx.EVT_MENU, self.OnOpen, id=wx.ID_OPEN)
        self.Bind(wx.EVT_MENU, self.OnSave, id=wx.ID_SAVE)
```

```
            self.Bind(wx.EVT_MENU, self.OnSave, id=wx.ID_SAVEAS)
            self.Bind(wx.EVT_MENU, self.OnExit, id=wx.ID_EXIT)
            self.Bind(wx.EVT_CLOSE, self.OnExit)

    def _SetupMenus(self):
        """Make the frames menus"""
        menub = wx.MenuBar()
        fmenu = wx.Menu()
        fmenu.Append(wx.ID_OPEN, "Open\tCtrl+O")
        fmenu.AppendSeparator()
        fmenu.Append(wx.ID_SAVE, "Save\tCtrl+S")
        fmenu.Append(wx.ID_SAVEAS, "Save As\tCtrl+Shift+S")
        fmenu.AppendSeparator()
        fmenu.Append(wx.ID_EXIT, "Exit\tCtrl+Q")
        menub.Append(fmenu, "File")
        self.SetMenuBar(menub)
```

Here are the event handlers for the `MenuItems` we added to the Frame's MenuBar above. These event handlers are used mostly to just delegate to the method that performs the action the user requested.

```
    #---- Event Handlers ----#

    def OnOpen(self, event):
        """Handle Open"""
        if event.GetId() == wx.ID_OPEN:
            self.DoOpen()
        else:
            event.Skip()

    def OnSave(self, event):
        """Handle Save/SaveAs"""
        evt_id = event.GetId()
        if evt_id in (wx.ID_SAVE,
                      wx.ID_SAVEAS):
            if self.file:
                self.Save(self.file)
            else:
                self.DoSaveAs()
        else:
            event.Skip()

    def OnExit(self, event):
        """Handle window close event"""
```

```
            # Give warning about unsaved changes
            if self.txtctrl.IsModified():
                message = ("There are unsaved changes.\n\n"
                           "Would you like to save them?")
                style = wx.YES_NO|wx.ICON_WARNING|wx.CENTRE
                result = wx.MessageBox(message,
                                       "Save Changes?",
                                       style=style)
                if result == wx.YES:
                    if self.file is None:
                        self.DoSaveAs()
                    else:
                        self.Save(self.file)
        event.Skip()


    #---- End Event Handlers ----#


    #---- Implementation ----#
```

Here, in the DoOpen method, we make the first use of the FileDialog in OPEN mode to allow the user to select the file they wish to open:

```
        def DoOpen(self):
            """Show file open dialog and open file"""
            wildcard = "Text Files (*.txt)|*.txt"
            dlg = wx.FileDialog(self,
                                message="Open a File",
                                wildcard=wildcard,
                                style=wx.FD_OPEN)
            if dlg.ShowModal() == wx.ID_OK:
                path = dlg.GetPath()
                with open(path, "rb") as handle:
                    text = handle.read()
                    self.txtctrl.SetValue(text)
                    self.file = path
            dlg.Destroy()
```

In DoSaveAs, we see the second use of the FileDialog to allow the user to choose where to save the file to, by creating the dialog in SAVE mode.

```
        def DoSaveAs(self):
            """Show SaveAs dialog"""
            wildcard = "Text Files (*.txt)|*.txt"
            dlg = wx.FileDialog(self,
                                message="Save As",
```

```
                                    wildcard=wildcard,
                                    style=wx.FD_SAVE
                                        |wx.FD_OVERWRITE_PROMPT)
            if dlg.ShowModal() == wx.ID_OK:
                path = dlg.GetPath()
                self.Save(path)
                self.file = path
            dlg.Destroy()

        def Save(self, path):
            """Save the file"""
            with open(path, "wb") as handle:
                text = self.txtctrl.GetValue()
                handle.write(text)
                self.txtctrl.SetModified(False)

        #---- End Implementation ----#

    #---- Main Execution ----#
    if __name__ == "__main__":
        app = FileEditorApp(False)
        app.MainLoop()
```

How it works...

Just to provide a feel of how quickly you can create a usable application in wxPython, let's just look at the recipe above. In roughly 100 lines of code, we have basically implemented a Windows Notepad clone. Since this recipe was about the `FileDialog`, let's just focus in on the `DoOpen` and `DoSaveAs` methods of our text editor application, to see how it works.

The `FileDialog` has two basic modes: Open and Save. The mode of the dialog depends upon which style flags it was created with. Our `DoOpen` method creates it with the `FD_OPEN` style flag, which puts it into Open mode. Open mode differs from Save mode in that it only allows you to select a file and not enter a name in order to create a new one.

In both of our uses of the `FileDialog` in this application, we used the same set of optional parameters for creating it. The `wildcards` parameter accepts a specially-formatted string to specify the file filter list in the dialog. This string must be formatted as follows:

```
"All Files (*)|*|Text Files (*.txt;*.in)|*.txt;*.in"
```

The fields in this string are interpreted as follows:

Description1 | *wildcard1* | *Description2* | *wildcard1;wildcard2*

Each field is a description followed by the pipe character as a separator, and then the `wx.ID_OK` wildcards to associate with that description. Multiple wildcards are separated by a semicolon.

Once the dialog is set up, its usage is quite simple. It just needs to be shown by using `ShowModal`. Then, if the user closed it with the affirmative, we just need to call the dialog's `GetPath` method in order to get the path that was selected or entered into the dialog by the user.

There's more...

The `FileDialog`'s constructor takes a number of parameters to customize its behavior; see below for more information on how to setup a `FileDIalog`.

Default paths

The `FileDialog` has a few extra parameters that we did not use in our application, and that can be used to customize its initial state. The first is the `defaultDir` parameter, which takes a directory path as a value. This path must exist, and will ensure that the dialog is shown with that directory selected initially. The other additional parameter is `defaultFile`, which takes the name of a file as a value. This will be put as the default value in the dialog's filename field.

Style flags

The style flags and their descriptions are shown in the following table:

Style Flags	Description
`wx.FD_DEFAULT_STYLE`	Same as `wx.FD_OPEN`
`wx.FD_OPEN`	Create it as an Open dialog. Cannot be combined with `wx.FD_SAVE`.
`wx.FD_SAVE`	Create it as a Save dialog. Cannot be combined with `wx.FD_OPEN`.
`wx.FD_OVERWRITE_PROMPT`	Prompt for confirmation if the path already exists. For Save dialog only.
`wx.FD_FILE_MUST_EXIST`	Allow users to select only files that actually exist. For Open dialog only.
`wx.FD_MULTIPLE`	Allow multiple files to be selected. For Open dialog only. Should use the dialogs `GetPaths` method to get the list of selected paths.
`wx.FD_PREVIEW`	Show a preview of the selected file.
`wx.FD_CHANGE_DIR`	Change the current working directory to where the user selected the file(s). If not using the `defaultDir` parameter, the next time the dialog is opened, it will open to the last-used location.

- The *Utilizing Stock IDs* recipe in *Chapter 1, Getting Started with wxPython* explains the usage of the built-in IDs.

- The *Handling events* recipe in *Chapter 2, Responding to Events* covers the basics of event handling.

- The *Adding Menus and MenuBars* recipe in *Chapter 3, Basic Building Blocks of a User Interface* discusses how to add menus to a Frame.

Searching text with a FindReplaceDialog

The `FindReplaceDialog` is a common dialog for getting information from the user in order to perform find and replace actions in an application. The `FindReplaceDialog` is always used as a modeless dialog, and emits events when its buttons are clicked that notify the parent window of the action that the user wishes to perform. This recipe will extend the previous recipe (`FileDialog`) to show how to add the Find and Replace functionality to an application using the `FindReplaceDialog`.

How to do it...

Here we will show how we subclassed the `FileEditorFrame` to add find and replace functionality with the `FindReplaceDialog`:

```
import wx
# FileDialog Recipe sample module
import filedialog

class FindReplaceEditorFrame(filedialog.FileEditorFrame):
    def __init__(self, *args, **kwargs):
        super(FindReplaceEditorFrame, self).__init__(*args,
                                                     **kwargs)

        # Attributes
        self.finddlg = None
        self.finddata = wx.FindReplaceData()

        # Setup
        menub = self.GetMenuBar()
        editmenu = wx.Menu()
        editmenu.Append(wx.ID_FIND, "Find\tCtrl+F")
        editmenu.Append(wx.ID_REPLACE, "Replace\tCtrl+R")
        menub.Append(editmenu, "Edit")
```

```
# Event Handlers
self.Bind(wx.EVT_MENU,
          self.OnFindMenu,
          id=wx.ID_FIND)
self.Bind(wx.EVT_MENU,
          self.OnFindMenu,
          id=wx.ID_REPLACE)
self.Bind(wx.EVT_FIND, self.OnFind)
self.Bind(wx.EVT_FIND_NEXT, self.OnFind)
self.Bind(wx.EVT_FIND_REPLACE, self.OnReplace)
self.Bind(wx.EVT_FIND_REPLACE_ALL, self.OnReplaceAll)
self.Bind(wx.EVT_FIND_CLOSE, self.OnFindClose)
```

This method is a helper method that creates the FindReplaceDialog in the correct mode, depending on which action the user selects from the Menu:

```
def _InitFindDialog(self, mode):
    if self.finddlg:
        self.finddlg.Destroy()

    style = (wx.FR_NOUPDOWN
             |wx.FR_NOMATCHCASE
             |wx.FR_NOWHOLEWORD)
    if mode == wx.ID_REPLACE:
        style |= wx.FR_REPLACEDIALOG
        title = "Find/Replace"
    else:
        title = "Find"
    dlg = wx.FindReplaceDialog(self,
                               self.finddata,
                               title,
                               style)
    self.finddlg = dlg


# ---- Event Handlers ----#
```

This first event handler is used to handle the events when a menu item is selected, and will be used to create and show the appropriate version of the FindReplaceDialog:

```
def OnFindMenu(self, event):
    evt_id = event.GetId()
    if evt_id in (wx.ID_FIND, wx.ID_REPLACE):
        self._InitFindDialog(evt_id)
        self.finddlg.Show()
    else:
        event.Skip()
```

These next four event handlers handle events that are generated by the `FindReplaceDialog`
in response to user actions:

```python
def OnFind(self, event):
    """Find text"""
    findstr = self.finddata.GetFindString()
    if not self.FindString(findstr):
        wx.Bell() # beep at the user for no match

def OnReplace(self, event):
    """Replace text"""
    rstring = self.finddata.GetReplaceString()
    fstring = self.finddata.GetFindString()
    cpos = self.GetInsertionPoint()
    start, end = cpos, cpos
    if fstring:
        if self.FindString(fstring):
            start, end = self.txtctrl.GetSelection()
    self.txtctrl.Replace(start, end, rstring)

def OnReplaceAll(self, event):
    """Do a replace all"""
    rstring = self.finddata.GetReplaceString()
    fstring = self.finddata.GetFindString()
    text = self.txtctrl.GetValue()
    newtext = text.replace(fstring, rstring)
    self.txtctrl.SetValue(newtext)

def OnFindClose(self, event):
    if self.finddlg:
        self.finddlg.Destroy()
        self.finddlg = None

#---- End Event Handlers ----#

#---- Implementation ----#
```

Finally, here we have a very simple method of searching for a given string in the `TextCtrl`,
and setting the selection if a match is found:

```python
def FindString(self, findstr):
    """Find findstr in TextCtrl and set selection"""
    text = self.txtctrl.GetValue()
    csel = self.txtctrl.GetSelection()
    if csel[0] != csel[1]:
```

```
        cpos = max(csel)
    else:
        cpos = self.txtctrl.GetInsertionPoint()

    if cpos == self.txtctrl.GetLastPosition():
        cpos = 0

    # Do a simple case insensitive search
    # to find the next match
    text = text.upper()
    findstr = findstr.upper()
    found = text.find(findstr, cpos)
    if found != -1:
        end = found + len(findstr)
        self.txtctrl.SetSelection(end, found)
        self.txtctrl.SetFocus()
        return True
    return False
```

Running the previous code will result in a window like the following being shown:

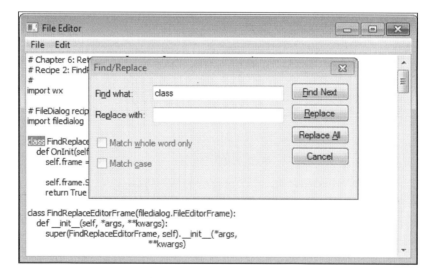

How it works...

In this recipe, we took the `FileEditorFrame` class that we created in the last recipe and extended it to have find and replace functionality, by using the `FindReplaceDialog`. So let's take a look at how we made use of the `FindReplaceDialog` by walking through what we added to this class from top to bottom.

In our `FindReplaceEditorFrame` class's `__init__` method, we added two instance attributes, `finddlg` and `finddata`. Since the `FindReplaceDialog` is modeless, we need to keep track of it in our class so we can properly clean it up later, to ensure that it will get assigned to the `finddlg` attribute when it is created. The second attribute, `finddata`, holds a reference to the `FindReplaceData` that is used for initializing the dialog, as well as for passing data back and forth between the dialog, and its parent window. We keep a reference to this item for two firstly, one it allows convenient access to the dialogs flags and user entered find and replace field strings, and secondly, by using the same `FindReplaceData` object each time, the dialog will be initialized with the same settings that the user last used it with. The last thing to take note of in `__init__` is the event binding: we bound to five of the events that the `FindReplaceDialog` can emit as a user interacts with it.

The next new method is the `_InitFindDialog` method. This method is what we use to initialize the `FindReplaceDialog` in response to the **Find** or **Replace** menu item events. Since our application is only going to support a simple one-direction, case-insensitive search, we disabled all the extra options in the dialog with the appropriate style flags. Then we simply create the dialog with the `FR_REPLACEDIALOG` flag if we are in replace mode, or without it if we are not, and finally assign the new dialog instance to our `finddlg` attribute.

The next section to look at is our `FindReplaceDialog` event handlers. This is where we handle the requested actions made by the user that is using the dialog. `OnFind` handles the situation where the user clicks the **Find** or **Find Next** buttons in the dialog. Here, we first get the string that was entered into the dialog by using our `finddata` attribute to access it. Then we perform a simple search in the text of the base class's `TextCtrl`, selecting the match if one is found, or use `wx.Bell` to make the computer beep at the user if no match is found.

`OnReplace` is called in response to the `FindReplaceDialogs` **Replace** button in the `FindReplaceDialog` being clicked. Here we get both the entered find and replace strings from the `FindReplaceData`. We then try to find a match and replace that match with the entered replace string. `OnReplaceAll` is called in response to the dialog's **Replace All** button being clicked, and does basically the same thing as `OnReplace`, but applies it to all matches in the `TextCtrl` text.

The last event handler is `OnFindClose`. This is called when the user closes the `FindReplaceDialog`. We need to handle this event so that we can clean up the dialog by calling `Destroy` on it. That's it. Now we have a text editor application that has find and replace functionality!

There's more...

For simplicity's sake, this recipe disabled the dialog's extra find options. When these options are selected in the dialog, they can be checked for, just like the find and replace strings, by using the `FindReplaceData` object. It will have the selected option's flags set in the value returned from `GetFlags`, which is a bitmask of the `FindReplaceData` flags. Due to the way in which these flags and the dialog's style flags are named, it can be a little confusing to know which are which, so please refer to the following two tables to distinguish between these two different, yet similarly-named sets of flags.

FindReplaceDialog style flags

These flags are flags that should be passed to the dialog's constructor's style parameter:

Flags	Description
wx.FR_NOMATCHCASE	Disable the "match case" checkbox
wx.FR_NOUPDOWN	Disable the "up" and "down" radio buttons
wx.FR_NOWHOLEWORD	Disable the "whole word" checkbox
wx.FR_REPLACEDIALOG	Create the dialog in Replace mode

FindReplaceData flags

The following flags are flags that can be set in FindReplaceData to set the initial state of the dialog and to identify the user's selected find preferences.

Flags	Description
wx.FR_DOWN	The "down" radio button is selected
wx.FR_MATCHCASE	The "match case" checkbox is selected
wx.FR_WHOLEWORD	The "whole word" checkbox is selected

See also

 ▸ See the *Selecting files with a FileDialog* recipe for the base example that this recipe extends.

 ▸ The *Understanding event propagation* recipe in *Chapter 2, Responding to Events* contains more information on how events are delivered to different windows.

Getting images with ImageDialog

ImageDialog is a custom dialog class provided by the wx.lib.imagebrowser module. It is similar in purpose to the default FileDialog, but is specialized for allowing the user to select and preview images. This recipe shows how to use this dialog to retrieve a user-selected image and load it into a StaticBitmap for display in the application's main window.

How to do it...

Here we will create a very simple image viewer application that allows the user to select an image to view with the ImageDialog:

```
import wx
import wx.lib.imagebrowser as imagebrowser

class ImageDialogApp(wx.App):
```

```
    def OnInit(self):
        self.frame = ImageDialogFrame(None,
                                      title="ImageDialog")
        self.frame.Show()
        return True

class ImageDialogFrame(wx.Frame):
    def __init__(self, *args, **kwargs):
        super(ImageDialogFrame, self).__init__(*args,
                                               **kwargs)

        # Attributes
        self.panel = ImageDialogPanel(self)

class ImageDialogPanel(wx.Panel):
    def __init__(self, *args, **kwargs):
        super(ImageDialogPanel, self).__init__(*args,
                                               **kwargs)

        # Attributes
        self.lastpath = None
        self.bmp = wx.StaticBitmap(self)
        self.btn = wx.Button(self, label="Choose Image")

        # Layout
        vsizer = wx.BoxSizer(wx.VERTICAL)
        hsizer = wx.BoxSizer(wx.HORIZONTAL)
        vsizer.Add(self.bmp, 0, wx.ALIGN_CENTER)
        vsizer.AddSpacer((5, 5))
        vsizer.Add(self.btn, 0, wx.ALIGN_CENTER)
        hsizer.AddStretchSpacer()
        hsizer.Add(vsizer, 0, wx.ALIGN_CENTER)
        hsizer.AddStretchSpacer()
        self.SetSizer(hsizer)

        # Event Handlers
        self.Bind(wx.EVT_BUTTON, self.OnShowDialog, self.btn)

    def OnShowDialog(self, event):
        # Create the dialog with the path cached
        # from the last time it was opened
        dlg = imagebrowser.ImageDialog(self, self.lastpath)
        if dlg.ShowModal() == wx.ID_OK:
            # Save the last used path
            self.lastpath = dlg.GetDirectory()
            imgpath = dlg.GetFile()
            bitmap = wx.Bitmap(imgpath)
```

```
                  if bitmap.IsOk():
                      self.bmp.SetBitmap(bitmap)
                      self.bmp.Layout()
                      self.bmp.Refresh()
              dlg.Destroy()

  if __name__ == '__main__':
      app = ImageDialogApp(False)
      app.MainLoop()
```

Running the previous code and clicking on the Choose Image button will result in the following dialog being shown:

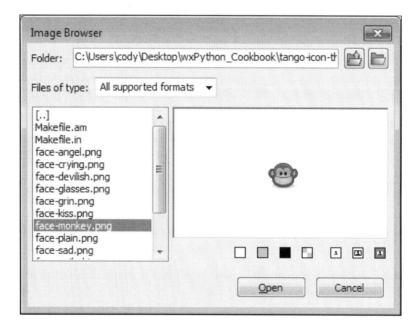

How it works...

In this recipe we created a simple little image viewer application that allows the user to use the `ImageDialog` to choose an image that is on the computer's hard drive, and have this image displayed in the application's window.

This application follows the common pattern of most simple applications. So let's take a detailed look at how we used the `ImageDialog`. First, we had to import the `wx.lib.imagebrowser` module, as the `ImageDialog` is not a part of the standard wx module. In our `ImageDialogFrame` class, we added three instance attributes. The first is to hold the path that was last used by the `ImageDialog`. We did this as a way to improve the usability of the application so that we can open the dialog to the last path the user used the next time they open it. The second attribute is a `StaticBitmap` object, which we will use to display the image that the user selects with the `ImageDialog`. Note that we used a `StaticBitmap` in this example for simplicity. To better support larger-sized images, it would be better to draw the image on the `Panel` ourselves. This approach will be covered by topics in *Chapter 8, Drawing to the Screen*. The last attribute is just a button that will be used to trigger the event to show the `ImageDialog`.

Our `OnShowDialog` method in this recipe creates the `ImageDialog` and initializes it to the last path used. The first time, it will be None, which defaults to the current working directory. The dialog is then shown, in order to allow the user to navigate to and select an image to display. If they click on the dialog's **Open** button, the dialog will return `wx.ID_OK`. At this point, we first get and save a reference to the last directory that the dialog was at so that we can restore it next time the dialog is shown. Then all that is left is to create the Bitmap and call the `StaticBitmap`'s `SetBitmap` method to change the image that is displayed. After this, it is necessary to call `Layout` on the `Panel`, to make sure the sizers can compensate for the new `Bitmap`'s size, and then we finally call `Refresh` on the `StaticBitmap` to make sure it is completely repainted.

There's more...

The only other option available in the current version of the `ImageDialog` is the ability to change the list of supported file filters. This can be done by passing to the dialog's `ChangeFileTypes` method a list of tuples that contain the file type's description and wildcard string.

```
dlg.ChangeFileTypes([('png, '*.png'), ('jpeg', '*.jpg')])
```

See also

▶   The *Using Bitmaps* recipe in *Chapter 1, Getting Started* with wxPython has additional examples of using Bitmaps and the `StaticBitmap` class.

Using the Print dialogs

Adding printing support to an application can be a difficult task, as there are a number of tasks that need to be handled. These include selecting and configuring a printer, translating your on-screen presentation to paper, and ultimately sending the data to the printer.

In wxPython, there are three dialog classes related to printing: the `PageSetupDialog`, `PreviewFrame`, and `Printer` classes. In addition to these classes, there are a number of supporting classes that must be used in conjunction with these dialogs, in order to add printing support to an application. This recipe shows some of the basics of how to use the wx printing framework, by creating a class that encapsulates the usage of the three printing dialogs and allows an application to print a `Bitmap`.

How to do it...

In order to simplify and condense the many different steps required to support printing in an application, we will start by defining a class to encapsulate the different tasks into a few simple method calls:

```python
class BitmapPrinter(object):
    """Manages PrintData and Printing"""
    def __init__(self, parent):
        """Initializes the Printer
        @param parent: parent window
        """
        super(BitmapPrinter, self).__init__()

        # Attributes
        self.parent = parent
        self.print_data = wx.PrintData()

    def CreatePrintout(self, bmp):
        """Creates a printout object
        @param bmp: wx.Bitmap
        """
        assert bmp.IsOk(), "Invalid Bitmap!"
        data = wx.PageSetupDialogData(self.print_data)
        return BitmapPrintout(bmp, data)
```

The `PageSetup` method handles the display of the printer setup dialog, and storage of the settings in the `print_data` attributes:

```python
    def PageSetup(self):
        """Show the PrinterSetup dialog"""
        # Make a copy of our print data for the setup dialog
        dlg_data = wx.PageSetupDialogData(self.print_data)
        print_dlg = wx.PageSetupDialog(self.parent, dlg_data)
        if print_dlg.ShowModal() == wx.ID_OK:
            # Update the printer data with the changes from
            # the setup dialog.
            newdata = dlg_data.GetPrintData()
            self.print_data = wx.PrintData(newdata)
            paperid = dlg_data.GetPaperId()
            self.print_data.SetPaperId(paperid)
        print_dlg.Destroy()
```

In Preview, we create the `PrintPreview` dialog to give a preview of what the printout will look like:

```python
def Preview(self, bmp):
    """Show the print preview
    @param bmp: wx.Bitmap
    """
    printout = self.CreatePrintout(bmp)
    printout2 = self.CreatePrintout(bmp)
    preview = wx.PrintPreview(printout, printout2,
                              self.print_data)
    preview.SetZoom(100)
    if preview.IsOk():
        pre_frame = wx.PreviewFrame(preview,
                                    self.parent,
                                    "Print Preview")
        # The default size of the preview frame
        # sometimes needs some help.
        dsize = wx.GetDisplaySize()
        width = self.parent.GetSize()[0]
        height = dsize.GetHeight() - 100
        pre_frame.SetInitialSize((width, height))
        pre_frame.Initialize()
        pre_frame.Show()
    else:
        # Error
        wx.MessageBox("Failed to create print preview",
                      "Print Error",
                      style=wx.ICON_ERROR|wx.OK)
```

Finally, in the `Print` method, we show the `Printer` dialog to allow the user to request a printout of a `Bitmap`, and send it to the printer to be printed:

```python
def Print(self, bmp):
    """Prints the document"""
    pdd = wx.PrintDialogData(self.print_data)
    printer = wx.Printer(pdd)
    printout = self.CreatePrintout(bmp)
    result = printer.Print(self.parent, printout)
    if result:
        # Store copy of print data for future use
        dlg_data = printer.GetPrintDialogData()
        newdata = dlg_data.GetPrintData()
        self.print_data = wx.PrintData(newdata)
```

```
    elif printer.GetLastError() == wx.PRINTER_ERROR:
        wx.MessageBox("Printer error detected.",
                      "Printer Error",
                      style=wx.ICON_ERROR|wx.OK)
    printout.Destroy()
```

Here we will implement the `Printout` object for printing `Bitmaps`. The `Printout` object is the object that is responsible for managing the print job and drawing the bitmap to the printer's device context:

```python
class BitmapPrintout(wx.Printout):
    """Creates an printout of a Bitmap"""
    def __init__(self, bmp, data):
        super(BitmapPrintout, self).__init__()

        # Attributes
        self.bmp = bmp
        self.data = data

    def GetPageInfo(self):
        """Get the page range information"""
        # min, max, from, to # we only support 1 page
        return (1, 1, 1, 1)

    def HasPage(self, page):
        """Is a page within range"""
        return page <= 1

    def OnPrintPage(self, page):
        """Scales and Renders the bitmap
        to a DC and prints it
        """
        dc = self.GetDC() # Get Device Context to draw on

        # Get the Bitmap Size
        bmpW, bmpH = self.bmp.GetSize()

        # Check if we need to scale the bitmap to fit
        self.MapScreenSizeToPageMargins(self.data)
        rect = self.GetLogicalPageRect()
        w, h = rect.width, rect.height
        if (bmpW > w) or (bmpH > h):
            # Image is large so apply some scaling
```

```
         self.FitThisSizeToPageMargins((bmpW, bmpH),
                                        self.data)

    x, y = 0, 0
else:
    # try to center it
    x = (w - bmpW) / 2
    y = (h - bmpH) / 2

# Draw the bitmap to DC
dc.DrawBitmap(self.bmp, x, y)

return True
```

How it works...

The `BitmapPrinter` class encapsulates the three main print-related tasks that an application may need to support: printer setup, print preview, and printing. This class is the interface that the application which wants to allow printing `Bitmap`s will use for all of its printing needs. All that the application requires is a `Bitmap`, and all that it needs to do is to use one of the three methods, `PageSetup`, `Preview`, and `Print`. So let's take a look at how this class and these three methods work.

The constructor takes one argument for a parent window. This will be used as the parent window for all of the dialogs. This will typically be an application's main window. We also create and store a reference to a `PrintData` object in the constructor. All of the print dialogs use `PrintData` in one form or another. This allows us to save any print configuration changes a user may make while using one of the dialogs.

`PageSetup` is used to create and show the `PageSetupDialog`. To use the `PageSetupDialog`, we first create a `PageSetupDialogData` object by passing our `PrintData` object to its constructor, so it will use any settings that may already be persisted in our data object. We then simply create the dialog by passing in the `PageSetupDialogData` object. If the dialog is closed by the OK button, we then get the `PrintData` from the dialog and make a copy of it to store. It is important to make a copy, because when the `PageSetupDialog` is destroyed it will delete the data.

`Preview` creates a preview of what the printout will look like, and shows it with the `PreviewFrame`. The `PreviewFrame` requires a `PrintPreview` object. To create the `PrintPreview` object, it must be passed two `Printout` objects and a `PrintData` object. A `Printout` object is what does the actual work of rendering what will be printed by the printer. We will come back to the details about how the `Printout` works when we get to our `BitmapPrintout` class. The first `Printout` object is used for the `PreviewFrame`, and the second one is used for the actual printing if the user clicks on the `PreviewFrame`'s Print button.

`Print` creates a `Printer` object that will show the printer dialog when its `Print` method is called. Like the `Preview` object, the `Printer` object is created with some `PrintData` and an instance of a `Printout` object. When the print dialog's Print button is clicked, it will use the `Printout` object to tell the physical printer what to draw on the paper.

The `BitmapPrintout` class implements a `Printout` object that is used for printing a single bitmap to a single sheet of paper at a time. `Printout` objects must always be subclassed in order to implement the application-specific requirements of the data that needs to be printed as the base class only provides an interface of virtual methods to override in the subclass. In our class, we overrode the three following methods: `GetPageInfo`, `HasPage`, and `OnPrintPage`. The first two are for returning information about the number of pages that will be printed; since we are only supporting one page, these are quite trivial in this recipe. The `OnPrintPage` method is what does the actual drawing to the printer's device context. This method gets called to do the drawing of each page that will be printed.

Drawing the `Printout` is done by using the device context object returned by the call to `GetDC`. The use of device contexts are covered in detail in *Chapter 8, Drawing to the Screen* so just too keep things simple all we did here was just to set the scale of the canvas calculations to try and center the image on the paper, and then used the DC's `DrawBitmap` method to draw the `Bitmap` to the device context. For an example of the `BitmapPrinter` class in action, see the sample code that accompanies this chapter.

There's more...

Included below is some additional information about the print framework.

Printout

The `wx.Printout` object has a number of other overrideable methods that may be of use for different types of documents. The following table is a reference to some of these other interface methods.

Interface methods	Description
`OnBeginDocument(start, end)`	Called at the beginning of each copy of a document that is in the print job. If this method is overridden, the base class's method must still be called in it.
`OnEndDocument()`	Called at the end of printing each copy of a document in the print job. If this method is overridden, the base class method must be called in it.
`OnBeginPrinting()`	Called once and only once at the beginning of a print job.
`OnEndPrinting()`	Called once and only once at the end of a print job.
`OnPreparePrinting()`	Called before any other use of the `Printout` object. This is usually where the calculations about things such as the number of pages in a document are done.

Bug notice

There is a bug in wxPython 2.8 where the page orientation (Portrait or Landscape) cannot be retrieved from the `PageSetup` or `Print` dialog's `PrintData`.

See also

▸ The *Understanding inheritance limitations* recipe in *Chapter 1, Getting Started with wxPython* includes a detailed explanation of how to override virtual methods in wxPython classes.

▸ The *Screen drawing* recipe in *Chapter 8, Drawing to the Screen* discusses the use of Device Contexts (DCs) and their drawing commands.

7

Window Layout and Design

In this chapter, we will cover:

- ▶ Using a `BoxSizer`
- ▶ Understanding proportions, flags, and borders
- ▶ Laying out controls with the `GridBagSizer`
- ▶ Standard dialog button layout
- ▶ Using XML resources
- ▶ Making a custom resource handler
- ▶ Using the `AuiFrameManager`

Introduction

Once you have an idea of how the interface of your applications should look, it comes the time to put it all together. Being able to take your vision and translate it into code can be a tricky and often tedious task. A window's layout is defined on a two dimensional plane with the origin being the window's top-left corner. All positioning and sizing of any widgets, no matter what it's onscreen appearance, is based on rectangles. Clearly understanding these two basic concepts goes a long way towards being able to understand and efficiently work with the toolkit.

Traditionally in older applications, window layout was commonly done by setting explicit static sizes and positions for all the controls contained within a window. This approach, however, can be rather limiting as the windows will not be resizable, they may not fit on the screen under different resolutions, trying to support localization becomes more difficult because labels and other text will differ in length in different languages, the native widgets will often be different sizes on different platforms making it difficult to write platform independent code, and the list goes on.

So, you may ask what the solution to this is. In wxPython, the method of choice is to use the `Sizer` classes to define and manage the layout of controls. Sizers are classes that manage the size and positioning of controls through an algorithm that queries all of the controls that have been added to the Sizer for their recommended best minimal sizes and their ability to stretch or not, if the amount of available space increases, such as if a user makes a dialog bigger. Sizers also handle cross-platform widget differences, for example, buttons on GTK tend to have an icon and be generally larger than the buttons on Windows or OS X. Using a `Sizer` to manage the button's layout will allow the rest of the dialog to be proportionally sized correctly to handle this without the need for any platform-specific code.

So let us begin our adventure into the world of window layout and design by taking a look at a number of the tools that wxPython provides in order to facilitate this task.

Using a BoxSizer

A `BoxSizer` is the most basic of `Sizer` classes. It supports a layout that goes in a single direction—either a vertical column or a horizontal row. Even though it is the most basic to work with, a `BoxSizer` is one of the most useful `Sizer` classes and tends to produce more consistent cross-platform behavior when compared to some of the other `Sizers` types. This recipe creates a simple window where we want to have two text controls stacked in a vertical column, each with a label to the left of it. This will be used to illustrate the most simplistic usage of a `BoxSizer` in order to manage the layout of a window's controls.

How to do it...

Here we define our top level Frame, which will use a BoxSizer to manage the size of its Panel:

```
class BoxSizerFrame(wx.Frame):
    def __init__(self, parent, *args, **kwargs):
        super(BoxSizerFrame, self).__init__(*args, **kwargs)

        # Attributes
        self.panel = BoxSizerPanel(self)

        # Layout
        sizer = wx.BoxSizer(wx.VERTICAL)
        sizer.Add(self.panel, 1, wx.EXPAND)
        self.SetSizer(sizer)
        self.SetInitialSize()
```

The `BoxSizerPanel` class is the next layer in the window hierarchy, and is where we will perform the main layout of the controls:

```
class BoxSizerPanel(wx.Panel):
    def __init__(self, parent, *args, **kwargs):
        super(BoxSizerPanel, self).__init__(*args, **kwargs)
```

```
    # Attributes
    self._field1 = wx.TextCtrl(self)
    self._field2 = wx.TextCtrl(self)

    # Layout
    self._DoLayout()
```

Just to help reduce clutter in the __init__ method, we will do all the layout in a separate _DoLayout method:

```
def _DoLayout(self):
    """Layout the controls"""
    vsizer = wx.BoxSizer(wx.VERTICAL)
    field1_sz = wx.BoxSizer(wx.HORIZONTAL)
    field2_sz = wx.BoxSizer(wx.HORIZONTAL)

    # Make the labels
    field1_lbl = wx.StaticText(self, label="Field 1:")
    field2_lbl = wx.StaticText(self, label="Field 2:")

    # Make the first row by adding the label and field
    # to the first horizontal sizer
    field1_sz.AddSpacer(50)
    field1_sz.Add(field1_lbl)
    field1_sz.AddSpacer(5) # put 5px of space between
    field1_sz.Add(self._field1)
    field1_sz.AddSpacer(50)

    # Do the same for the second row
    field2_sz.AddSpacer(50)
    field2_sz.Add(field2_lbl)
    field2_sz.AddSpacer(5)
    field2_sz.Add(self._field2)
    field2_sz.AddSpacer(50)

    # Now finish the layout by adding the two sizers
    # to the main vertical sizer.
    vsizer.AddSpacer(50)
    vsizer.Add(field1_sz)
    vsizer.AddSpacer(15)
    vsizer.Add(field2_sz)
    vsizer.AddSpacer(50)

    # Finally assign the main outer sizer to the panel
    self.SetSizer(vsizer)
```

How it works...

The previous code shows the basic pattern of how to create a simple window layout programmatically, using sizers to manage the controls. First let's start by taking a look at the `BoxSizerPanel` class's `_DoLayout` method, as this is where the majority of the layout in this example takes place.

First, we started off by creating three `BoxSizer` classes: one with a vertical orientation, and two with a horizontal orientation. The layout we desired for this window requires us to use three `BoxSizer` classes and this is why. If you break down what we want to do into simple rectangles, you will see that:

1. We wanted two `TextCtrl` objects each with a label to the left of them which can simply be thought of as two horizontal rectangles.

2. We wanted the `TextCtrl` objects stacked vertically in the window which is just a vertical rectangle that will contain the other two rectangles.

This is illustrated by the following screenshot (borders are drawn in and labels are added to show the area managed by each of `Panel`'s three `BoxSizer`s):

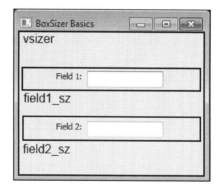

In the section where we populate the first horizontal sizer (`field1_sz`), we use two of the `BoxSizer` methods to add items to the layout. The first is `AddSpacer`, which does simply as its named and adds a fixed amount of empty space in the left-hand side of the sizer. Then we use the `Add` method to add our `StaticText` control to the right of the spacer, and continue from here to add other items to complete this row. As you can see, these methods add items to the layout from left to right in the sizer. After this, we again do the same thing with the other label and `TextCtrl` in the second horizontal sizer.

The last part of the Panel's layout is done by adding the two horizontal sizers to the vertical sizer. This time, since the sizer was created with a `VERTICAL` orientation, the items are added from top to bottom. Finally, we use the `Panel`'s `SetSizer` method to assign the main outer `BoxSizer` as the `Panel`'s sizer.

The `BoxSizerFrame` also uses a `BoxSizer` to manage the layout of its `Panel`. The only difference here is that we used the `Add` method's `proportion` and `flags` parameters to tell it to make the Panel expand to use the entire space available. After setting the Frame's sizer, we used its `SetInitialSize` method, which queries the window's sizer and its descendents to get and set the best minimal size to set the window to. We will go into more detail about these other parameters and their effects in the next recipe.

There's more...

Included below is a little more additional information about adding spacers and items to a sizer's layout.

Spacers

The `AddSpacer` will add a square-shaped spacer that is X pixels wide by X pixels tall to the `BoxSizer`, where X is the value passed to the `AddSpacer` method. Spacers of other dimensions can be added by passing a `tuple` as the first argument to the `BoxSizer`'s `Add` method.

```
someBoxSizer.Add((20,5))
```

This will add a 20x5 pixel spacer to the sizer. This can be useful when you don't want the vertical space to be increased by as much as the horizontal space, or vice versa.

AddMany

The `AddMany` method can be used to add an arbitrary number of items to the sizer in one call. `AddMany` takes a `list` of `tuples` that contain values that are in the same order as the `Add` method expects.

```
someBoxSizer.AddMany([(staticText,),
                      ((10, 10),),
                      (txtCtrl, 0, wx.EXPAND)]))
```

This will add three items to the sizer: the first two items only specify the one required parameter, and the third specifies the `proportion` and `flags` parameters.

See also

▶ The *Understanding proportions, flags, and borders* recipe in this chapter expands into further detail about the behavioral attributes of `SizerItems`.

Understanding proportions, flags, and borders

Through the use of the optional parameters in a sizer's various `Add` methods, it is possible to control the relative proportions, alignment, and padding around every item that is managed by the sizer. Without using these additional settings, all the items in the sizer will just use their "best" minimum size and will be aligned to the top-left of the rectangle of space that the sizer provides. This means that the controls will not stretch or contract when the window is resized. Also, for example, if in a horizontal row of items in a `BoxSizer` one of the items has a greater height than some of the other items in that same row, they may not be aligned as desired (see the following diagram).

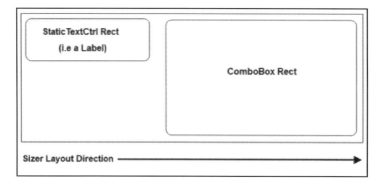

This diagram illustrates an alignment issue that can occur when some controls have a different-sized rectangle than the one next to it. This is a realistic example of a problem that can occur on GTK (Linux), as its `ComboBoxes` tend to be much taller than a `StaticTextCtrl`. So where on other platforms these two controls may appear to be properly center-aligned, they will look like this on Linux.

This recipe will re-implement the previous recipe's `BoxSizerPanel`, using these additional `Add` parameters to improve its layout, in order to show how these parameters can be used to influence how the sizer manages each of the controls that have been added to it.

Getting Started

Before getting started on this recipe, make sure you have reviewed the previous recipe, *Using a BoxSizer*, as we will be modifying its `_DoLayout` method in this recipe to define some additional behaviors that the sizers should apply to its layout.

How to do it...

Here, we will make some modifications to the `SizerItems` proportions, flags, and borders to change the behavior of the layout:

```
def _DoLayout(self):
    """Layout the controls"""
    vsizer = wx.BoxSizer(wx.VERTICAL)
    field1_sz = wx.BoxSizer(wx.HORIZONTAL)
    field2_sz = wx.BoxSizer(wx.HORIZONTAL)

    # Make the labels
    field1_lbl = wx.StaticText(self, label="Field 1:")
    field2_lbl = wx.StaticText(self, label="Field 2:")

    # 1) HORIZONTAL BOXSIZERS
    field1_sz.Add(field1_lbl, 0,
                  wx.ALIGN_CENTER_VERTICAL|wx.RIGHT, 5)
    field1_sz.Add(self._field1, 1, wx.EXPAND)

    field2_sz.Add(field2_lbl, 0,
                  wx.ALIGN_CENTER_VERTICAL|wx.RIGHT, 5)
    field2_sz.Add(self._field2, 1, wx.EXPAND)

    # 2) VERTICAL BOXSIZER
    vsizer.AddStretchSpacer()
    BOTH_SIDES = wx.EXPAND|wx.LEFT|wx.RIGHT
    vsizer.Add(field1_sz, 0, BOTH_SIDES|wx.TOP, 50)
    vsizer.AddSpacer(15)
    vsizer.Add(field2_sz, 0, BOTH_SIDES|wx.BOTTOM, 50)
    vsizer.AddStretchSpacer()

    # Finally assign the main outer sizer to the panel
    self.SetSizer(vsizer)
```

How it works...

This recipe just shows what we changed in the previous recipe's `_DoLayout` method to take advantage of some of these extra options. The first thing to notice in the section where we add the controls to the horizontal sizers is that we no longer have the `AddSpacer` calls. These have been replaced by specifying a border in the `Add` calls. When adding each of the labels we added two sizer flags, `ALIGN_CENTER_VERTICAL` and `RIGHT`. The first flag is an alignment flag that specifies the desired behavior of the alignment and the second is a border flag that specifies where we want the border parameter to be applied. In this case, the sizer will align the `StaticText` in the center of the vertical space and add a 5px padding to the right side of it.

Next, where we add the `TextCtrl` objects to the sizer, we specified a `1` for the proportion and `EXPAND` for the sizer flag. Setting the proportion greater than the default of `0` will tell the sizer to give that control proportionally more of the space in the sizer's managed area. A proportion value greater than 0 in combination with the `EXPAND` flag which tells the control to get bigger as space is available will let it stretch as the dialog is resized to a bigger size. Typically you will only need to specify `0` or `1` for the proportion parameter, but under some complex layouts it may be necessary to give different controls a relatively different amount of the total available space. For example, in a layout with two controls if both are given a proportion of 1, they would each get 50 percent of the space. Changing the proportion of one of the controls to 2 would change the space allocation to a 66/33 percent balance.

We also made some changes to the final layout with the vertical sizer. First, instead of using the regular `AddSpacer` function to add some static spacers to the layout, we changed it to use `AddStretchSpacer` instead. `AddStretchSpacer` is basically the equivalent of doing `Add((-1,-1), 1, wx.EXPAND)`, which just adds a spacer of indeterminate size that will stretch as the window size is changed. This allows us to keep the controls in the center of the dialog as its vertical size changes.

Finally, when adding the two horizontal sizers to the vertical sizer, we used some flags to apply a static 50px of spacing around the `LEFT`, `RIGHT`, and `TOP` or `BOTTOM` of the sizers. It's also important to notice that we once again passed the `EXPAND` flag. If we did not do this, the vertical sizer would not allow those two items to expand which in turn would nullify us adding the `EXPAND` flag for the `TextCtrl` objects. Try running this and the previous sample side-by-side and resizing each window to see the difference in behavior.

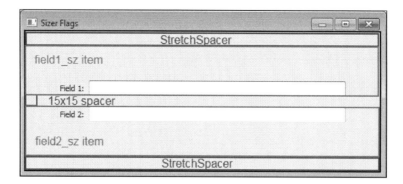

The previous screenshot has had some lines drawn over it to show the five items that are managed by the main top level `VERTICAL` sizer `vsizer`.

There's more...

There are a number of flags that can be used to affect the layout in various ways. The following three tables list the different categories of these flags that can be combined in the flag's bitmask:

Alignment flags

This table shows a listing of all the alignment flags and a description of what each one does:

Alignment flags	Description
wx.ALIGN_TOP	Align the item to the top of the available space
wx.ALIGN_BOTTOM	Align the item to the bottom of the available space
wx.ALIGN_LEFT	Align the item to the left of the available space
wx.ALIGN_RIGHT	Align the item to the right of the available space
wx.ALIGN_CENTER_VERTICAL wx.ALIGN_CENTRE_VERTICAL	Align the item in the center of the vertical space
wx.ALIGN_CENTER_HORIZONTAL wx.ALIGN_CENTRE_HORIZONTAL	Align the item in the center of the horizontal space

Border flags

The following flags can be used to control which side(s) of the control the border argument of the Sizer's `Add` method is applied to:

Border flags	Description
wx.TOP	Apply the border to the top of the item
wx.BOTTOM	Apply the border to the bottom of item
wx.LEFT	Apply the border to the left of the item
wx.RIGHT	Apply the border to the right of the item
wx.ALL	Apply the border to all sides of the item

Behavior flags

The sizer flags in this table can be used to control how a control is resized within a sizer:

Behaviour flags	Description
wx.EXPAND	Item will expand to fill the space provided to it (wx.GROW is the same)
wx.SHAPED	Similar to EXPAND but maintains the item's aspect ratio
wx.FIXED_MINSIZE	Don't let the item become smaller than its initial minimum size
wx.RESERVE_SPACE_EVEN_IF_HIDDEN	Don't allow the sizer to reclaim an item's space when it is hidden

See also

▶ See the *Using a BoxSizer* recipe in this chapter for the basics of using a `BoxSizer`.

▶ The *Laying out controls with the GridBagSizer* recipe in this chapter shows how to use one of the more complex sizer classes.

Laying out controls with the GridBagSizer

There are a number of other types of sizers in wxPython, besides the `BoxSizer`, that are designed to help simplify different kinds of layouts. The `GridSizer`, `FlexGridSizer`, and `GridBagSizer` can be used to lay items out in a grid-like manner. The `GridSizer` provides a fixed grid layout where items are added into different "cells" in the grid. The `FlexGridSizer` is just like the `GridSizer`, except that the columns in the grid can be different widths. Finally, the `GridBagSizer` is similar to the `FlexGridSizer` but also allows items to span over multiple "cells" in the grid, which makes it possible to achieve layouts that can usually only be achieved by nesting several `BoxSizers`. This recipe will discuss the use of the `GridBagSizer`, and use it to create a dialog that could be used for viewing the details of a log event.

How to do it...

Here we will create a custom `DetailsDialog` that could be used for viewing log messages or system events. It has two fields in it for displaying the type of message and the verbose message text:

```python
class DetailsDialog(wx.Dialog):
    def __init__(self, parent, type, details, title=""):
        """Create the dialog
        @param type: event type string
        @param details: long details string
        """
        super(DetailsDialog, self).__init__(parent, title=title)

        # Attributes
        self.type = wx.TextCtrl(self, value=type,
                                style=wx.TE_READONLY)
        self.details = wx.TextCtrl(self, value=details,
                                   style=wx.TE_READONLY|
                                         wx.TE_MULTILINE)

        # Layout
        self.__DoLayout()
        self.SetInitialSize()
```

```
def __DoLayout(self):
    sizer = wx.GridBagSizer(vgap=8, hgap=8)

    type_lbl = wx.StaticText(self, label="Type:")
    detail_lbl = wx.StaticText(self, label="Details:")

    # Add the event type fields
    sizer.Add(type_lbl, (1, 1))
    sizer.Add(self.type, (1, 2), (1, 15), wx.EXPAND)

    # Add the details field
    sizer.Add(detail_lbl, (2, 1))
    sizer.Add(self.details, (2, 2), (5, 15), wx.EXPAND)

    # Add a spacer to pad out the right side
    sizer.Add((5, 5), (2, 17))
    # And another to the pad out the bottom
    sizer.Add((5, 5), (7, 0))

    self.SetSizer(sizer)
```

How it works...

The `GridBagSizer`'s `Add` method of `GridBagSizer` takes some additional parameters compared to the other types of sizers. It is necessary to specify the grid position and optionally the number of columns and rows to span. We used this in our details dialog in order to allow the `TextCtrl` fields to span multiple columns and multiple rows in the case of the details field. The way this layout works can get a little complicated, so let's go over our `__DoLayout` method line-by-line to see how each of them affect the dialog's layout.

First, we create out `GridBagSizer`, and in its constructor we specify how much padding we want between the rows and columns. Next, we start adding our items to the sizer. The first item that we add is the type `StaticText` label, which we added at row 1, column 1. This was done to leave some padding around the outside edge. Next, we added the `TextCtrl` to the right of the label at row 1, column 2. For this item, we also specified the span parameter to tell the item to span 1 row and 15 columns. The column width is proportionally based upon the size of the first column in the grid.

Next we add the details fields, starting with the details label, which is added at row 2, column 1, in order to line up with the type `StaticText` label. Since the details text may be long, we want it to span multiple rows. Hence, for its span parameter we specified for it to span 5 rows and 15 columns.

Finally, so that the padding around our controls on the bottom and right-hand side matches the top and left, we need to add a spacer to the right and bottom to create an extra column and row. Notice that for this step we need to take into account the span parameters of the previous items we added, so that our items do not overlap. Items cannot occupy the same column or row as any other item in the sizer. So first we add a spacer to row 2, column 17, to create a new column on the right-hand side of our `TextCtrl` objects. We specified column 17 because the `TextCtrl` objects start at column 2 and span 15 columns. Likewise, we did the same when adding one to the bottom, to take into account the span of the details text field. Note that instead of offsetting the first item in the grid and then adding spacers, it would have been easier to nest our `GridBagSizer` inside of a `BoxSizer` and specify a border. The approach in this recipe was done just to illustrate the need to account for an item's span when adding additional items to the grid:

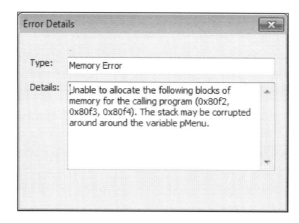

See the sample code that accompanies this chapter for a small application that uses this dialog.

See also

> ▶ The *Understanding proportions, flags, and borders* recipe in this chapter describes the use of sizer flags in detail.

Standard dialog button layout

Each platform has different standards for how different dialog buttons are placed in the dialog. This is where the `StdDialogButtonSizer` comes into play. It can be used to add standard buttons to a dialog, and automatically take care of the specific platform standards for where the button is positioned. This recipe shows how to use the `StdDialogButtonSizer` to quickly and easily add standard buttons to a `Dialog`.

How to do it...

Here is the code for our custom message box class that can be used as a replacement for the standard `MessageBox` in cases where the application wants to display custom icons in their pop-up dialogs:

```
class CustomMessageBox(wx.Dialog):
    def __init__(self, parent, message, title="",
                 bmp=wx.NullBitmap, style=wx.OK):
        super(CustomMessageBox, self).__init__(parent, title=title)

        # Attributes
        self._flags = style
        self._bitmap = wx.StaticBitmap(self, bitmap=bmp)
        self._msg = wx.StaticText(self, label=message)

        # Layout
        self.__DoLayout()
        self.SetInitialSize()
        self.CenterOnParent()

    def __DoLayout(self):
        vsizer = wx.BoxSizer(wx.VERTICAL)
        hsizer = wx.BoxSizer(wx.HORIZONTAL)

        # Layout the bitmap and caption
        hsizer.AddSpacer(10)
        hsizer.Add(self._bitmap, 0, wx.ALIGN_CENTER_VERTICAL)
        hsizer.AddSpacer(8)
        hsizer.Add(self._msg, 0, wx.ALIGN_CENTER_VERTICAL)
        hsizer.AddSpacer(10)

        # Create the buttons specified by the style flags
        # and the StdDialogButtonSizer to manage them
        btnsizer = self.CreateButtonSizer(self._flags)

        # Finish the layout
        vsizer.AddSpacer(10)
        vsizer.Add(hsizer, 0, wx.ALIGN_CENTER_HORIZONTAL)
        vsizer.AddSpacer(8)
        vsizer.Add(btnsizer, 0, wx.EXPAND|wx.ALL, 5)

        self.SetSizer(vsizer)
```

How it works...

Here, we created a custom `MessageBox` clone that can accept a custom `Bitmap` to display instead of just the standard icons available in the regular `MessageBox` implementation. This class is pretty simple, so let's jump into the `__DoLayout` method to see how we made use of the `StdDialogButtonSizer`.

In `__DoLayout`, we first created some regular `BoxSizers` to do the main part of the layout, and then in one single line of code we created the entire layout for our buttons. To do this, we used the `CreateButtonSizer` method of the base `wx.Dialog` class. This method takes a bitmask of flags that specifies the buttons to create, then creates them, and adds them to a `StdDialogButtonSizer` that it returns. All we need to do after this is to add the sizer to our dialog's main sizer and we are done!

The following screenshots show how the `StdDialogButtonSizer` handles the differences in platform standards.

For example, the **OK** and **Cancel** buttons on a dialog are ordered as **OK/Cancel** on Windows:

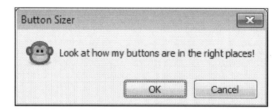

On Macintosh OS X, the standard layout for the buttons is **Cancel/OK**:

There's more...

Here is a quick reference to the flags that can be passed as a bitmask to the `CreateButtonSizer` method in order to create the buttons that the button sizer will manage:

Flags	Description
wx.OK	Creates an OK button
wx.CANCEL	Creates a Cancel button
wx.YES	Creates a Yes button

Flags	Description
`wx.NO`	Creates a No button
`wx.HELP`	Creates a Help button
`wx.NO_DEFAULT`	Sets the No button as the default

See also

▸ The *Creating Stock Buttons* recipe in *Chapter 3, Basic Building Blocks of a User Interface* discusses how to create common buttons from built-in IDs.

▸ The *Using a BoxSizer* recipe in this chapter discusses the basics of window layout using `BoxSizers`.

Using XML resources

XRC is a way of creating and design window layouts with XML resource files. The hierarchical nature of XML parallels that of an application's window hierarchy, which makes it a very sensible data format to serialize a window layout with. This recipe shows how to create and load a simple dialog with two `CheckBoxe` objects and two `Button` objects on it, from an XML resource file.

How to do it...

Here is the XML for our dialog that we have in a file called `xrcdlg.xrc`:

```
<?xml version="1.0" ?>
<resource>
  <object class="wxDialog" name="xrctestdlg">
    <object class="wxBoxSizer">
      <orient>wxVERTICAL</orient>
      <object class="spacer">
        <option>1</option>
        <flag>wxEXPAND</flag>
      </object>
      <object class="sizeritem">
        <object class="wxCheckBox">
          <label>CheckBox Label</label>
        </object>
        <flag>wxALL|wxALIGN_CENTRE_HORIZONTAL</flag>
        <border>5</border>
      </object>
      <object class="spacer">
        <option>1</option>
        <flag>wxEXPAND</flag>
```

```
          </object>
        <object class="sizeritem">
          <object class="wxBoxSizer">
            <object class="sizeritem">
              <object class="wxButton" name="wxID_OK">
                <label>Ok</label>
              </object>
              <flag>wxALL</flag>
              <border>5</border>
            </object>
            <object class="sizeritem">
              <object class="wxButton" name="wxID_CANCEL">
                <label>Cancel</label>
              </object>
              <flag>wxALL</flag>
              <border>5</border>
            </object>
            <orient>wxHORIZONTAL</orient>
          </object>
          <flag>wxALIGN_BOTTOM|wxALIGN_CENTRE_HORIZONTAL</flag>
          <border>5</border>
        </object>
      </object>
    <title>Xrc Test Dialog</title>
    <style>wxDEFAULT_DIALOG_STYLE|wxRESIZE_BORDER</style>
  </object>
</resource>
```

When loaded, the above XML will generate the following dialog:

This is a minimal program to load this XML resource to make and show the dialog it represents:

```
import wx
import wx.xrc as xrc
app = wx.App()
frame = wx.Frame(None)
resource = xrc.XmlResource("xrcdlg.xrc")
dlg = resource.LoadDialog(frame, "xrctestdlg")
dlg.ShowModal()
app.MainLoop()
```

How it works...

The XML in this recipe was created with the help of `xrced`, which is an XML resource editor tool that is a part of the wxPython tools package. The `object` tag is used to represent a class object. Nesting other objects inside is how the parent child relationship is represented with the XML. The `class` attribute of the `object` tag is what is used to specify the type of class to create. The values should be a class name and in the case of wxPython provided classes, they use the `wxWidgets` names, which are prefixed with "wx". To work with `XmlResource` classes, it is highly recommended to use a tool like `xrced` to generate the XML.

In order to load the XML to create the object(s) that are used for representation, you need to import the `wx.xrc` package, which provides the `XmlResource` class. There are a few ways to use `XmlResource` to perform the transformations on the XML. In this example, we created our `XmlResource` object by passing the path to our `xrc` file in its constructor. This object has a number of load methods for instantiating different types of objects. We want to load a dialog, so we called its `LoadDialog` method, passing a parent window as the first argument and then the name of the dialog we want to load from the XML. It will then instantiate an instance of that dialog and return it so that we can show it.

There's more...

Included below are some additional references to features available when using the XRC library.

Loading other types of resources

The `XmlResource` object has methods for loading many different kinds of resources from XML. Here is quick reference to some of the additional methods:

Methods	Description
`LoadBitmap(name)`	Loads and returns the Bitmap identified by name
`LoadDialog(parent, name)`	Loads and returns the Dialog identified by name
`LoadFrame(parent, name)`	Loads and returns the Frame identified by name
`LoadIcon(name)`	Loads and returns the Icon identified by name
`LoadMenu(name)`	Loads and returns the Menu identified by name
`LoadMenuBar(parent, name)`	Loads and returns the MenuBar identified by name
`LoadPanel(parent, name)`	Loads and returns the Panel identified by name
`LoadToolBar(parent, name)`	Loads and returns the ToolBar identified by name

Specifying standard IDs

In order to give an object a standard ID in XRC, it should be specified in the `object` tag's `name` attribute, using the `wxWidgets` naming for the ID (that is, `wxID_OK` without the '.').

See also

▶ The *Making a custom resource handler* recipe in this chapter contains some additional information on using XRC.

Making a custom resource handler

Although XRC has built-in support for a large number of the standard controls, any non-trivial application will use its own subclasses and/or custom widgets. Creating a custom `XmlResource` class will allow these custom classes to be loaded from an XML resource file. This recipe shows how to create an XML resource handler for a custom `Panel` class and then use that handler to load the resource.

Getting Started

This recipe discusses how to customize and extend the handling of XML resources. Please review the *Using XML resources* recipe in this chapter to learn the basics of how XRC works.

How to do it...

In the following code, we will show how to create a custom XML resource handler for a Panel and then how to use XRC to load that resource into a Frame:

```python
import wx
import wx.xrc as xrc

# Xml to load our object
RESOURCE = r"""<?xml version="1.0"?>
<resource>
<object class="TextEditPanel" name="TextEdit">
</object>
</resource>
"""
```

Here, in our Frame subclass, we simply create an instance of our custom resource handler and use it to load our custom Panel:

```python
class XrcTestFrame(wx.Frame):
    def __init__(self, *args, **kwargs):
        super(XrcTestFrame, self).__init__(*args, **kwargs)

        # Attributes
        resource = xrc.EmptyXmlResource()
```

```
handler = TextEditPanelXmlHandler()
resource.InsertHandler(handler)
resource.LoadFromString(RESOURCE)
self.panel = resource.LoadObject(self,
                                 "TextEdit",
                                 "TextEditPanel")


# Layout
sizer = wx.BoxSizer(wx.VERTICAL)
sizer.Add(self.panel, 1, wx.EXPAND)
self.SetSizer(sizer)
```

Here is the Panel class that our custom resource handler will be used to create. It is just a simple Panel with a TextCtrl and two Buttons on it:

```
class TextEditPanel(wx.Panel):
    """Custom Panel containing a TextCtrl and Buttons
    for Copy and Paste actions.
    """
    def __init__(self, *args, **kwargs):
        super(TextEditPanel, self).__init__(*args, **kwargs)

        # Attributes
        self.txt = wx.TextCtrl(self, style=wx.TE_MULTILINE)
        self.copy = wx.Button(self, wx.ID_COPY)
        self.paste = wx.Button(self, wx.ID_PASTE)

        # Layout
        self._DoLayout()

        # Event Handlers
        self.Bind(wx.EVT_BUTTON, self.OnCopy, self.copy)
        self.Bind(wx.EVT_BUTTON, self.OnPaste, self.paste)

    def _DoLayout(self):
        """Layout the controls"""
        vsizer = wx.BoxSizer(wx.VERTICAL)
        hsizer = wx.BoxSizer(wx.HORIZONTAL)

        vsizer.Add(self.txt, 1, wx.EXPAND)
        hsizer.AddStretchSpacer()
        hsizer.Add(self.copy, 0, wx.RIGHT, 5)
        hsizer.Add(self.paste)
        hsizer.AddStretchSpacer()
        vsizer.Add(hsizer, 0, wx.EXPAND|wx.ALL, 10)
```

```
        # Finally assign the main outer sizer to the panel
        self.SetSizer(vsizer)

    def OnCopy(self, event):
        self.txt.Copy()

    def OnPaste(self, event):
        self.txt.Paste()
```

Finally, here is our custom XML resource handler class, where we just have to override two methods to implement the handling for our `TextEditPanel` class:

```
class TextEditPanelXmlHandler(xrc.XmlResourceHandler):
    """Resource handler for our TextEditPanel"""
    def CanHandle(self, node):
        """Required override. Returns a bool to say
        whether or not this handler can handle the given class
        """
        return self.IsOfClass(node, "TextEditPanel")

    def DoCreateResource(self):
        """Required override to create the object"""
        panel = TextEditPanel(self.GetParentAsWindow(),
                              self.GetID(),
                              self.GetPosition(),
                              self.GetSize(),
                              self.GetStyle("style",
                                            wx.TAB_TRAVERSAL),
                              self.GetName())
        self.SetupWindow(panel)
        self.CreateChildren(panel)
        return panel
```

How it works...

The `TextEditPanel` is our custom class that we want to create a custom resource handler for. The `TextEditPanelXmlHandler` class is a minimal resource handler that we created to be able to load our class from XML. This class has two required overrides that need to be implemented for it to function properly. The first is `CanHandle`, which is called by the framework to check if the handler can handle a given node type. We used the `IsOfClass` method to check if the node was of the same type as our `TextEditPanel`. The second is `DoCreateResource`, which is what is called to create our class. To create the class, all of its arguments can be retrieved from the resource handler.

The `XrcTestFrame` class is where we made use of our custom resource handler. First, we created an `EmptyXmlResource` object and used its `InsertHandler` method to add our custom handler to it. Then we loaded the XML from the `RESOURCE` string that we defined using the handler's `LoadFromString` method. After that, all there was to do was load the object using the resource's `LoadObject` method, which takes three arguments: the `parent` window of the object to be loaded, the `name` of the object in the XML resource, and the `classname`.

See also

▶ See the *Understanding inheritance limitations* recipe in *Chapter 1, Getting Started with wxPython* for some additional information about overriding virtual methods in wxPython classes.

▶ See the *Using XML resources* recipe in this chapter for more examples of using XML to create screen layouts.

Using the AuiFrameManager

The `AuiFrameManager` is part of the Advanced User Interface (`wx.aui`) library added to wxPython in 2.8. It allows a Frame to have a very user customizable interface. It automatically manages children windows in panes that can be undocked and turned into separate floating windows. There are also some built-in features to help with persisting and restoring the window's layout during running the application. This recipe will create a Frame base class that has AUI support and will automatically save its perspective and reload it when the application is next launched.

How to do it...

The following code will define a base class that encapsulates some of the usage of an `AuiManager`:

```
import wx
import wx.aui as aui

class AuiBaseFrame(wx.Frame):
    """Frame base class with builtin AUI support"""
    def __init__(self, parent, *args, **kwargs):
        super(AuiBaseFrame, self).__init__(*args, **kwargs)

        # Attributes
        auiFlags = aui.AUI_MGR_DEFAULT
        if wx.Platform == '__WXGTK__' and \
           aui.AUI_MGR_DEFAUL & aui.AUI_MGR_TRANSPARENT_HINT:
            # Use venetian blinds style as transparent can
            # cause crashes on Linux when desktop compositing
```

```
                  # is used.  (wxAUI bug in 2.8)
                  auiFlags -= aui.AUI_MGR_TRANSPARENT_HINT
                  auiFlags |= aui.AUI_MGR_VENETIAN_BLINDS_HINT
             self._mgr = aui.AuiManager(self, flags=auiFlags)

             # Event Handlers
             self.Bind(wx.EVT_CLOSE, self.OnAuiBaseClose)
```

`OnAuiBaseClose` will be called when the Frame closes. We use this as the point to get the current window layout perspective and save it for the next time the application is launched:

```
         def OnAuiBaseClose(self, event):
             """Save perspective on exit"""
             appName = wx.GetApp().GetAppName()
             assert appName, "No App Name Set!"
             config = wx.Config(appName)
             perspective = self._mgr.SavePerspective()
             config.Write("perspective", perspective)
             event.Skip() # Allow event to propagate
```

`AddPane` simply wraps getting access to the Frame's `AuiManager` and adds the given pane and `auiInfo` to it:

```
         def AddPane(self, pane, auiInfo):
             """Add a panel to be managed by this Frame's
             AUI Manager.
             @param pane: wx.Window instance
             @param auiInfo: AuiInfo Object
             """
             # Delegate to AuiManager
             self._mgr.AddPane(pane, auiInfo)
             self._mgr.Update() # Refresh the layout
```

The next method is simply a convenience method for creating and adding the main center pane to the managed window:

```
         def SetCenterPane(self, pane):
             """Set the main center pane of the frame.
             Convenience method for AddPane.
             @param pane: wx.Window instance
             """
             info = aui.AuiPaneInfo()
             info = info.Center().Name("CenterPane")
             info = info.Dockable(False).CaptionVisible(False)
             self._mgr.AddPane(pane, info)
```

This final method is used to load the last saved window layout from the last time the window was opened:

```
def LoadDefaultPerspective(self):
    appName = wx.GetApp().GetAppName()
    assert appName, "Must set an AppName!"
    config = wx.Config(appName)
    perspective = config.Read("perspective")
    if perspective:
        self._mgr.LoadPerspective(perspective)
```

How it works...

In this recipe, we created a class to help encapsulate some of the `AuiManager`'s functionality. So let's take a look at some of the functionality that this class provides, and how it works.

The `__init__` method is where we create the `AuiManager` object that will manage the panes that we want to add to the Frame. The `AuiManager` accepts a number of possible flags to dictate its behavior. We employed a small workaround for a bug on Linux platforms that use desktop compositing. Using the transparent docking hints can cause an AUI application to crash in this scenario, so we replaced it with the venetian blind style instead.

`OnAuiBaseClose` is used as an event handler for when the `Frame` closes. We use this as a hook to automatically store the current layout of the `AuiManager`, which is called a perspective, for the next application launch. To implement this feature, we have created a requirement that the App object's `SetName` method was called to set the application name because we need this in order to use `wx.Config`. The `wx.Config` object is simply an interface used to access the Registry on Windows or an application configuration file on other platforms. `SavePerspective` returns a string encoded with all of the information that the `AuiManager` needs in order to restore the current window layout. The application can then simply call our `LoadDefaultPerspective` method when the application starts up, in order to restore the user's last window layout.

The other two methods in this class are quite simple and are provided simply for convenience to delegate to the `AuiManager` of the `Frame`. The `AddPane` method of the `AuiManager` is how to add panes to be managed by it. The `pane` argument needs to be a window object that is a child of the `Frame`. In practice, this is usually some sort of `Panel` subclass. The `auiInfo` argument is an `AuiPaneInfo` object. This is what the `AuiManager` uses to determine how to manage the pane. See the sample code that accompanies this recipe for an example of this class in action.

There's more...

Here is a quick reference to the flags that can be used in the flags bitmask for the
`AuiManager` in order to customize its behavior and the styles of some of its components:

Flags	Description
AUI_MGR_DEFAULT	Equivalent of AUI_MGR_ALLOW_FLOATING|AUI_MGR_ TRANSPARENT_HINT|AUI_MGR_HINT_ FADE|AUI_MGR_NO_VENETIAN_BLINDS_ FADE
AUI_MGR_ALLOW_FLOATING	Allow for floating panes
AUI_MGR_ALLOW_ACTIVE_PANE	Highlight the caption bar of the currently-active pane
AUI_MGR_HINT_FADE	Fade docking hints out of view
AUI_MGR_LIVE_RESIZE	Resize panes while the sash between them is being dragged
AUI_MGR_NO_VENETIAN_BLINDS_FADE	Disable the venetian blind fade in/out
AUI_MGR_RECTANGLE_HINT	Show a simple rectangle docking hint when dragging floating panes
AUI_MGR_TRANSPARENT_DRAG	Make floating panes partially-transparent when they are being dragged
AUI_MGR_TRANSPARENT_HINT	Show a partially-transparent light blue docking hint when dragging floating panels
AUI_MGR_VENETIAN_BLINDS_HINT	Use a venetian blind style docking hint for floating panels

8
Drawing to the Screen

In this chapter, we will cover:

- ▶ Screen drawing
- ▶ Drawing shapes
- ▶ Utilizing `SystemSettings`
- ▶ Using a `GraphicsContext`
- ▶ Drawing with `RendererNative`
- ▶ Reducing flicker in drawing routines

Introduction

Being able to display objects on a computer's display is one of the most basic functionalities of a GUI toolkit. In wxPython, objects are shown on the display through drawing commands issued to a **Device Context** (**DC**). Underneath the hood, all controls are represented as bitmaps that are drawn on the screen's display. The interface provided by a DC allows for the customization of a control's appearance. When used in combination with events, they are also the basis for creating new controls.

These rudimentary tools open a number of doors and possibilities that allow the application designer to fill the gaps in what the toolkit provides in order to meet the specific needs of an application. Now that the tool has been presented, it is time to pick it up and put it to use.

Screen drawing

All windows that are visible on the screen issue some drawing commands to a Device Context (often referred to as a DC) to tell the system what kind of pixel information to display on the screen. Some control's classes, such as `wx.Control`, `wx.Window`, and `wx.Panel` allow for user-defined control of what is drawn on the screen through the use of `wx.EVT_PAINT`. This recipe provides an introduction to screen drawing by creating a simple little slideshow widget that will load a PNG or JPG file from a directory, and then draw that image on the screen along with some label text below it, to show which image is out of the set.

How to do it...

Here we will look at our `ImageCanvas` widget. Starting with its constructor we `Bind` to `EVT_PAINT` so that we can get call backs from the framework when a part of our window has been marked as needing to be redrawn:

```
import os
import wx

class ImageCanvas(wx.PyPanel):
    def __init__(self, parent):
        super(SlideShowPanel, self).__init__(parent)

        # Attributes
        self.idx = 0 # Current index in image list
        self.images = list() # list of images found to display

        # Event Handlers
        self.Bind(wx.EVT_PAINT, self.OnPaint)
```

Here we override `DoGetBestSize` so that the widget can be resized depending upon the size of the image that is displayed in it:

```
    def DoGetBestSize(self):
        """Virtual override for PyPanel"""
        newsize = wx.Size(0, 0)
        if len(self.images):
            imgpath = self.images[self.idx]
            bmp = wx.Bitmap(imgpath)
            newsize = bmp.GetSize()
            newsize = newsize + (20, 20) # some padding
        else:
```

```
        tsize = self.GetTextExtent("No Image!")
        newsize = tsize + (20, 20)

    # Ensure new size is at least 300x300
    return wx.Size(max(300, newsize[0]),
                   max(300, newsize[1]))
```

Here, in `OnPaint`, we handle `EVT_PAINT` and create a `PaintDC` to draw the current image on the Panel:

```
    def OnPaint(self, event):
        """Draw the image on to the panel"""
        dc = wx.PaintDC(self) # Must create a PaintDC

        # Get the working rectangle
        rect = self.GetClientRect()

        # Setup the DC
        dc.SetTextForeground(wx.BLACK)

        # Do the drawing
        if len(self.images):
            # Draw the current image
            imgpath = self.images[self.idx]
            bmp = wx.Bitmap(imgpath)
            bsize = bmp.GetSize()
            # Try and center the image
            # Note: assumes image is smaller than canvas
            xpos = (rect.width - bsize[0]) / 2
            ypos = (rect.height - bsize[1]) / 2
            dc.DrawBitmap(bmp, xpos, ypos)
            # Draw a label under the image saying what
            # number in the set it is.
            imgcount = len(self.images)
            number = "%d / %d" % (self.idx+1, imgcount)
            tsize = dc.GetTextExtent(number)
            xpos = (rect.width - tsize[0]) / 2
            ypos = ypos + bsize[1] + 5 # 5px below image
            dc.DrawText(number, xpos, ypos)
        else:
            # Display that there are no images
            font = self.GetFont()
            font.SetWeight(wx.FONTWEIGHT_BOLD)
            dc.SetFont(font)
            dc.DrawLabel("No Images!", rect, wx.ALIGN_CENTER)
```

Finally, we add a few methods for client code to interact with in order to change the image and set the image source directory:

```python
def Next(self):
    """Goto next image"""
    self.idx += 1
    if self.idx >= len(self.images):
        self.idx = 0 # Go back to zero
    self.Refresh() # Causes a repaint

def Previous(self):
    """Goto previous image"""
    self.idx -= 1
    if self.idx < 0:
        self.idx = len(self.images) - 1 # Goto end
    self.Refresh() # Causes a repaint

def SetImageDir(self, imgpath):
    """Set the path to where the images are"""
    assert os.path.exists(imgpath)
    # Find all the images in the directory
    self.images = [ os.path.join(imgpath, img)
                    for img in os.listdir(imgpath)
                    if img.lower().endswith('.png') or
                        img.lower().endswith('.jpg') ]
    self.idx = 0
```

How it works...

That was pretty easy, so let's take a quick walkthrough to see how everything works. First we derived our `ImageCanvas` panel from `PyPanel` so that we could get access to some of its virtual methods. Next, in the constructor, we `Bind` our paint handler to `EVT_PAINT` so that we will get `PaintEvent` notifications.

The next method, `DoGetBestSize`, is a virtual override. The framework will call this method when it wants us to tell it what our best size is. This occurs when the layout is being calculated. We base the best size on the size of the current image, but reserve a minimum rectangle of 300x300 pixels just to ensure that we have some space to work with.

Next we get to `OnPaint`. This is where the main focus of this recipe unfolds. The first thing to notice is that we create a `PaintDC`. This is a required step. If a `PaintDC` is not created within an `EVT_PAINT` handler, then on platforms such as Windows there will be errors when refreshing the window. The `PaintDC` provides the interface to the DC, which will allow us to draw on the screen.

Most of the work in OnPaint is just calculating where to position what we want to draw. We do this by first getting the rectangle that we have to work in, which is simply returned by calling GetClientRect. From here, in the case where we have some images to display, we do some simple calculations to center the current image, and then use the DC's DrawBitmap method to draw our Bitmap object to the screen. Then we proceed to draw some text under the image to show what number the image is in the set. To do this, we use GetTextExtent to get the on-screen size that our string will require to be drawn with the current font. In the case where there are no images, we simply use the DC's DrawLabel function with the ALIGN_CENTER flag to draw a warning label in the middle of the rectangle.

To facilitate cycling through the images in the directory specified by calling SetImageDir, we have two methods: Next and Previous. These methods simply increment or decrement the index we are looking at in the list, and then call Refresh. Refresh will cause the system to issue a new PaintEvent. When this happens, our OnPaint handler will be called and will draw the new image. See the sample code that accompanies this recipe for a sample application using our ImageCanvas widget.

See also

▸ The *Using Bitmaps* recipe in *Chapter 1, Getting Started with wxPython* discusses the basics of using Bitmaps in an application.

▸ The *Understanding inheritance limitations* recipe in *Chapter 1, Getting Started with wxPython* explains the usage of the Py classes and how to override their virtual methods.

Drawing shapes

Besides being able to draw text and bitmaps, DC's are also able to draw arbitrary shapes and lines. These rudimentary tools are what make it possible to create entirely custom widgets and controls, and to perform tasks such as drawing diagrams. This recipe explores these additional abilities of the PaintDC by creating a simple smiley face control.

How to do it...

Here we will define our simple smiley face control that is derived from PyControl:

```
class Smiley(wx.PyControl):
    def __init__(self, parent, size=(50,50)):
        super(Smiley, self).__init__(parent,
                                     size=size,
                                     style=wx.NO_BORDER)

        # Event Handlers
        self.Bind(wx.EVT_PAINT, self.OnPaint)
```

Here in, `OnPaint` is where we will draw our Smiley face onto the `PyControl`'s background:

```
def OnPaint(self, event):
    """Draw the image on to the panel"""
    dc = wx.PaintDC(self) # Must create a PaintDC

    # Get the working rectangle we can draw in
    rect = self.GetClientRect()

    # Setup the DC
    dc.SetPen(wx.BLACK_PEN) # for drawing lines / borders
    yellowbrush = wx.Brush(wx.Colour(255, 255, 0))
    dc.SetBrush(yellowbrush) # Yellow fill
```

First we will start by drawing the circle for the head, by finding the center of the control's rectangle and using `DrawCircle` to draw a yellow circle with a black border, using the current Pen and Brush that was set above:

```
cx = (rect.width / 2) + rect.x
cy = (rect.width / 2) + rect.y
radius = min(rect.width, rect.height) / 2
dc.DrawCircle(cx, cy, radius)
```

The next step is to draw the eyes. This smiley face is going to have blue, square-shaped eyes. To do this, we first calculate the size of the eyes as 1/8th of the total face area, set the brush to blue, and then use the DC's `DrawRectangle` method to draw each of the eyes:

```
eyesz = (rect.width / 8, rect.height / 8)
eyepos = (cx / 2, cy / 2)
dc.SetBrush(wx.BLUE_BRUSH)
dc.DrawRectangle(eyepos[0], eyepos[1],
                 eyesz[0], eyesz[1])
eyepos = (eyepos[0] + (cx - eyesz[0]), eyepos[1])
dc.DrawRectangle(eyepos[0], eyepos[1],
                 eyesz[0], eyesz[1])
```

Last but not least is to draw the smile onto the face. To do this, we set the brush back to yellow and then use the DC's `DrawArc` method to draw a slice of a circle. Since all we want is the bottom part of the arc to use as the smile, we finish by drawing a yellow rectangle over the top part of the slice, to cover up the wedge:

```
dc.SetBrush(yellowbrush)
startpos = (cx / 2, (cy / 2) + cy)
endpos = (cx + startpos[0], startpos[1])
dc.DrawArc(startpos[0], startpos[1],
           endpos[0], endpos[1], cx, cy)
```

```
dc.SetPen(wx.TRANSPARENT_PEN)
dc.DrawRectangle(startpos[0], cy,
                 endpos[0] - startpos[0],
                 startpos[1] - cy)
```

How it works...

In this recipe, we made use of a `Pen`, a `Brush`, and some of the rudimentary drawing routines that `PaintDC` provides us with. Let's take a look at our `OnPaint` method, to see how everything works.

First, we start off by setting up our DCs drawing tools. We set a black `Pen`, which will be used by the DC when it draws lines. We then set a yellow `Brush`. A `Brush` is used to fill the area inside of a shape when it is drawn. Next, we proceed to draw the face, which is a circle. To do this, we simply needed to find the center of our drawing area and then call the `DrawCircle` method with the center point and radius that we desire. The DC will then use our `Pen` and `Brush` to create a yellow circle with a black border drawn around it.

Next, for the eyes, we decided to draw them as blue squares. So we changed to a blue `Brush` and called the `DrawRectangle` routine to draw the squares. This method's first two arguments are where the top left corner of the rectangle will be drawn from. The second two are the width and height of the rectangle.

The final step is to draw the smile, which is just a simple arc. To perform this step, we need to figure out where we want the arc's two end points to be, which we just based on the center point of our circle. Then we called the `DrawArc` method, which will draw a slice of a circle. Because it draws a slice, there will be two unwanted lines from the center point extending to the start and end points of the arc. To get rid of this, we drew a yellow rectangle over the top of these two lines to erase it and only leave the arc which makes up the smile.

There's more...

Here is a quick reference to the basic drawing functions of a `PaintDC`.

Functions	Description
`DrawArc(x1,y1,x2,y2,` `        xcenter,ycenter)`	Draws a section of a circle with an arc from x1,y1 to x2,y2 centered from xcenter,ycenter.
`DrawBitmap(bmp,x,y,` `           useMask=False)`	Draws a bitmap at position x,y.
`DrawCheckMark(x,y,width,` `              height)`	Draws a checkmark in the given rectangle.
`DrawCircle(x,y,radius)`	Draws a circle with center point x,y and the given radius.

Functions	Description
`DrawEllipse(x,y,width,height)`	Draws an ellipse in the given rectangle.
`DrawEllipticArc(x,y,w,h, start,end)`	Draw the arc of an ellipse in the given rectangle. The start and end parameters are angles that specify the start and end of the arc relative to the 3 o'clock position in the rectangle.
`DrawIcon(icon, x, y)`	Draw an icon at x,y.
`DrawImageLabel(lbl,bmp,rect, align)`	Draw a label and a bitmap in the given rectangle, using the given alignment flags.
`DrawLabel(text,rect,align)`	Draw the text in the rectangle with the given alignment flags.
`DrawLine(x1,y1,x2,y2)`	Draw a line with the current pen from x1,y1 to x2,y2.
`DrawPoint(x,y)`	Draw a point at x,y with the current pen.
`DrawPolygon(points,x,y)`	Draw a polygon based on the list of points at position x,y.
`DrawRectangle(x,y,w,h)`	Draw a rectangle of size w,h at position x,y.
`DrawRotatedText(text,x,y, angle)`	Draw text at position x,y rotated to the given angle.
`DrawRoundedRectangle(x,y,w,h, angle)`	Draw a rectangle with rounded corners.
`DrawSpline(points)`	Draw a spline using the list of points.
`DrawText(text,x,y)`	Draw text at position x,y.

See also

▸ See the *Screen drawing* recipe in this chapter for the basics of creating and using a `DeviceContext`.

Utilizing SystemSettings

The `SystemSettings` object allows a program to query the system for information about default colors and fonts. Being able to know this information can be very helpful when creating custom drawings, as it makes it possible to use the same colors and fonts that the native system components are using, so that your custom control or window decoration can blend in and look like it belongs with the other native components that share the same window with it. In this recipe, we will use `SystemSettings` to create a custom control that is similar to a `StaticBox` but with a caption that is similar to the title bar of the `Frame` bar.

How to do it...

For this custom control, we will again start by deriving from `PyPanel` so that we have access to its `DoGetBestSize` method:

```
class CaptionBox(wx.PyPanel):
    def __init__(self, parent, caption):
        super(CaptionBox, self).__init__(parent,
                                         style=wx.NO_BORDER)

        # Attributes
        self._caption = caption
        self._csizer = wx.BoxSizer(wx.VERTICAL)

        # Setup
        self.__DoLayout()

        # Event Handlers
        self.Bind(wx.EVT_PAINT, self.OnPaint)

    def __DoLayout(self):
        msizer = wx.BoxSizer(wx.HORIZONTAL)
        self._csizer.AddSpacer(12) # extra space for caption
        msizer.Add(self._csizer, 0, wx.EXPAND|wx.ALL, 8)
        self.SetSizer(msizer)

    def DoGetBestSize(self):
        size = super(CaptionBox, self).DoGetBestSize()
        # Compensate for wide caption labels
        tw = self.GetTextExtent(self._caption)[0]
        size.SetWidth(max(size.width, tw+20))
        return size

    def AddItem(self, item):
        """Add a window or sizer item to the CaptionBox"""
        self._csizer.Add(item, 0, wx.ALL, 5)
```

Here, in our `EVT_PAINT` handler, we draw a simple caption at the top of the panel, and a border around the rest, using the caption color that we retrieve from the `SystemSettings` singleton:

```
    def OnPaint(self, event):
        """Draws the Caption and border around the controls"""
        dc = wx.PaintDC(self)
```

```
# Get the working rectangle we can draw in
rect = self.GetClientRect()

# Get the sytem color to draw the caption
ss = wx.SystemSettings
color = ss.GetColour(wx.SYS_COLOUR_ACTIVECAPTION)
txtcolor = ss.GetColour(wx.SYS_COLOUR_CAPTIONTEXT)
dc.SetTextForeground(txtcolor)

# Draw the border
rect.Inflate(-2, -2)
dc.SetPen(wx.Pen(color))
dc.SetBrush(wx.TRANSPARENT_BRUSH)
dc.DrawRectangleRect(rect)

# Add the Caption
rect = wx.Rect(rect.x, rect.y,
               rect.width, 16)
dc.SetBrush(wx.Brush(color))
dc.DrawRectangleRect(rect)
rect.Inflate(-5, 0)
dc.SetFont(self.GetFont())
dc.DrawLabel(self._caption, rect, wx.ALIGN_LEFT)
```

How it works...

In this recipe, we derived our new `CaptionBox` class from `PyPanel`. This was done because this control is going to be a container of other controls, and the use of `PyPanel` will allow the use of sizers to manage the layout and sizing of the control.

As a part of the initial layout of the Panel in `__DoLayout`, we reserved 20 pixels of space on the top and 8 pixels around the other sides, for the caption and border. This was done by putting in a spacer at the top plus an additional 8 pixel border around the `BoxSizer` that will be used to layout the `CaptionBox`'s children controls. Also as part of the layout management, we overrode `DoGetBestSize` in order to handle cases where the caption text is wider than the box's children windows. When using this class, its `AddItem` method must be used to add its children controls to it.

Now let's check out how we draw the control. In `OnPaint`, the first thing we do is use the `SystemSettings` singleton to get the system-defined colours for a caption's background and text, which will allow the control to fit in and match other controls no matter what theme or operating system it is run on. Next, we shrink the drawing `Rect` by 2 pixels in both directions to define the controls border. After this, all there is to do is set the Pen to the caption color and call `DrawRect` to draw the border. The caption bar is also drawn in a similar fashion by creating a smaller rectangle in the upper space we had reserved in the layout and drawing a solid rectangle by setting the `Brush` to the caption color. All that leaves is the final step of drawing the caption text on the rectangle we just drew. See the following screenshot, which shows two `CaptionBoxes`:

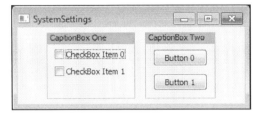

There's more

In addition to being able to provide colors, the `SystemSettings` object can also provide system fonts and metrics. The three methods `GetColour`, `GetFont`, and `GetMetric` all take an index parameter that is one of the `wx.SYS_*` constants.

See also

▶ See the *Screen drawing* recipe in this chapter for details of how to create and use a Device Context.

Using a GraphicsContext

The `GraphicsContext` is a new feature in wxPython2.8. It provides access to the platform's higher-level drawing functionality. It provides features such as anti-aliasing, a floating point precision coordinate system, alpha blending, gradient brushes, and a handful of advanced methods. This recipe uses it to create a custom control that is like `StaticText`, but has a gradient-filled, pill-shaped background.

How to do it...

Much like the other recipes in this chapter, we will derive our new control from `PyControl` so that we can override its `DoGetBestSize` method to size the control to our label:

```
class PodLabel(wx.PyControl):
    def __init__(self, parent, label, color):
        super(PodLabel, self).__init__(parent,
                                       style=wx.NO_BORDER)
        # Attributes
        self._label = label
        self._color = color
```

```
            # Event Handlers
            self.Bind(wx.EVT_PAINT, self.OnPaint)

    def DoGetBestSize(self):
        txtsz = self.GetTextExtent(self._label)
        size = wx.Size(txtsz[0] + 10, txtsz[1] + 6)
        return size
```

This time in `OnPaint`, we will create a GCDC from our `PaintDC` and do the drawing with the GCDC and its `GraphicsContext`:

```
    def OnPaint(self, event):
        """Draws the Caption and border around the controls"""
        dc = wx.PaintDC(self)
        gcdc = wx.GCDC(dc)
        gc = gcdc.GetGraphicsContext()

        # Get the working rectangle we can draw in
        rect = self.GetClientRect()

        # Setup the GraphicsContext
        pen = gc.CreatePen(wx.TRANSPARENT_PEN)
        gc.SetPen(pen)
        rgb = self._color.Get(False)
        alpha = self._color.Alpha() *.2 # fade to transparent
        color2 = wx.Colour(*rgb, alpha=alpha)
        x1, y1 = rect.x, rect.y
        y2 = y1 + rect.height
        gradbrush = gc.CreateLinearGradientBrush(x1, y1,
                                                 x1, y2,
                                                 self._color,
                                                 color2)
        gc.SetBrush(gradbrush)

        # Draw the background
        gc.DrawRoundedRectangle(rect.x, rect.y,
                                rect.width, rect.height,
                                rect.height/2)
        # Use the GCDC to help draw the aa text
        gcdc.DrawLabel(self._label, rect, wx.ALIGN_CENTER)
```

How it works...

In order to draw this control in `OnPaint`, we took the `PaintDC` and wrapped it in a `GCDC`. A `GCDC` is a device context interface that uses a `GraphicsContext` internally. Using this interface makes it possible to use a `GraphicsContext` in a similar way to using a regular device context.

When setting up the `Pen` and `Brush`, we used a transparent pen in order to not draw a border round the control. Drawing a gradient-colored background with a `GraphicsContext` is made simple with the use of the `GraphicsBrush` returned by the `CreateLinearGradientBrush` method of `GraphicsContext`. This method will create a brush that draws a gradient from the first set of coordinates to the second set, starting with the first color and blending it to the second. In this case, our second color only differs in its alpha level, so the gradient will fade to partially-transparent, which will show the panel behind it.

All that is left now is to just call the `GraphicsContext`'s `DrawRoundedRectangle` method, to draw a nice pill-shaped background that is filled with the gradient defined by the `GraphicsBrush` we created earlier. Then all that is left is to draw the label text on top of the background. To do this, we used the `DrawLabel` method of `GCDC` which is just like the `DrawLabel` method of `PaintDC` but uses the `GraphicsContext` under the hood to draw smooth, anti-aliased text. The following screenshot shows an example dialog with three instances of the `PodLabel` control on it. As can be seen, using the `GraphicsContext` has allowed the control to be drawn with smooth, anti-aliased edges and a gradient background that fades and becomes transparent near the bottom by taking advantage of the alpha blending of `GraphicsContext`.

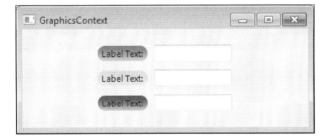

See also

- The *Screen drawing* recipe in this chapter discusses the use of Device Contexts.
- See the *Drawing shapes* recipe in this chapter for an overview of the basic drawing routines.
- See the *Reducing flicker in drawing routines* recipe in this chapter for more examples of using a `GraphicsContext`.

Drawing with RendererNative

RendererNative is a class that contains a collection of functions that encapsulate the drawing of a native UI component. It allows you to draw things such as native-looking Button and CheckBox objects in a device context without needing to know any of the details about how it is done. This is a very powerful and useful class when you need to create generic widgets but want and maintain the native look and feel of the platform's own widgets. This recipe uses RendererNative to create a custom button class for showing a drop-down menu.

How to do it...

This custom Button class will use RendererNative to do its drawing, based on the location and state of the mouse:

```python
class DropArrowButton(wx.PyControl):
    def __init__(self, parent, id=wx.ID_ANY,
                 label="", pos=wx.DefaultPosition,
                 size=wx.DefaultSize, style=0,
                 validator=wx.DefaultValidator,
                 name="DropArrowButton"):
        style |= wx.BORDER_NONE
        super(DropArrowButton, self).__init__(parent, id,
                                              pos, size,
                                              style,
                                              validator, name)

        # Attributes
        self._label = label
        self._menu = None
        self._state = 0

        # Event Handlers
        self.Bind(wx.EVT_LEFT_DOWN, self.OnLeftDown)
        self.Bind(wx.EVT_LEFT_UP, self.OnLeftUp)
        self.Bind(wx.EVT_LEAVE_WINDOW,
                  lambda event:
                  self.SetState(0))
        self.Bind(wx.EVT_ENTER_WINDOW,
                  lambda event:
                  self.SetState(wx.CONTROL_CURRENT))
        self.Bind(wx.EVT_PAINT, self.OnPaint)
```

We override `DoGetBestSize` and use the size of the label string as the basis for calculating the button's size:

```
def DoGetBestSize(self):
    size = self.GetTextExtent(self._label)
    size = (size[0]+16, size[1]+16) # Drop Arrow
    size = (size[0]+8, size[1]+4) # Padding
    self.CacheBestSize(size)
    return size
```

Here we add handlers for `EVT_LEFT_DOWN` and `EVT_LEFT_UP` to change the state of the control, and to show our pop-up menu:

```
def OnLeftDown(self, event):
    """Show the drop menu"""
    self.SetState(wx.CONTROL_PRESSED)
    if self._menu:
        size = self.GetSizeTuple()
        self.PopupMenu(self._menu, (0, size[1]))

def OnLeftUp(self, event):
    """Send a button click event"""
    if self._state != wx.CONTROL_PRESSED:
        return

    self.SetState(wx.CONTROL_CURRENT)
```

Here, in `OnPaint`, we create the required `PaintDC` and get a reference to the `RendererNative` singleton, which we will use to help us draw the Button's background:

```
def OnPaint(self, event):
    """Draw the Conrol"""
    dc = wx.PaintDC(self)
    gc = wx.GCDC(dc) # AA text

    # Get the renderer singleton
    render = wx.RendererNative.Get()

    # Get the working rectangle we can draw in
    rect = self.GetClientRect()

    # Draw the button
    render.DrawPushButton(self, gc, rect, self._state)
    # Draw the label on the button
    lblrect = wx.Rect(rect.x+4, rect.y+2,
                      rect.width-24, rect.height-4)
    gc.DrawLabel(self._label, lblrect, wx.ALIGN_CENTER)
```

```
# Draw drop arrow
droprect = wx.Rect((rect.x+rect.width)-20,
                        rect.y+2, 16, rect.height-4)
state = self._state
if state != wx.CONTROL_PRESSED:
    state = wx.CONTROL_CURRENT
render.DrawDropArrow(self, gc, droprect, state)
```

Finally, we have an API to allow the client code to set the Button's pop-up menu:

```
def SetMenu(self, menu):
    """Set the buttons drop menu
    @param menu: wx.Menu
    """
    if self._menu:
        self._menu.Destroy()
    self._menu = menu

def SetState(self, state):
    self._state = state
    self.Refresh()
```

How it works...

In this recipe, we created a completely new custom button control that looks just like a regular native button but has a drop-down arrow and will show a `Menu` when clicked on. Using `RendererNative` to handle most of the drawing has greatly simplified the creation of this nice-looking control, so let's take a look at how it all came together.

Let's start by looking at the `OnPaint` method, since it is where the control gets drawn. First, we created the required `PaintDC`, and then we used this to create a `GCDC` that will allow us to draw anti-aliased text just like the native control has. Then we get a reference to the `RendererNative` singleton by calling the classes `Get` method. Next, we start drawing the control. All the `RenderNative` methods take the same four arguments: the window we are drawing on, a DC, the `Rect`, and the renderer flags. `DrawPushButton` will draw a native button control with the given DC in the state specified by the renderer flag's bitmask. We pass in one of three flags in this example: 0 for the default state, `CONTROL_CURRENT` for the hover-over state, and `CONTROL_PRESSED` for when the control is pressed. We finish up the rest with `DrawLabel` and `DrawDropArrow` to draw the button's label with a down arrow to the right of it.

To make this behave like a button, we bind to a number of mouse events in the `__init__` method of our control. `EVT_ENTER_WINDOW` and `EVT_LEAVE_WINDOW` are used to toggle the hover-over state by changing the control flag between `CONTROL_CURRENT` and 0. `EVT_LEFT_DOWN` is used to set the `CONTROL_PRESSED` state, and finally `EVT_LEFT_UP` is used to show the pop-up menu. After each state change, `Refresh` is called to re-invoke the `OnPaint` handler and draw the control in its new state.

There's more...

Included below are some quick reference tables that list the drawing commands for `RendererNative`, and the state flags that affect how it draws the control.

Drawing Methods

The following table is a quick reference to the `RendererNative` methods. All the methods take the same first four arguments: `window`, `DC`, `rect`, and `flags`.

`RendererNative` methods	Description
DrawCheckBox	Draws a `CheckBox`
DrawChoice	Draws a `Choice` control
DrawComboBox	Draws a `ComboBox`
DrawComboBoxDropButton	Draws a `ComboBox` button
DrawDropArrow	Draws a drop arrow
DrawHeaderButton	Draws a `ListCtrl` column header
DrawItemSelectionRect	Draws a selection rectangle
DrawPushButton	Draws a `Button`
DrawRadioButton	Draws a `RadioButton`
DrawSplitterBorder	Draws the border of a `SplitterWindow` sash
DrawSplitterSash	Draws a `SplitterWindow` sash
DrawTextCtrl	Draws a `TextCtrl`
DrawTreeItemButton	Draws a `TreeCtrl` node button

Control Flags

The following flags can be passed as a part of a bitmask to the draw method's `flags` parameter. Not passing any flags, or passing `0` for the `flags` parameter, results in the control being drawn in its default state:

Flags	Description
CONTROL_CHECKABLE	Control can be checked (for `DrawCheckBox`)
CONTROL_CHECKED	Control is checked (for `DrawCheckBox`)
CONTROL_CURRENT	Mouse is over the control
CONTROL_DISABLED	Control is disabled
CONTROL_EXPANDED	Only for `DrawTreeItemButton`
CONTROL_FOCUSED	Control has the keyboard focus
CONTROL_ISDEFAULT	Is default control (for `DrawPushButton`)

Flags	Description
CONTROL_PRESSED	Button is pressed
CONTROL_SELECTED	Control is selected
CONTROL_UNDETERMINED	CheckBox is in undetermined state

See also

▶ See the *Playing with the mouse* recipe in *Chapter 2, Responding to Events* for some additional examples of working with MouseEvents.

Reducing flicker in drawing routines

Flicker occurs when the redrawing of the window leads to a visible flashing in the user interface. Even simple drawing routines, when done improperly, can lead to flicker. Luckily there are a number of things that can be done to combat and minimize flicker, which will then lead to an improved look and feel in an application's interface. This recipe shows a few snippets of three techniques that can be used to reduce flicker in drawing routines. The sample code that accompanies this chapter includes a sample application that uses all of these techniques in a simple animated wristwatch control.

How to do it...

We will start with one of the simplest techniques, which is to avoid unnecessary background erasure events by binding to EVT_ERASE_BACKGROUND:

```
self.Bind(wx.EVT_ERASE_BACKGROUND, self.OnErase)
```

Then we need do nothing in the handler for it, in order to prevent it from erasing the background:

```
def OnErase(self, event):
    # Do nothing, reduces flicker by removing
    # unneeded background erasures and redraws
    pass
```

The next technique is to use a buffered PaintDC in the OnPaint handler, so that all the individual drawing steps are performed off-screen, and then the finished product is displayed on the screen in one step:

```
def OnPaint(self, event):
    """Draw the image on to the panel"""
    # Create a Buffered PaintDC
    dc = wx.AutoBufferedPaintDCFactory(self)
```

The third technique is to just redraw the bare minimum of the screen when possible, by using the `Refresh` method's `rect` argument to tell it the part of the window that needs to be updated:

```
self.Refresh(rect=RectToUpdate)
```

How it works...

The first technique that was shown creates an empty event handler and bind it to the `EVT_ERASE_BACKGROUND` event. This is usually the first thing to try when you are running into flicker issues in your drawing routines. By doing nothing in the event handler, we prevent the system from clearing the background, so that when we draw it again in `OnPaint` it will draw over the existing background. This reduces the visibility of the redraw because the background won't flash to white in between `EVT_ERASE_BACKGROUND` and `EVT_PAINT`.

The second technique uses an `AutoBufferedPaintDCFactory` in order to create a buffered `PaintDC` instead of a regular `PaintDC` in the `OnPaint` handler. Buffered DCs do all the drawing in an off-screen `Bitmap` and then `Blit` the whole new `Bitmap` to the screen in one operation. This greatly reduces flicker because the screen gets updated in one single change instead of many individual changes when drawing to the screen directly in an unbuffered DC.

The final technique shown was to only redraw the minimal part of the screen that needs to be redrawn. This technique can be used when a control needs to manually redraw only a part of itself due to a state change. For example, imagine a control that consists of some label text and an image. If the control has the behavior to change the label color on mouse over, it could call Refresh on itself using the `rect` argument to specify just the label's rectangle in the control, so that only that part of the control is updated, minimizing the area of the screen that is redrawn.

See also

▸ The *Handling events* recipe in *Chapter 2, Responding to Events* explains the basics of event handling.

▸ See the *Using a GraphicsContext* recipe in this chapter for more detailed information on using the `GraphicsContext` class for drawing gradients.

▸ See the *Using Timers* recipe in *Chapter 11, Using Threads and Timers to Create Responsive Interfaces* for more information on using timers.

9
Design Approaches and Techniques

In this chapter, we will cover:

- ▶ Creating Singletons
- ▶ Implementing an observer pattern
- ▶ Strategy pattern
- ▶ Model View Controller
- ▶ Using mixin classes
- ▶ Using decorators

Introduction

Programming is all about patterns. There are patterns at every level, from the programming language itself, to the toolkit, to the application. Being able to discern and choose the optimal approach to use to solve the problem at hand can at times be a difficult task. The more patterns you know, the bigger your toolbox, and the easier it will become to be able to choose the right tool for the job.

Different programming languages and toolkits often lend themselves to certain patterns and approaches to problem solving. The Python programming language and wxPython are no different, so let's jump in and take a look at how to apply some common design approaches and techniques to wxPython applications.

Creating Singletons

In object oriented programming, the Singleton pattern is a fairly simple concept of only allowing exactly one instance of a given object to exist at a given time. This means that it only allows for only one instance of the object to be in memory at any given time, so that all references to the object are shared throughout the application. Singletons are often used to maintain a global state in an application since all occurances of one in an application reference the same exact instance of the object. Within the core wxPython library, there are a number of singleton objects, such as ArtProvider, ColourDatabase, and SystemSettings. This recipe shows how to make a singleton Dialog class, which can be useful for creating non-modal dialogs that should only have a single instance present at a given time, such as a settings dialog or a special tool window.

How to do it...

To get started, we will define a metaclass that can be reused on any class that needs to be turned into a singleton. We will get into more detail later in the *How it works* section. A metaclass is a class that creates a class. It is passed a class to it's __init__ and __call__ methods when someone tries to create an instance of the class.

```
class Singleton(type):
    def __init__(cls, name, bases, dict):
        super(Singleton, cls).__init__(name, bases, dict)
        cls.instance = None

    def __call__(cls, *args, **kw):
        if not cls.instance:
            # Not created or has been Destroyed
            obj = super(Singleton, cls).__call__(*args, **kw)
            cls.instance = obj
            cls.instance.SetupWindow()

        return cls.instance
```

Here we have an example of the use of our metaclass, which shows how easy it is to turn the following class into a singleton class by simply assigning the Singleton class as the __metaclass__ of SingletonDialog. The only other requirement is to define the SetupWindow method that the Singleton metaclass uses as an initialization hook to set up the window the first time an instance of the class is created.

Note that in Python 3+ the __metaclass__ attribute has been replaced with a metaclass keyword argument in the class definition.

```
class SingletonDialog(wx.Dialog):
    __metaclass__ = Singleton

    def SetupWindow(self):
        """Hook method for initializing window"""
        self.field = wx.TextCtrl(self)
        self.check = wx.CheckBox(self, label="Enable Foo")

        # Layout
        vsizer = wx.BoxSizer(wx.VERTICAL)
        label = wx.StaticText(self, label="FooBar")
        hsizer = wx.BoxSizer(wx.HORIZONTAL)
        hsizer.AddMany([(label, 0, wx.ALIGN_CENTER_VERTICAL),
                        ((5, 5), 0),
                        (self.field, 0, wx.EXPAND)])
        btnsz = self.CreateButtonSizer(wx.OK)
        vsizer.AddMany([(hsizer, 0, wx.ALL|wx.EXPAND, 10),
                        (self.check, 0, wx.ALL, 10),
                        (btnsz, 0, wx.EXPAND|wx.ALL, 10)])
        self.SetSizer(vsizer)
        self.SetInitialSize()
```

How it works...

There are a number of ways to implement a Singleton in Python. In this recipe, we used a metaclass to accomplish the task. This is a nicely contained and easily reusable pattern to accomplish this task. The `Singleton` class that we defined can be used by any class that has a `SetupWindow` method defined for it. So now that we have done it, let's take a quick look at how a singleton works.

The Singleton metaclass dynamically creates and adds a class variable called `instance` to the passed in class. So just to get a picture of what is going on, the metaclass would generate the following code in our example:

```
class SingletonDialog(wx.Dialog):
    instance = None
```

Then the first time the metaclass's `__call__` method is invoked, it will then assign the instance of the class object returned by the super class's `__call__` method, which in this recipe is an instance of our `SingletonDialog`. So basically, it is the equivalent of the following:

```
SingletonDialog.instance = SingletonDialog(*args,**kwargs)
```

Any subsequent initializations will cause the previously-created one to be returned, instead of creating a new one since the class definition maintains the lifetime of the object and not an individual reference created in the user code.

Our `SingletonDialog` class is a very simple Dialog that has `TextCtrl`, `CheckBox`, and `Ok Button` objects on it. Instead of invoking initialization in the dialog's `__init__` method, we instead defined an interface method called `SetupWindow` that will be called by the Singleton metaclass when the object is initially created. In this method, we just perform a simple layout of our controls in the dialog. If you run the sample application that accompanies this topic, you can see that no matter how many times the show dialog button is clicked, it will only cause the existing instance of the dialog to be brought to the front. Also, if you make changes in the dialog's `TextCtrl` or `CheckBox`, and then close and reopen the dialog, the changes will be retained since the same instance of the dialog will be re-shown instead of creating a new one.

Implementing an observer pattern

The observer pattern is a design approach where objects can subscribe as observers of events that other objects are publishing. The publisher(s) of the events then just broadcasts the events to all of the subscribers. This allows the creation of an extensible, loosely-coupled framework of notifications, since the publisher(s) don't require any specific knowledge of the observers. The `pubsub` module provided by the `wx.lib` package provides an easy-to-use implementation of the observer pattern through a publisher/subscriber approach. Any arbitrary number of objects can subscribe their own callback methods to messages that the publishers will send to make their notifications. This recipe shows how to use the `pubsub` module to send configuration notifications in an application.

How to do it...

Here, we will create our application configuration object that stores runtime configuration variables for an application and provides a notification mechanism for whenever a value is added or modified in the configuration, through an interface that uses the observer pattern:

```
import wx
from wx.lib.pubsub import Publisher

# PubSub message classification
MSG_CONFIG_ROOT = ('config',)

class Configuration(object):
    """Configuration object that provides
    notifications.
    """
    def __init__(self):
        super(Configuration, self).__init__()
```

```
        # Attributes
        self._data = dict()

    def SetValue(self, key, value):
        self._data[key] = value
        # Notify all observers of config change
        Publisher.sendMessage(MSG_CONFIG_ROOT + (key,),
                              value)

    def GetValue(self, key):
        """Get a value from the configuration"""
        return self._data.get(key, None)
```

Now, we will create a very simple application to show how to subscribe observers to configuration changes in the `Configuration` class:

```
class ObserverApp(wx.App):
    def OnInit(self):
        self.config = Configuration()
        self.frame = ObserverFrame(None,
                                   title="Observer Pattern")
        self.frame.Show()
        self.configdlg = ConfigDialog(self.frame,
                                      title="Config Dialog")
        self.configdlg.Show()
        return True

    def GetConfig(self):
        return self.config
```

This dialog will have one configuration option on it to allow the user to change the applications font:

```
class ConfigDialog(wx.Dialog):
    """Simple setting dialog"""
    def __init__(self, *args, **kwargs):
        super(ConfigDialog, self).__init__(*args, **kwargs)

        # Attributes
        self.panel = ConfigPanel(self)

        # Layout
        sizer = wx.BoxSizer(wx.VERTICAL)
        sizer.Add(self.panel, 1, wx.EXPAND)
        self.SetSizer(sizer)
        self.SetInitialSize((300, 300))
```

```
class ConfigPanel(wx.Panel):
    def __init__(self, parent):
        super(ConfigPanel, self).__init__(parent)

        # Attributes
        self.picker = wx.FontPickerCtrl(self)

        # Setup
        self.__DoLayout()

        # Event Handlers
        self.Bind(wx.EVT_FONTPICKER_CHANGED,
                  self.OnFontPicker)

    def __DoLayout(self):
        vsizer = wx.BoxSizer(wx.VERTICAL)
        hsizer = wx.BoxSizer(wx.HORIZONTAL)

        vsizer.AddStretchSpacer()
        hsizer.AddStretchSpacer()
        hsizer.AddWindow(self.picker)
        hsizer.AddStretchSpacer()
        vsizer.Add(hsizer, 0, wx.EXPAND)
        vsizer.AddStretchSpacer()
        self.SetSizer(vsizer)
```

Here, in the `FontPicker`'s event handler, we get the newly-selected font and call `SetValue` on the `Configuration` object owned by the `App` object in order to change the configuration, which will then cause the `('config', 'font')` message to be published:

```
def OnFontPicker(self, event):
    """Event handler for the font picker control"""
    font = self.picker.GetSelectedFont()
    # Update the configuration
    config = wx.GetApp().GetConfig()
    config.SetValue('font', font)
```

Now, here, we define the application's main window that will subscribe it's `OnConfigMsg` method as an observer of all `('config',)` messages, so that it will be called whenever the configuration is modified:

```
class ObserverFrame(wx.Frame):
    """Window that observes configuration messages"""
    def __init__(self, *args, **kwargs):
        super(ObserverFrame, self).__init__(*args, **kwargs)
```

```
            # Attributes
            self.txt = wx.TextCtrl(self, style=wx.TE_MULTILINE)
            self.txt.SetValue("Change the font in the config "
                              "dialog and see it update here.")

            # Observer of configuration changes
            Publisher.subscribe(self.OnConfigMsg, MSG_CONFIG_ROOT)

        def __del__(self):
            # Unsubscribe when deleted
            Publisher.unsubscribe(self.OnConfigMsg)
```

Here is the observer method that will be called when any message beginning with `'config'` is sent by the `pubsub` `Publisher`. In this sample application, we just check for the (`'config'`, `'font'`) message and update the font of the `TextCtrl` object to use the newly-configured one:

```
        def OnConfigMsg(self, msg):
            """Observer method for config change messages"""
            if msg.topic[-1] == 'font':
                # font has changed so update controls
                self.SetFont(msg.data)
                self.txt.SetFont(msg.data)


    if __name__ == '__main__':
        app = ObserverApp(False)
        app.MainLoop()
```

How it works...

This recipe shows a convenient way to manage an application's configuration by allowing the interested parts of an application to subscribe to updates when certain parts of the configuration are modified. Let's start with a quick walkthrough of how pubsub works.

Pubsub messages use a tree structure to organize the categories of different messages. A message type can be defined either as a tuple (`'root'`, `'child1'`, `'grandchild1'`) or as a dot-separated string (`'root.child1.grandchild1'`). Subscribing a callback to (`'root'`,) will cause your callback method to be called for all messages that start with (`'root'`,). This means that if a component publishes (`'root'`, `'child1'`, `'grandchild1'`) or (`'root'`, `'child1'`), then any method that is subscribed to (`'root'`,) will also be called.

Pubsub basically works by storing the mapping of message types to callbacks in static memory in the `pubsub` module. In Python, modules are only imported once any other part of your application that uses the `pubsub` module shares the same singleton `Publisher` object.

In our recipe, the `Configuration` object is a simple object for storing data about the configuration of our application. Its `SetValue` method is the important part to look at. This is the method that will be called whenever a configuration change is made in the application. In turn, when this is called, it will send a pubsub message of `('config',) + (key,)` that will allow any observers to subscribe to either the root item or more specific topics determined by the exact configuration item.

Next, we have our simple `ConfigDialog` class. This is just a simple example that only has an option for configuring the application's font. When a change is made in the `FontPickerCtrl` in the `ConfigPanel`, the `Configuration` object will be retrieved from the `App` and will be updated to store the newly-selected `Font`. When this happens, the `Configuration` object will publish an update message to all subscribed observers.

Our `ObserverFrame` is an observer of all `('config',)` messages by subscribing its `OnConfigMsg` method to `MSG_CONFIG_ROOT`. `OnConfigMsg` will be called any time the `Configuration` object's `SetValue` method is called. The `msg` parameter of the callback will contain a `Message` object that has a `topic` and `data` attribute. The `topic` attribute will contain the tuple that represents the message that triggered the callback and the `data` attribute will contain any data that was associated with the `topic` by the publisher of the message. In the case of a `('config', 'font')` message, our handler will update the `Font` of the `Frame` and its `TextCtrl`.

See also

 ▸ See the *Creating Singletons* recipe in this chapter for an explanation of how singleton objects like the Publisher from this recipe work.

 ▸ See the *Making a tool window* recipe in *Chapter 10, Creating Components and Extending Functionality* for another example of the publisher pattern in action.

Strategy pattern

The strategy pattern is an approach that allows for an application to choose the strategy or behavior that will be used at run time. It accomplishes this by encapsulating different algorithms and making them usable by the client regardless of what the underlying behavior of the algorithm is. This is probably one of the most fundamental design patterns in programming, and you're probably already using it in one form or another without even knowing it. This recipe shows how to create a reusable `Dialog` class that uses the strategy pattern to allow for the main content to vary depending on the strategy used.

How to do it...

First, we will start by defining a base interface with all of the strategies that our dialog class will use:

```
class BaseDialogStrategy:
    """Defines the strategy interface"""
    def GetWindowObject(self, parent):
        """Must return a Window object"""
        raise NotImplementedError, "Required method"

    def DoOnOk(self):
        """@return: bool (True to exit, False to not)"""
        return True

    def DoOnCancel(self):
        """@return: bool (True to exit, False to not)"""
        return True
```

Now let's define our simple Ok/Cancel dialog, which will use a strategy derived from our `BaseDialogStrategy` class to allow its main content area to vary depending on the strategy used:

```
class StrategyDialog(wx.Dialog):
    """Simple dialog with builtin OK/Cancel button and
    strategy based content area.
    """
    def __init__(self, parent, strategy, *args, **kwargs):
        super(StrategyDialog, self).__init__(parent,
                                             *args,
                                             **kwargs)

        # Attributes
        self.strategy = strategy
        self.pane = self.strategy.GetWindowObject(self)

        # Layout
        self.__DoLayout()

        # Event Handlers
        self.Bind(wx.EVT_BUTTON, self.OnButton)
```

Here, in the following methods of our `StrategyDialog`, we just delegate to the current strategy to allow it to define the behavior of the dialog:

```python
def __DoLayout(self):
    sizer = wx.BoxSizer(wx.VERTICAL)
    sizer.Add(self.pane, 1, wx.EXPAND)
    btnsz = self.CreateButtonSizer(wx.OK|wx.CANCEL)
    sizer.Add(btnsz, 0, wx.EXPAND|wx.ALL, 8)
    self.SetSizer(sizer)

def GetStrategy(self):
    return self.strategy

def OnButton(self, event):
    evt_id = event.GetId()
    bCanExit = False
    if evt_id == wx.ID_OK:
        bCanExit = self.strategy.DoOnOk()
    elif evt_id == wx.ID_OK:
        bCanExit = self.strategy.DoOnCancel()
    else:
        evt.Skip()

    if bCanExit:
        self.EndModal(evt_id)
```

Now let's implement a simple strategy that can be used to get the dialog to display a control for selecting a file:

```python
class FileTreeStrategy(BaseDialogStrategy):
    """File chooser strategy"""
    def GetWindowObject(self, parent):
        assert not hasattr(self, 'dirctrl')
        self.dirctrl = wx.GenericDirCtrl(parent)
        return self.dirctrl

    def DoOnOk(self):
        path = self.dirctrl.GetPath()
        if path:
            wx.MessageBox("You selected: %s" % path)
            return True
        else:
            wx.MessageBox("No file selected!")
            return False
```

Then, in an application, all that needs to be done to create a dialog that uses this strategy would be the following:

```
# Note: 'self' is some window object (i.e a Frame)
strategy = FileTreeStrategy()
dlg = StrategyDialog(self, strategy, title="Choose File")
dlg.ShowModal()
```

How it works...

Since all strategies that our dialog will use must be interchangeable, it is important to define an interface that they will implement. So, in our `BaseDialogStrategy` class, we defined a simple three-method interface that our `StrategyDialog` will delegate to.

The `StrategyDialog` is basically just a simple generic shell that delegates all decisions regarding its appearance and behavior to the strategy. When the dialog is initialized, it asks the strategy for a window object that will be used as the main content area of the dialog. The dialog then creates and adds some standard OK/Cancel buttons to the interface.

When a user clicks on one of these buttons, the `StrategyDialog` will then simply delegate to its strategy, to allow the strategy to handle the user action. This allows us to reuse this dialog class in many different ways, by simply implementing different strategies.

See also

▸ See the *Model View Controller* recipe in this chapter for some more examples of a strategy pattern.

Model View Controller

Model View Controller (**MVC**) is a design pattern that creates a clear separation of concerns within a program's architecture. It breaks down into three layers: the **Model**, which is the application's data objects and business logic at the bottom, the **View** at the top, which typically consists of controls for displaying and editing data, and finally the **Controller** in the middle, which is responsible for mediating the flow of data from the Model to the View and vice versa:

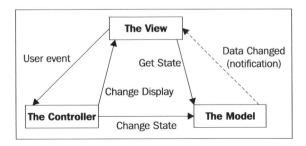

MVC is really one big monster pattern made up of other, simpler patterns working together. The Model implements an observer pattern to keep interested parties updated on changes, which allows it to be implemented separately from the View and Controller. The View and the Controller, on the other hand, implement a strategy pattern where the Controller is a strategy that implements the behavior of the View.

In this recipe, we explore how to create a simple number generator application that implements this pattern in wxPython.

How to do it...

Since there are multiple components that need to work together, having defined interfaces is an important step in the process, so first let us define some base classes that define the interface for our number generator's model and controller.

Beginning with our Model's interface, we provide a class that simply requires its `Generate` method to be overridden in order to provide the implementation-specific behavior. We have also built in a simple observer pattern mechanism to allow the view to subscribe to update notifications in the model:

```python
class ModelInterface(object):
    """Defines an interface for a simple value
    generator model.
    """
    def __init__(self):
        super(ModelInterface, self).__init__()

        # Attributes
        self.val = 0
        self.observers = list()

    def Generate(self):
        """Interface method to be implemented by
        subclasses.
        """
        raise NotImplementedError

    def SetValue(self, val):
        self.val = val
        self.NotifyObservers()

    def GetValue(self):
        return self.val
```

```
def RegisterObserver(self, callback):
    """Register an observer callback
    @param: callable(newval)
    """
    self.observers.append(callback)

def NotifyObservers(self):
    """Notify all observers of current value"""
    for observer in self.observers:
        observer()
```

Next we have the base interface definition for the controllers of our framework's view to derive from. This just defines one simple `DoGenerateNext` method that must be overridden by the specific implementation:

```
class ControllerInterface(object):
    """Defines an interface a value generator
    controller.
    """
    def __init__(self, model):
        super(ControllerInterface, self).__init__()

        # Attributes
        self.model = model
        self.view = TheView(None, self, self.model,
                            "Fibonacci Generator")

        # Setup
        self.view.Show()

    def DoGenerateNext(self):
        """User action request next value"""
        raise NotImplementedError
```

Now let's define some subclasses that implement the interface and provide the specialization.

Beginning with our `FibonacciModel` class, we define a model that will generate Fibonacci numbers:

```
class FibonacciModel(ModelInterface):
    def Generate(self):
        cval = self.GetValue()
        # Get the next one
        for fib in self.fibonacci():
            if fib > cval:
                self.SetValue(fib)
                break
```

```
@staticmethod
def fibonacci():
    """Fibonacci generator method"""
    a, b = 0, 1
    while True:
        yield a
        a, b = b, a + b
```

Then our `FibonacciController` provides the controller specialization, which in this example just makes one update to the user interface, to disable the button while the model is calculating the next value:

```
class FibonacciController(ControllerInterface):
    def DoGenerateNext(self):
        self.view.EnableButton(False)
        self.model.Generate()
```

Now that the model and controller have been defined, let's take a look at our view, which is composed of a `Frame`, a `Panel` that has a `TextCtrl` for displaying the current value stored in the model, and a `Button` for retrieving the next value in the sequence defined by the model:

```
class TheView(wx.Frame):
    def __init__(self, parent, controller, model, title):
        """The view for """
        super(TheView, self).__init__(parent, title=title)

        # Attributes
        self.panel = ViewPanel(self, controller, model)

        # Layout
        sizer = wx.BoxSizer(wx.VERTICAL)
        sizer.Add(self.panel, 1, wx.EXPAND)
        self.SetSizer(sizer)
        self.SetInitialSize((300, 300))

    def EnableButton(self, enable=True):
        self.panel.button.Enable(enable)
```

Here, the `ViewPanel` is where we interface with the model and controller. We retrieve the initial value from the model on initialization and then register as an observer of changes in the model:

```
class ViewPanel(wx.Panel):
    def __init__(self, parent, controller, model):
        super(ViewPanel, self).__init__(parent)
```

```
        # Attributes
        self.model = model
        self.controller = controller
        initial = str(self.model.GetValue())
        self.text = wx.TextCtrl(self, value=initial)
        self.button = wx.Button(self, label="Generate")

        # Layout
        self.__DoLayout()

        # Setup
        self.model.RegisterObserver(self.OnModelUpdate)

        # Event Handlers
        self.Bind(wx.EVT_BUTTON, self.OnAction)

    def __DoLayout(self):
        vsizer = wx.BoxSizer(wx.VERTICAL)
        hsizer = wx.BoxSizer(wx.HORIZONTAL)

        vsizer.AddStretchSpacer()
        vsizer.Add(self.text, 0, wx.ALIGN_CENTER|wx.ALL, 8)
        hsizer.AddStretchSpacer()
        hsizer.AddWindow(self.button)
        hsizer.AddStretchSpacer()
        vsizer.Add(hsizer, 0, wx.EXPAND)
        vsizer.AddStretchSpacer()
        self.SetSizer(vsizer)
```

Here is our observer method that will be called when the model is updated with a new value:

```
    def OnModelUpdate(self):
        """Observer method"""
        value = self.model.GetValue()
        self.text.SetValue(str(value))
        self.button.Enable(True)
```

This event handler is for the `Button`, and it delegates to the controller in order to allow the controller to perform the implementation-specific action:

```
    def OnAction(self, event):
        self.controller.DoGenerateNext()
```

Finally, we put it all together and implement an application:

```
class ModelViewApp(wx.App):
    def OnInit(self):
        self.model = FibonacciModel()
        self.controller = FibonacciController(self.model)
        return True


if __name__ == '__main__':
    app = ModelViewApp(False)
    app.MainLoop()
```

How it works...

Using MVC to design an application's framework takes a fair amount of discipline. As can be seen in this simple example, there is quite a bit of extra "stuff" that needs to be done. As described before, MVC separates concerns into three main roles:

1. The Model
2. The View
3. The Controller

So let's take a look at how these roles came together in our sample recipe.

First the Model: This has the ability to store a value and to generate the next one in the sequence when its `Generate` method is called. In this recipe, we implemented a Model that calculates and stores Fibonacci numbers. The important part to take away from this is that the Model does not have any direct knowledge of the View or the Controller.

Next let's jump to the View, which just displays a `TextCtrl` field and a `Button`. It does not know any of the details of how the Controller or Model works. It only interacts with them through a defined interface. When the user clicks the `Button`, it asks the Controller to decide what to do. In order to know when the Model has changed, it registers a callback function with the Model, as an observer of when the Model's `SetValue` method is called.

Now to the Controller which is the glue that holds the Model and View together. The Controller is primarily charged with implementing the View's behavior in regards to the Model's state. Our simple Controller for this recipe only has one interface method that is called in response to a `Button` click in the View. This action first disables the `Button`, and then tells the Model to generate the next number in the sequence.

There's more...

You may be wondering "what's the point?" of all that extra rigmarole to create such a simple application. Well since the Model is completely separate from the View, it can be more easily unit tested in an automated test suite. In addition to this, since the View is just simply a view and does not implement any behavior, it can easily be reused if, for example, we wanted to add a Prime Number generator model to our application.

Maintainability is also improved since all three parts are separated and can be worked on individually without interfering with the other components. Because of these benefits, many other toolkits, such as Django and web2py make use of this pattern.

See also

▶ See the *Implementing an observer pattern* recipe in this chapter for another approach to using an observer pattern.

▶ See the *Strategy pattern* recipe in this chapter for more information on using strategies.

Using mixin classes

A mixin class is a design approach that is similar to the strategy pattern, but directly uses inheritance in order to add extended/common functionality to a new class. This recipe shows how to create a mixin class that adds debug logging facilities to any class that uses it.

How to do it...

First, let's start by creating our `LoggerMixin` class, which will provide the logging functionality to classes that need to have logging. It simply provides a `Log` method that will write the passed in string to a file:

```python
import os
import time
import wx

class LoggerMixin:
    def __init__(self, logfile="log.txt"):
        """@keyword logfile: path to log output file"""
        # Attributes
        self.logfile = logfile

    def Log(self, msg):
        """Write a message to the log.
```

```
        Automatically adds timestamp and originating class
        information.
        """
        if self.logfile is None:
            return

        # Open and write to the log file
        with open(self.logfile, 'ab') as handle:
            # Make a time stamp
            ltime = time.localtime(time.time())
            tstamp = "%s:%s:%s" % (str(ltime[3]).zfill(2),
                                   str(ltime[4]).zfill(2),
                                   str(ltime[5]).zfill(2))
            # Add client info
            client = getattr(self, 'GetName',
                             lambda: "unknown")()
            # Construct the final message
            output = "[%s][%s] %s%s" % (tstamp, client,
                                        msg, os.linesep)
            handle.write(output)
```

Then, to use the LoggerMixin in an application, it can simply be mixed in to any class to give it a Log method:

```
    class MixinRecipeFrame(wx.Frame, LoggerMixin):
        """Main application window"""
        def __init__(self, parent, *args, **kwargs):
            wx.Frame.__init__(self, parent, *args, **kwargs)
            LoggerMixin.__init__(self)
            self.Log("Creating instance...")

            # Attributes
            self.panel = MixinRecipePanel(self)

            # Layout
            sizer = wx.BoxSizer(wx.VERTICAL)
            sizer.Add(self.panel, 1, wx.EXPAND)
            self.SetSizer(sizer)
            self.SetInitialSize((300, 300))
```

How it works...

The mixin class in this recipe is the `LoggerMixin` class. It will add a `Log` method to the classes that use it, which will take a simple string as an argument and write it to the specified log file with a timestamp and ID that shows where the message came from.

A mixin works by using multiple inheritance in order to add additional functionality to a class. The `LoggerMixin` mixin class can be used with any Python class, but it expects (but doesn't require) that the class it is being mixed into has a `GetName` method to use for getting the ID portion of the log message:

```
[17:42:24][unknown] OnInit called
[17:42:24][frame] Creating instance...
[17:42:24][panel] Begin Layout
[17:42:24][panel] End Layout
[17:42:26][panel] Button -203: Clicked
[17:42:26][panel] Button -203: Clicked
[17:42:27][panel] Button -203: Clicked
```

There's more

There are a number of handy mixin classes provided by the `wx.lib.mixins` package. Here is a quick rundown on some of the mixins that are available and what functionality they provide.

ListCtrl mixins

All of the following mixins classes are intended for use with a `ListCtrl` subclass and are provided by the `wx.lib.mixins.listctrl` module:

Mixins classes	Description
CheckListCtrlMixin	Adds `CheckBox` functionality to the first column of a `ListCtrl`
ColumnSorterMixin	Handles sorting of items in the `ListCtrl` when its column header is clicked
ListCtrlAutoWidthMixin	Automatically resizes the last column of a `ListCtrl` to fill any remaining space
ListRowHighlighter	Automatically changes the background color on alternating rows in the `ListCtrl` to give it a stripped appearance
TextEditMixin	Adds the ability to show an editable text field in any column of a `ListCtrl`

TreeCtrl mixins

All of the following mixin classes are for use with a `TreeCtrl` subclass, and are provided by the `wx.lib.mixins.treectrl` module:

Mixins classes	Description
DragAndDrop	Helps to simplify the addition of Drag and Drop support to a `TreeCtrl`
ExpansionState	Helper to save and restore the expansion state of nodes in a `TreeCtrl`
VirtualTree	Allow the `TreeCtrl` to be virtualized so that nodes are added and removed on demand, instead of having to construct the whole tree up front

Using decorators

Due to the window hierarchy, there are some architectural issues that can be presented to the programmer that lead to some tedious and unnecessary code duplication due to the need to have delegate accessor methods or properties at each level of the containment hierarchy. Typically, any Frame or Dialog in an application is structured as shown in the following diagram:

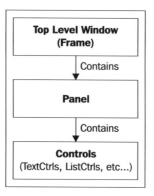

When needing to retrieve or modify the data that is shown in the window, it is the widgets and **Controls** that need to be accessed. These are contained by the **Panel** which is in turn contained by the **Top Level Window**. Since the Panel is responsible for its children, it will often have methods for modifying and accessing the data that is maintained by its children's controls. Because of this, the top-level window class often needs to have duplicate methods that simply delegate to the Panel's methods for getting and setting the window's data. These delegate methods are needed because the top-level window is the object that is instantiated at the application level and the application should not need to know the details of the top-level window's `Panel` in order to use it.

This recipe shows how to create a simple decorator method that takes advantage of Python's dynamic nature in order to expose a select method of a custom Panel class to its top-level window container.

How to do it...

This decorator class takes the name of a class as an argument and will dynamically define the `delegate` method in the targeted child `Panel` of the top level window:

```
class expose(object):
    """Expose a panels method to a to a specified class
    The panel that is having its method exposed by this
    decorator must be a child of the class its exposing
    itself too.
    """
    def __init__(self, cls):
        """@param cls: class to expose the method to"""
        super(expose, self).__init__()
        self.cls = cls
```

Here is where the magic occurs. We use `setattr` to dynamically add a function with the same name as the function being decorated to the targeted class. When called from the targeted class, the new method will walk through the window's children to find its `Panel`, and will delegate the call to the child class's method:

```
    def __call__(self, funct):
        """Dynamically bind and expose the function
        to the toplevel window class.
        """
        fname = funct.func_name
        def delegate(*args, **kwargs):
            """Delegate method for panel"""
            self = args[0] # The TLW
            # Find the panel this method belongs to
            panel = None
            for child in self.GetChildren():
                if isinstance(child, wx.Panel) and \
                    hasattr(child, fname):
                    panel = child
                    break
            assert panel is not None, "No matching child!"
            # Call the panels method
            return getattr(panel, fname)(*args[1:], **kwargs)
```

```
# Bind the new delegate method to the tlw class
delegate.__name__  = funct.__name__
delegate.__doc__   = funct.__doc__
setattr(self.cls, fname, delegate)

# Return original function to the current class
return funct
```

The example code that accompanies this chapter has a sample application that shows how to use this decorator.

How it works...

This recipe isn't so much a design pattern as it is a technique to help make writing new `Dialog` and `Frame` classes quicker and also to reduce code duplication. To do this, we created a decorator class for exposing methods from child `Panel` classes to their parent top-level window. Let's start with a look at the `expose` decorator to see how it works its magic.

The `expose` decorator takes a single argument, which is the class that the method should be exposed to. A reference to this is saved in the constructor for later use when the decorator is applied in its `__call__` method. The `__call__` method creates a method called `delegate` which will search for the first child panel that has a method with the same name as the one that is being exposed. If it finds an appropriate panel, then it simply calls the panel's method and returns its value. Next, it uses `setattr` to insert the newly-generated `delegate` method with an alias matching the `Panel`'s method into the namespace of the class specified in the decorator's constructor. At this point, the method is available for use in the top-level window that `expose` was called with. Finally, we just return the unaltered original function to the `Panel` class it belongs to.

Just to be clear, this decorator, as it is defined in this recipe, can only be used by `Panel` subclasses that have a known relationship of being the only child of their parent window. This is typical of how most `Frame` and `Dialog` subclasses are constructed, as can be seen in the example `CommentDialog` class that is included in this chapter's sample code.

See also

- ▸ See the *Understanding the window hierarchy* recipe in *Chapter 1, Getting Started with wxPython* for an additional explanation of the containment hierarchy of different objects.

10
Creating Components and Extending Functionality

In this chapter, we will cover:

- ▶ Customizing the `ArtProvider`
- ▶ Adding controls to a `StatusBar`
- ▶ Making a tool window
- ▶ Creating a `SearchBar`
- ▶ Working with `ListCtrl` mixins
- ▶ `StyledTextCtrl` custom highlighting
- ▶ Creating a custom control

Introduction

Once you've been working with wxPython for a while, you may find that you need some functionality or behavior that is not provided by default with the common controls. So in order to get this, you need some level of customization, or even the creation of a completely new type of control may become necessary in order to provide the interface that your application and users need.

There is a fair amount of flexibility built into many controls to change their behavior through the use of their style flags. In this chapter however, we will explore some object-oriented approaches for creating new controls as well as extending the functionality of some of the standard controls through inheritance. So let's get going and jump into some recipes.

Customizing the ArtProvider

The `ArtProvider` is a singleton object that can be used by any component that wants to display system theme provided bitmaps. In wxPython 2.8, only the GTK (Linux) port has a native implementation of this object, so other platforms use the icons that are built into wxPython. These built-in icons are a bit dated and out-of-place looking to say the least. This recipe shows how to create a custom `ArtProvider` to handle the display of custom icons on Windows and OS X while still retaining the native system theme icons on Linux.

How to do it...

Here we define our custom `ArtProvider` implementation, which just requires us to override the `CreateBitmap` method, which is used to load our custom icons:

```
class TangoArtProvider(wx.ArtProvider):
    def __init__(self):
        super(TangoArtProvider, self).__init__()

        # Attributes
        self.bmps = [bmp.replace('.png', '')
                       for bmp in os.listdir('tango')
                       if bmp.endswith('.png')]

    def CreateBitmap(self, id,
                     client=wx.ART_OTHER,
                     size=wx.DefaultSize):

        # Return NullBitmap on GTK to allow
        # the default artprovider to get the
        # system theme bitmap.
        if wx.Platform == '__WXGTK__':
            return wx.NullBitmap

        # Non GTK Platform get custom resource
        # when one is available.
        bmp = wx.NullBitmap
        if client == wx.ART_MENU or size == (16,16):
            if id in self.bmps:
                path = os.path.join('tango', id+'.png')
                bmp = wx.Bitmap(path)
        else:
```

```
        # TODO add support for other bitmap sizes
        pass


    return bmp
```

Then all that we need to do in order to use the custom `TangoArtProvider` in an application is to push it onto the `ArtProvider` stack:

```
class ArtProviderApp(wx.App):
    def OnInit(self):
        # Push our custom ArtProvider on to
        # the provider stack.
        wx.ArtProvider.PushProvider(TangoArtProvider())
        title = "Tango ArtProvider"
        self.frame = ArtProviderFrame(None,
                                          title=title)
        self.frame.Show()
        return True
```

How it works...

The `ArtProvider` singleton maintains a stack of `ArtProvider` objects that are chained together. When calling `GetBitmap` on the `ArtProvider`, it will first ask the one at the top of the stack for the requested `Bitmap`. If that one returns `NullBitmap`, it will ask the next one, and so on and so forth until either the `Bitmap` is found or the bottom of the stack is reached.

All that needs to be done to create a custom `ArtProvider` is to create a subclass that overrides the `CreateBitmap` method. Our `TangoArtProvider` overrides this method and provides a small set of icons from the free Tango (`http://tango.freedesktop.org`) icon set. We simply have a folder with some PNG images in it that we map to some of the wxPython `ART_*` IDs and then load them from disk into a `Bitmap` when requested.

See also

> ▶ See the *Creating Singletons* recipe in *Chapter 9, Design Approaches and Techniques* for an explanation of what singletons, such as the `ArtProvider`, are.

Adding controls to a StatusBar

The `StatusBar` is a common component found in many applications for the display of short information messages at the bottom of the main windows content area. The standard `StatusBar` supports the display of multiple status text fields. This recipe shows how to create an advanced `StatusBar` that has a `Gauge` built-in to it in order to show progress during long-running tasks. Just as a sneak peak of what we are going to create, take a look at the following screenshot to see the `ProgressStatusBar` in action:

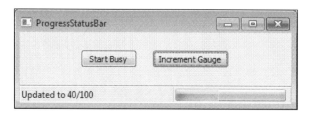

How to do it...

First, we will create our `ProgressStatusBar` class by creating a subclass of `StatusBar`. In the constructor, we create the `Gauge` for showing the progress and a `Timer` to use for updating the `Gauge`:

```
class ProgressStatusBar(wx.StatusBar):
    """Custom StatusBar with a built-in progress bar"""
    def __init__(self, parent, id_=wx.ID_ANY,
                 style=wx.SB_FLAT,
                 name="ProgressStatusBar"):
        super(ProgressStatusBar, self).__init__(parent,
                                                id_,
                                                style,
                                                name)

        # Attributes
        self._changed = False   # position has changed ?
        self.busy = False       # Bar in busy mode ?
        self.timer = wx.Timer(self)
        self.prog = wx.Gauge(self, style=wx.GA_HORIZONTAL)
        self.prog.Hide() # Hide on init

        # Layout
        self.SetFieldsCount(2)
        self.SetStatusWidths([-1, 155])
```

```
        # Event Handlers
        self.Bind(wx.EVT_IDLE,
                  lambda evt: self.__Reposition())
        self.Bind(wx.EVT_TIMER, self.OnTimer)
        self.Bind(wx.EVT_SIZE, self.OnSize)

    def __del__(self):
        if self.timer.IsRunning():
            self.timer.Stop()
```

The following helper method is used to make sure that the Gauge control is repositioned into the right-most status field when its Frame changes position or size:

```
    def __Reposition(self):
        """Repositions the gauge as necessary"""
        if self._changed:
            lfield = self.GetFieldsCount() - 1
            rect = self.GetFieldRect(lfield)
            prog_pos = (rect.x + 2, rect.y + 2)
            self.prog.SetPosition(prog_pos)
            prog_size = (rect.width - 8, rect.height - 4)
            self.prog.SetSize(prog_size)
        self._changed = False

    def OnSize(self, evt):
        self._changed = True
        self.__Reposition()
        evt.Skip()
```

The Timer event handler is used for handling when the Gauge is being used in indeterminate mode to pulse the Gauge:

```
    def OnTimer(self, evt):
        if not self.prog.IsShown():
            self.Stop()

        if self.busy:
            # In busy (indeterminate) mode
            self.prog.Pulse()
```

Starting here with the `Run` method, we have added some public methods for manipulating the `StatusBar`'s `Gauge` from user code.

```python
def Run(self, rate=100):
    if not self.timer.IsRunning():
        self.timer.Start(rate)

def GetProgress(self):
    return self.prog.GetValue()

def SetProgress(self, val):
    if not self.prog.IsShown():
        self.ShowProgress(True)

    # Check if we are finished
    if val == self.prog.GetRange():
        self.prog.SetValue(0)
        self.ShowProgress(False)
    else:
        self.prog.SetValue(val)

def SetRange(self, val):
    if val != self.prog.GetRange():
        self.prog.SetRange(val)

def ShowProgress(self, show=True):
    self.__Reposition()
    self.prog.Show(show)

def StartBusy(self, rate=100):
    self.busy = True
    self.__Reposition()
    self.ShowProgress(True)
    if not self.timer.IsRunning():
        self.timer.Start(rate)

def StopBusy(self):
    self.timer.Stop()
    self.ShowProgress(False)
    self.prog.SetValue(0)     # Reset progress value
    self.busy = False

def IsBusy(self):
    """Is the gauge busy?"""
    return self.busy
```

See the sample code that accompanies this chapter for a sample application of the `ProgressStatusBar` in action.

How it works...

The main trick to this recipe is the need to manually maintain the size and position of the `Gauge` control so that it stays in the same relative place on the `StatusBar`, regardless of how the window is moved or resized. We handled this with our `__Reposition` method that simply positions and sizes the `Gauge` based on the right-most field in the `StatusBar`. Then we just call this method whenever we hide or show the Gauge, or when the window is resized, and during `OnIdle` as necessary.

The `ProgressStatusBar` class supports two modes of operation for the progress gauge. The `Gauge` can either be shown in busy mode (indeterminate) or in incremental mode. In busy mode, we just start and run a `Timer` to `Pulse` the `Gauge` in the event handler. In incremental mode, the `Gauge`'s range is first set with `SetRange` and then its progress is updated incrementally by the application as necessary by calling `SetProgress`.

See also

- ▸ See the *Creating a custom SplashScreen* recipe in Chapter 5, *Providing Information and Alerting Users* for another example of using the Gauge control and Timers.

Making a tool window

A `ToolWindow` is a little floating window that often functions like a `ToolBar` by having many different tool icons on it that can be clicked to initiate various actions. These types of windows are often seen in paint applications for holding pallets and other tools. This recipe shows how to create a simple `ToolWindow` class.

How to do it...

First let's define the base `ToolWindow` class by deriving from `MiniFrame` so that it will be a small, floating, top-level window:

```python
import wx
import wx.lib.pubsub as pubsub

# message data will be tool id
MSG_TOOL_CLICKED = ('toolwin', 'clicked')

class ToolWindow(wx.MiniFrame):
    def __init__(self, parent, rows=1, columns=0, title=''):
```

```
        style = wx.CAPTION|wx.SYSTEM_MENU|\
               wx.SIMPLE_BORDER|wx.CLOSE_BOX
        super(ToolWindow, self).__init__(parent,
                                         title=title,
                                         style=style)

        # Attributes
        self.panel = ToolPanel(self, rows, columns)

        # Layout
        sizer = wx.BoxSizer(wx.VERTICAL)
        sizer.Add(self.panel, 1, wx.EXPAND)
        self.SetSizer(sizer)

    def AddTool(self, id, bmp, helplbl=''):
        """Add a tool to the window"""
        self.panel.AddTool(id, bmp, helplbl)
        self.Fit()
```

The `ToolPanel` class acts as the container and manager for the tools that are added to the `ToolWindow`:

```
class ToolPanel(wx.Panel):
    """Panel to hold the tools"""
    def __init__(self, parent, rows, columns):
        super(ToolPanel, self).__init__(parent)

        # Attributes
        self.sizer = wx.FlexGridSizer(rows, columns, 5, 5)

        # Setup
        self.SetSizer(self.sizer)

        # Event Handlers
        self.Bind(wx.EVT_BUTTON, self.OnButton)
```

The `AddTool` method takes the passed in ID and Bitmap and creates a `BitmapButton` to use as the tool, and then simply adds this to the sizer's layout:

```
    def AddTool(self, id, bmp, helplbl=''):
        tool = wx.BitmapButton(self, id, bmp)
        tool.SetToolTipString(helplbl)
        self.sizer.Add(tool)
        self.Layout()
```

The `OnButton` handler catches all button clicks in the `Panel` and then publishes a notification to all observers that have subscribed to tool messages:

```
def OnButton(self, event):
    """Notify clients when tool is clicked"""
    pubsub.Publisher.sendMessage(MSG_TOOL_CLICKED,
                                 event.GetId())
```

See the example code that accompanies this chapter for a sample text editor application that uses `ToolWindow`.

How it works...

Now that we have seen the code, let's take a quick walkthrough so we can see how it all works together.

Our `ToolWindow` class is composed of a `MiniFrame` and a `Panel` that will have `BitmapButton`s added to it when the client code calls its `AddTool` method. The `ToolWindow` has two arguments, `rows` and `columns`, that can specify the dimensions to use when laying out the tools in the `ToolPanel`'s `FlexGridSizer`. In order to ensure that the `ToolWindow` is the correct size and that all of its tools are visible, it is necessary to call `Layout` in the `ToolPanel`'s `AddTool` method, and then call `Fit` on the `ToolWindow` to ensure that the layout is recalculated and that the window is resized to best fit its contents.

When a tool is clicked on the `ToolWindow`, the event handler for the button simply uses `pubsub` to send a message containing the tool's ID to any observers of the `MSG_TOOL_CLICKED` topic. This method of notification was chosen because this way, if the application has multiple windows, they can all share the same `ToolWindow` instead of each creating their own instance of it.

See also

▶ See the *Implementing an observer pattern* recipe in *Chapter 9, Design Approaches and Techniques* for an in-depth discussion about using the observer pattern.

Creating a SearchBar

Search bars have become a fairly familiar component in many applications as an alternative to showing a `FindDialog` that can cover part of the screen, obscuring the search area. There is no built-in control in wxPython that implements this functionality, so this recipe shows how to create a simple `SearchBar` control.

How to do it...

Our `SearchBar` control will be a composite control composed of a `Panel` as the base, with a `SearchCtrl` on it to allow for the search text to be entered:

```python
class SearchBar(wx.Panel):
    def __init__(self, parent):
        style = wx.BORDER_RAISED
        super(SearchBar, self).__init__(parent,
                                        style=style)

        # Attributes
        self.search = wx.SearchCtrl(self,
                                    size=(250, -1),
                                    style=wx.TE_PROCESS_ENTER)
        self.lastfind = ''

        # Layout
        self.__DoLayout()

        # Event Handlers
        if wx.Platform in ['__WXMSW__', '__WXGTK__']:
            # Workaround for composite control on msw/gtk
            for child in self.search.GetChildren():
                if isinstance(child, wx.TextCtrl):
                    child.Bind(wx.EVT_KEY_UP, self.OnEnter)
                    break
        else:
            self.search.Bind(wx.EVT_KEY_UP, self.OnEnter)
        self.Bind(wx.EVT_SEARCHCTRL_CANCEL_BTN, self.OnCancel)

    def __DoLayout(self):
        sizer = wx.BoxSizer(wx.HORIZONTAL)
        sizer.Add(self.search, 0, wx.ALL, 2)
        self.SetSizer(sizer)
```

Here, in `OnCancel`, we handle the cancel button event of the `SearchCtrl` in order to clear the current search text and hide the cancel button:

```python
    def OnCancel(self, event):
        self.search.SetValue("")
        self.search.ShowCancelButton(False)
```

`OnEnter` will handle the keyboard events generated by the `SearchCtrl`. We use it to see when the user has pressed the return key to initiate a search. We do this by creating a `FindDialogEvent` to allow clients to bind to `EVT_FIND` and handle the searching:

```
def OnEnter(self, event):
    """Send a search event"""
    code = event.GetKeyCode()
    val = self.search.GetValue()
    if code == wx.WXK_RETURN and val:
        if val == self.lastfind:
            etype = wx.wxEVT_COMMAND_FIND
        else:
            etype = wx.wxEVT_COMMAND_FIND_NEXT
        fevent = wx.FindDialogEvent(etype)
        fevent.SetFindString(val)
        self.ProcessEvent(fevent)
        self.lastfind = val
    else:
        show = bool(val)
        self.search.ShowCancelButton(show)
```

Running the example application that accompanies this recipe will result in a window like the following being shown:

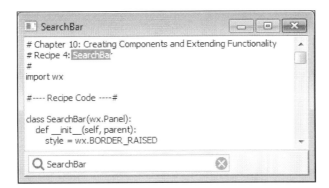

How it works...

This recipe shows how to make a very basic composite control. The `SearchBar` is just a simple `Panel` that has a `SearchCtrl` on it. To use it in a `Frame`, all that needs to be done is to create a vertical `BoxSizer` and add the `SearchBar` to this, so that it is positioned below or above the main content area in which the searches will take place. The Frame can then respond to the events that the `SearchBar` emits. We had to do a few things in order to support the sending of a find event when the user presses the *Return* key in the `SearchCtrl`. So let's take a look at that now.

In the `SearchBar`'s constructor we had to define some special case code for Windows and Linux to be able to bind our `EVT_KEY_UP` handler. This was necessary to work around a bug where the `KeyEvents` don't propagate properly due to the `SearchControl` being a composite control on those two platforms. On Macintosh, the `SearchCtrl` is a native widget so the event binding works normally. Next, in our `OnEnter` event handler, we check the value of the text in the control and generate either an `EVT_FIND` or `EVT_FIND_NEXT` event depending on the context of the search. Since these are command events, calling `self.ProcessEvent` will start the processing of our `FIND` event in the event handler chain allowing it to propagate until it is handled.

See also

> ► See the *Understanding event propagation* recipe in *Chapter 2, Responding to Events* for a discussion of how events work.

> ► See the *Using a BoxSizer* recipe in *Chapter 7, Window Layout and Design* for an explanation of how to use BoxSizers to perform window layout control.

Working with ListCtrl mixins

Like the `TreeCtrl`, there are a number of mixin classes available to extend the functionality of the standard `ListCtrl`. This recipe provides an introduction to using the `CheckListCtrlMixin`, `ListRowHighlighter`, and `ListCtrlAutoWidthMixin` mixin classes to create a `ListCtrl` that allows the selection of multiple items by using `CheckBoxes`.

How to do it...

Here, we will define our base `CheckListCtrl` class that uses three mixin classes to customize the control's look and feel, as well as add checkboxes:

```python
import wx
import wx.lib.mixins.listctrl as listmix

class CheckListCtrl(wx.ListCtrl,
                    listmix.CheckListCtrlMixin,
                    listmix.ListRowHighlighter,
                    listmix.ListCtrlAutoWidthMixin):
    def __init__(self, *args, **kwargs):
        wx.ListCtrl.__init__(self, *args, **kwargs)
        listmix.CheckListCtrlMixin.__init__(self)
        listmix.ListRowHighlighter.__init__(self)
        listmix.ListCtrlAutoWidthMixin.__init__(self)

        # Attributes
        self._observers = list()
```

Here, we override the `CheckListCtlrMixin`'s `OnCheckItem` method and implement an observer interface to notify clients when a `CheckBox` in the list is toggled:

```
def OnCheckItem(self, index, flag):
    """Overrides CheckListCtrlMixin.OnCheckItem
    callback"""
    # Notify observers that a checkbox was
    # checked/unchecked
    for observer in self._observers:
        observer(index, flag)
```

All that's remaining is to add a `GetItems` method to return the list of checked items, and another method to allow clients to register themselves as observers of when items are checked in the control:

```
def GetItems(self, checked=True):
    """Gets a list of all the (un)checked items"""
    indexes = list()
    for index in range(self.GetItemCount()):
        if self.IsChecked(index) == checked:
            indexes.append(index)
    return indexes

def RegisterObserver(self, callback):
    """Register OnCheckItem callback
    @param callaback: callable(index, checked)
    """
    self._observers.append(callback)
```

How it works...

In this recipe, we created a general use base class, `CheckListCtrl`, that will have the following extended features. It will have a `CheckBox` on each row in column 0, alternate rows will have their backgrounds highlighted, and the rightmost column of the `ListCtrl` will automatically be sized to fill the remaining space in the control. Each of these features are provided by the `CheckListCtrlMixin`, `ListRowHighlighter`, and `ListCtrlAutoWidthMixin` classes respectively.

The `CheckListCtrlMixin` provides an overridable method, `OnCheckItem`, that will be called when one of the `CheckBoxes` in the `ListCtrl` is clicked on. We overrode this method and added a way for client code to register observer callback methods with the control. In this way, if any client code that uses this control wants to be notified when a `CheckBox` is toggled, they can register their own observer methods.

The last part of our `CheckListCtrl` class is the `GetItems` method that was added to make it easy to get a list of the indexes of all the checked or unchecked items in the control. Please see the sample code that accompanies this topic for a sample application that uses this new control:

There's more...

The `wx.lib.mixins.listctrl` module provides a couple more mixin classes for the `ListCtrl`. Here is a quick reference to these other classes:

Mixin classes	Description
`ColumnSorterMixin`	Helps handle the sorting of the items in the control when a column header is clicked on.
`TextEditMixin`	Makes it possible to edit the text in any column of a multi-column `ListCtrl`.

See also

▶ See the *Listing data with a ListCtrl* recipe in *Chapter 4, Advanced Building Blocks of a User Interface* for another example of using the `ListCtrl`.

▶ See the *Implementing an observer pattern* recipe in *Chapter 9, Design Approaches and Techniques* for a discussion of using the observer pattern.

StyledTextCtrl custom highlighting

As discussed in the *StyledTextCtrl using lexers* section of Chapter 4, *Advanced Building Blocks of a User Interface*, the `StyledTextCtrl` is a powerful source code editing component that has support for syntax-highlighting many different types of source code. However, if you find that you need to support some highlighting in your application that the `StyledTextCtrl` doesn't have a built-in lexer for, you might think that you are out of luck. This isn't the case, though. Custom lexers can be added through the use of the special container lexer. This recipe shows how to write and use a custom lexer that does some simple highlighting.

How to do it...

As a part of this recipe, we will create a simple little framework that can be extended to do other kinds of highlighting. Let's start with the `BaseLexer` class, which defines a single method interface for handling the `EVT_STC_STYLENEEDED` event that is generated by the `StyledTextCtrl`:

```python
import wx
import wx.stc

class BaseLexer(object):
    """Defines simple interface for custom lexer objects"""
    def __init__(self):
        super(BaseLexer, self).__init__()

    def StyleText(self, event):
        raise NotImplementedError
```

Next we have our example implementation of the `VowelLexer`, which will provide text styling for all vowels in a document:

```python
class VowelLexer(BaseLexer):
    """Simple lexer to highlight vowels"""
    # Define some style IDs
    STC_STYLE_VOWEL_DEFAULT, \
    STC_STYLE_VOWEL_KW = range(2)
    def __init__(self):
        super(VowelLexer, self).__init__()

        # Attributes
        self.vowels = [ord(char) for char in "aeiouAEIOU"]
```

The `StyleText` method is what our custom `StyledTextCtrl` will delegate to in its `EVT_STC_STYLENEEDED` event handler. The `VowelLexer` supports two different styles: one for its default style and another one for vowels.

```python
    def StyleText(self, event):
        """Handle the EVT_STC_STYLENEEDED event"""
        stc = event.GetEventObject()
        # Last correctly styled character
        last_styled_pos = stc.GetEndStyled()
        # Get styling range for this call
        line = stc.LineFromPosition(last_styled_pos)
        start_pos = stc.PositionFromLine(line)
        end_pos = event.GetPosition()
```

```
                        # Walk the line and find all the vowels to style
                        while start_pos < end_pos:
                            stc.StartStyling(start_pos, 0x1f)
                            char = stc.GetCharAt(start_pos)
                            if char in self.vowels:
                                # Set Vowel Keyword style
                                style = VowelLexer.STC_STYLE_VOWEL_KW
                            else:
                                # Set Default style
                                style = VowelLexer.STC_STYLE_VOWEL_DEFAULT
                            # Set the styling byte information for 1 char from
                            # current styling position (start_pos) with the
                            # given style.
                            stc.SetStyling(1, style)
                            start_pos += 1
```

The `CustomSTC` class will provide the framework for using `BaseLexer`-derived classes to customize the highlighting of the text in the control:

```
    class CustomSTC(wx.stc.StyledTextCtrl):
        def __init__(self, *args, **kwargs):
            super(CustomSTC, self).__init__(*args, **kwargs)

            # Attributes
            self.custlex = None

            # Event Handlers
            self.Bind(wx.stc.EVT_STC_STYLENEEDED, self.OnStyle)

        def OnStyle(self, event):
            # Delegate to custom lexer object if one exists
            if self.custlex:
                self.custlex.StyleText(event)
            else:
                event.Skip()

        def SetLexer(self, lexerid, lexer=None):
            """Overrides StyledTextCtrl.SetLexer
            Adds optional param to pass in custom container
            lexer object.
            """
            self.custlex = lexer
            super(CustomSTC, self).SetLexer(lexerid)
```

Included with the sample code that accompanies this chapter is a simple application that uses the custom `VowelLexer` class defined above.

How it works...

In this recipe, we first built a little framework for creating custom lexers for the `StyledTextCtrl`. Starting with our `BaseLexer` class, we defined a simple interface for objects that will delegate the task of handling `EVT_STC_STYLENEEDED`. Next, we created the `VowelLexer` class, which is a simple subclass of `BaseLexer` that will highlight vowels in the text of a document. Applying styling in the `StyledTextCtrl` involves three basic steps. First, you need to call `StartStyling` to indicate the position in the buffer you wish to start styling text, then you need to determine what style byte to set, and finally you need to call `SetStyling` to set how many characters from the start position to style with the given style.

Now in order for the `StyledTextCtrl` to make use of these lexers, we needed to do a couple things that we have encapsulated in the `CustomSTC` class. The `StyledTextCtrl` needs to bind to `EVT_STC_STYLENEEDED` and set the `STC_LEX_CONTAINER` lexer. The `StyledTextCtrl` will generate `EVT_STC_STYLEDNEEDED` when the container lexer is the current lexer and when it detects that some of the text in the buffer may need to be restyled due to changes in its contents. To handle this in our `CustomSTC` class, we simply delegate the event to the current lexer object that was set by the call to our overridden `SetLexer` method.

Finally, we have a super-simple sample application that shows how our `CustomSTC` and `VowelLexer` can be used in an application. First, we needed to set up the styling by calling `SetStyleSpec` to set which colors will be applied for our lexer's two-style bytes. The `STC_STYLE_VOWEL_DEFAULT` will be styled with plain black text, and `STC_STYLE_VOWEL_KW` will be styled with red text. Then, all is left is to call `SetLexer` to set the `STC_LEX_CONTAINER` lexer and create an instance of our `VowelLexer` for the control to use. So give it a run and see that as you type into the buffer, all vowels should be colored red.

See also

▸ See the *StyledTextCtrl using lexers* recipe in *Chapter 4, Advanced Building Blocks of a User Interface* for another example of using the `StyleTextCtrl`.

Creating a custom control

At some point, you may need to invent an entirely new control to fit some specific requirement of your application. So in this recipe we will take a look at some techniques for creating a new control completely from scratch. We will create a custom `CheckBox` control that has its label below the `CheckBox`.

How to do it...

To get started, we will define the constructor of the `CustomCheckBox` control as a subclass of `PyControl`. In the constructor, we bind to a number of events that will let us define the behavior of the control:

```
class CustomCheckBox(wx.PyControl):
    """Custom CheckBox implementation where label is
    below the CheckBox.
    """
    def __init__(self, parent, id_=wx.ID_ANY, label=""):
        style = wx.BORDER_NONE
        super(CustomCheckBox, self).__init__(parent,
                                             id_,
                                             style=style)

        # Attributes
        self.InheritAttributes()
        self._hstate = 0
        self._checked = False
        self._ldown = False
        self.SetLabel(label)

        # Event Handlers
        self.Bind(wx.EVT_PAINT, self.OnPaint)
        self.Bind(wx.EVT_ERASE_BACKGROUND, self.OnErase)
        self.Bind(wx.EVT_LEFT_DOWN, self.OnLeftDown)
        self.Bind(wx.EVT_LEFT_UP, self.OnLeftUp)
        self.Bind(wx.EVT_ENTER_WINDOW,
                  lambda event:
                  self._SetState(wx.CONTROL_CURRENT))
        self.Bind(wx.EVT_LEAVE_WINDOW,
                  lambda event: self._SetState(0))
```

Next, we have this helper method to help manage what state the control is in with regards to the mouse:

```
    def _SetState(self, state):
        if self._hstate != state:
            if state == 0:
                self._ldown = False
            self._hstate = state
            self.Refresh()

    #-- Implementation --#
```

This is a virtual override of the `PyControl`'s `DoGetBestSize` method to control what the size of the control is:

```python
def DoGetBestSize(self):
    lblsz = self.GetTextExtent(self.GetLabel())
    width = max(lblsz[0], 16) + 4 # 2px padding l/r
    height = lblsz[1] + 16 + 6
    best_sz = wx.Size(width, height)
    self.CacheBestSize(best_sz)
    return best_sz


#-- Event Handlers --#
```

Next, we focus on the event handlers that will define the behavior of the control. First, in `OnPaint`, we do the drawing that gives the control its appearance:

```python
def OnPaint(self, event):
    dc = wx.AutoBufferedPaintDCFactory(self)
    gc = wx.GCDC(dc)
    renderer = wx.RendererNative.Get()

    # Setup GCDC
    rect = self.GetClientRect()
    bcolour = self.GetBackgroundColour()
    brush = wx.Brush(bcolour)
    gc.SetBackground(brush)
    gc.Clear()

    # Center checkbox
    cb_x = (rect.width - 16) / 2
    cb_y = 2 # padding from top
    cb_rect = wx.Rect(cb_x, cb_y, 16, 16)

    # Draw the checkbox
    state = 0
    if self._checked:
        state = wx.CONTROL_CHECKED
    if not self.IsEnabled():
        state |= wx.CONTROL_DISABLED
    renderer.DrawCheckBox(self, dc, cb_rect,
                          state|self._hstate)

    # Draw the label
    lbl_rect = wx.Rect(0, cb_rect.bottom, rect.width,
                       rect.height - cb_rect.height)
```

```
                gc.DrawLabel(self.GetLabel(),
                          lbl_rect,
                          wx.ALIGN_CENTER)

        def OnErase(self, event):
            pass # do nothing
```

The next two event handlers manage the mouse click state in the control to toggle the `CheckBox` state:

```
        def OnLeftDown(self, event):
            self._ldown = True
            event.Skip()

        def OnLeftUp(self, event):
            if self._ldown:
                self._ldown = False
                self._checked = not self._checked
                self.Refresh()
                # Generate EVT_CHECKBOX event
                etype = wx.wxEVT_COMMAND_CHECKBOX_CLICKED
                chevent = wx.CommandEvent(etype, self.GetId())
                chevent.SetEventObject(self)
                self.ProcessEvent(chevent)
            event.Skip()
```

Last but not least, we define a couple of methods to implement part of the `wx.CheckBox` interface:

```
        #---- Public Api ----#

        def SetValue(self, state):
            self._checked = state
            self.Refresh()

        def GetValue(self):
            return self._checked

        def IsChecked(self):
            return self.GetValue()
```

How it works...

This was a fairly simple control to implement, but it is a good example of some of the approaches to take when creating your own custom control. So let's break down each of the important parts and see how they affect the way in which the control works.

First, in the constructor, we define three attributes to manage the state of the control:

1. `self._hstate`: To hold the current highlight state of the control.
2. `self._checked`: To hold the `CheckBox` state.
3. `self._ldown`: To hold when the left mouse button was clicked down in the control.

Next, we `Bind` to the events that are necessary to draw the control and implement its behavior. We made use of two paint events and four different mouse events. First, let's take a look at the mouse event handlers that are used to implement the control's behavior.

In `OnLeftDown`, we simply set our `self._ldown` flag to `True` in order to indicate that the down-click action was initiated in this window and not elsewhere. Then, in the `OnLeftUp` handler, if the `self._ldown` flag is `True`, we toggle the `self._checked` flag to reflect the new `CheckBox` state, and then call `Refresh`. Calling `Refresh` will cause an `EVT_PAINT` event to be generated so that we can redraw the control in its new state with our `OnPaint` handler. After this, we also generate an `EVT_CHECKBOX` event in order to inform the application that the `CheckBox` state has changed. The remaining two mouse events are used to update the control's highlight state when the mouse enters or leaves the controls area.

`OnPaint` is where we draw the control and give it its appearance. We start in `OnPaint` by creating our drawing contexts and setting up the background. Next, we calculate the position to draw the `CheckBox` within the control's rectangle and use `RendererNative` to draw the `CheckBox` according to the control's current state. Then, all that is left is to draw the label below the `CheckBox` using our `GCDC`'s `DrawLabel` method.

To finish off the control, we added some methods to implement part of the regular interface for the `CheckBox` so that the application code using this control can get and set the `CheckBox` state:

See also

▶ See the *Understanding inheritance limitations* recipe in *Chapter 1, Getting Started with wxPython* for a discussion about overriding virtual methods.

▶ See the Understanding event propagation recipe in *Chapter 2, Responding to Events* for more information on working with events.

▶ See the *Drawing with RendererNative* recipe in *Chapter 8, Drawing to the Screen* for another example of using `RendererNative` for drawing native-looking controls.

▶ See the *Reducing flicker in drawing routines* recipe in *Chapter 8, Drawing to the Screen* for an explanation of how to reduce flicker in drawing routines.

11

Using Threads and Timers to Create Responsive Interfaces

In this chapter, we will cover:

- ▶ Non-Blocking GUI
- ▶ Understanding thread safety
- ▶ Threading tools
- ▶ Using Timers
- ▶ Capturing output

Introduction

It's all too familiar and an annoying issue when you are using an application and click on some button or control only to find that the application's UI all of a sudden appears to stop responding, the busy cursor shows up, and you are left there wondering if the application is still working, or if it has locked up and needs to be forced quit. This unpleasant experience is almost always the result of a function or action that takes a considerable amount of time to return after being called. If this function or action is called on the same thread that the GUI objects live on, it will block all the code that is running in the background and that is managing the GUI, leading to this locked up and unresponsive interface.

Being able to design an application in a way that prevents this situation from being presented to its users requires additional considerations in comparison to most traditional procedural approaches. This chapter explores this problem by providing solutions, and hopefully all the tools necessary, to build highly-responsive, multi-threaded applications in wxPython.

Non-Blocking GUI

In this recipe, we explore what a responsive interface is and try to gain a good understanding of what the problem is that the other recipes in this chapter will provide solutions to. The recipe creates a simple application with two buttons. Each button will perform exactly the same task. However, the way in which the application responds and provides feedback to the user after the button is clicked will differ greatly between the two buttons, due to how the control flow is carried out.

How to do it...

To illustrate the issue at hand, we will create a simple Fibonacci number calculator application. First, we will begin by defining a Thread class and the function that will be used to calculate the Nth Fibonacci number:

```python
import wx
import threading

class FibThread(threading.Thread):
    def __init__(self, window, n):
        super(FibThread, self).__init__()

        # Attributes
        self.window = window
        self.n = n

    def run(self):
        val = SlowFib(self.n)
        wx.CallAfter(self.window.output.SetValue, str(val))
        wx.CallAfter(self.window.StopBusy)

def SlowFib(n):
    """Calculate Fibonacci numbers
    using slow recursive method to demonstrate
    blocking the UI.
    """
    if n == 0:
        return 0
    elif n == 1:
        return 1
    else:
        return SlowFib(n-1) + SlowFib(n-2)
```

Now let's create the user interface for our Fibonacci number calculator:

```
class BlockingApp(wx.App):
    def OnInit(self):
        self.frame = BlockingFrame(None,
                                    title="Non-Blocking Gui")
        self.frame.Show()
        return True

class BlockingFrame(wx.Frame):
    """Main application window"""
    def __init__(self, *args, **kwargs):
        super(BlockingFrame, self).__init__(*args, **kwargs)

        # Attributes
        self.panel = BlockingPanel(self)

        # Layout
        sizer = wx.BoxSizer(wx.VERTICAL)
        sizer.Add(self.panel, 1, wx.EXPAND)
        self.SetSizer(sizer)
        self.SetInitialSize()
```

Here, in the `Panel`, is where most of the action will be taking place in this example. Here we lay out a simple interface with an input field and an output field, two buttons, and a progress bar:

```
class BlockingPanel(wx.Panel):
    def __init__(self, parent):
        super(BlockingPanel, self).__init__(parent)

        # Attributes
        self.timer = wx.Timer(self)
        self.input = wx.SpinCtrl(self, value="35", min=1)
        self.output = wx.TextCtrl(self)
        self.block = wx.Button(self, label="Blocking")
        self.noblock = wx.Button(self, label="Non-Blocking")
        self.prog = wx.Gauge(self)

        # Layout
        self.__DoLayout()

        # Event Handlers
        self.Bind(wx.EVT_BUTTON, self.OnButton)
        self.Bind(wx.EVT_TIMER, self.OnPulse, self.timer)

    def __DoLayout(self):
        vsizer = wx.BoxSizer(wx.VERTICAL)
        hsizer = wx.BoxSizer(wx.HORIZONTAL)
        gridsz = wx.GridSizer(2, 2, 5, 5)
```

```
        # Layout controls
        vsizer.Add(self.prog, 0, wx.EXPAND)
        gridsz.Add(wx.StaticText(self, label="fib(n):"))
        gridsz.Add(self.input, 0, wx.EXPAND)
        gridsz.Add(wx.StaticText(self, label="result:"))
        gridsz.Add(self.output, 0, wx.EXPAND)
        vsizer.Add(gridsz, 0, wx.EXPAND|wx.ALL, 10)
        hsizer.Add(self.block, 0, wx.ALL, 5)
        hsizer.Add(self.noblock, 0, wx.ALL, 5)
        vsizer.Add(hsizer, 0, wx.ALIGN_CENTER_HORIZONTAL)

        self.SetSizer(vsizer)
```

Here, in our handler for EVT_BUTTON, is where we do the calculations. First, we clear the current output and then start the progress Gauge. After that, we take one of two paths depending upon which Button was clicked. If the "Blocking" button, we do the calculations right here in the same thread. If the "Non-Blocking" button was clicked, we delegate the task to a background thread in order to allow the GUI to continue processing:

```
    def OnButton(self, event):
        input = self.input.GetValue()
        self.output.SetValue("") # clear output
        self.StartBusy() # give busy feedback
        if event.GetEventObject() == self.block:
            # Calculate value in blocking mode
            val = SlowFib(input)
            self.output.SetValue(str(val))
            self.StopBusy()
        else:
            # Non-Blocking mode
            task = FibThread(self, input)
            task.start()
```

These methods were added to control the progress Gauge and to update the state of the GUI, depending upon whether the application is busy calculating or not:

```
    def OnPulse(self, event):
        self.prog.Pulse() # Pulse busy feedback

    def StartBusy(self):
        self.timer.Start(100)
        self.block.Disable()
        self.noblock.Disable()

    def StopBusy(self):
        self.timer.Stop()
```

```
        self.prog.SetValue(0)
        self.block.Enable()
        self.noblock.Enable()

if __name__ == '__main__':
    app = BlockingApp(False)
    app.MainLoop()
```

How it works...

Running the previous code will result in the following application window being displayed:

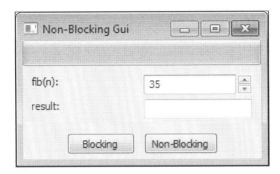

This application will calculate the Nth Fibonacci number specified by the first field. Using a number of 35 or higher will take from many seconds to several minutes to calculate by using the SlowFib function. Clicking on either of the two buttons will result in the same SlowFib function being called, and ultimately the same result being generated. So with this in mind, let's jump to the BlockingPanel's OnButton method to see what happens differently between the two buttons.

When OnButton is called, we first clear the result field and then Start the Timer to Pulse the Gauge at the top of the window to give the user feedback that we are busy calculating the result. If the Blocking button was clicked, we directly call the SlowFib function to get the result. At this point, the control flow of the application will be stuck waiting for SlowFib to return, which means that the MainLoop will be waiting on our OnButton method to return. Since OnButton will not return until SlowFib finishes, the framework will not be able to process any events for things such as repainting the window, mouse clicks, or our TimerEvent for pulsing the Gauge. Because of this, the Blocking button will still appear to be pressed, and the Frame and all of its controls will be completely unresponsive until SlowFib finishes and returns control to the MainLoop:

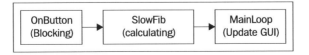

On the contrary, if you click on the Non-Blocking button we still run the same `SlowFib` function, but do it in a separate `Thread`. This allows `OnButton` to return immediately, returning control to the `MainLoop`. So since the `MainLoop` isn't stuck in `OnButton`, it is free to process other events, allowing our busy indicator to be updated, the buttons to be shown as disabled, and the `Frame` to be freely moved around the desktop. When the calculations finish on the `FibThread`, it uses the `CallAfter` function to send a message to call the required functions to update the GUI back on the main thread and then exits, leaving the GUI ready to start another calculation:

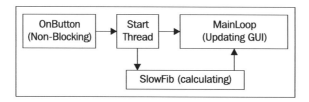

Both buttons will take about the same time to produce the result, but the Non-Blocking button allows the GUI to continue running smoothly and will give the user a better impression of knowing that the software is busy working and is not just locked up.

See also

- ▸ See the *Understanding thread safety* recipe in this chapter for more information on creating thread-safe GUIs.

- ▸ See the *Using Timers* recipe in this chapter for another approach to keeping the GUI responsive while performing a long-running task.

Understanding thread safety

Nearly all user interface toolkits are designed to run within a single thread of execution. Knowing how to interact with the GUI thread from other worker threads in a threaded application is an important task that needs to be performed with care in order to avoid seemingly unexplainable and random crashes in an application. This is as true in wxPython as any other typical GUI toolkit.

Maintaining thread safety in a wxPython application can be handled in a few different ways, but the use of events is most typical. The event queue monitored by the `MainLoop` provides a thread-safe way to pass data and actions from a background thread to be processed in the context of the GUI thread. This recipe shows how to use custom events and the `PostEvent` function to make updates to GUI objects that exist in the main GUI thread.

How to do it...

Since we will be using events to maintain thread safety in our sample application, we will first start by defining a custom event type:

```python
import wx
import time
import threading

# Define a new custom event type
wxEVT_THREAD_UPDATE = wx.NewEventType()
EVT_THREAD_UPDATE = wx.PyEventBinder(wxEVT_THREAD_UPDATE, 1)

class ThreadUpdateEvent(wx.PyCommandEvent):
    def __init__(self, eventType, id):
        super(ThreadUpdateEvent, self).__init__(eventType, id)

        # Attributes
        self.value = None

    def SetValue(self, value):
        self.value = value

    def GetValue(self):
        return self.value
```

The `CountingThread` class below will be used as this application's background worker thread and will use the previous event class to notify and make updates on the main GUI thread:

```python
class CountingThread(threading.Thread):
    """Simple thread that sends an update to its
    target window once a second with the new count value.
    """
    def __init__(self, targetwin, id):
        super(CountingThread, self).__init__()

        # Attributes
        self.window = targetwin
        self.id = id
        self.count = 0
        self.stop = False
```

```python
    def run(self):
        while not self.stop:
            time.sleep(1) # wait a second
            # Notify the main thread it's time
            # to update the ui
            if self.window:
                event = ThreadUpdateEvent(wxEVT_THREAD_UPDATE,
                                          self.id)
                event.SetValue(self.count)
                wx.PostEvent(self.window, event)
            self.count += 1

    def Stop(self):
        # Stop the thread
        self.stop = True

class ThreadSafetyApp(wx.App):
    def OnInit(self):
        self.frame = ThreadSafeFrame(None,
                                     title="Thread Safety")
        self.frame.Show()
        return True
```

Beginning here, with the ThreadSafeFrame class, we will create the application's GUI. The Frame will be the target for the updates from the CountingThread:

```python
class ThreadSafeFrame(wx.Frame):
    """Main application window"""
    def __init__(self, *args, **kwargs):
        super(ThreadSafeFrame, self).__init__(*args, **kwargs)

        # Attributes
        self.panel = ThreadSafePanel(self)
        self.threadId = wx.NewId()
        self.worker = CountingThread(self, self.threadId)

        # Layout
        sizer = wx.BoxSizer(wx.VERTICAL)
        sizer.Add(self.panel, 1, wx.EXPAND)
        self.SetSizer(sizer)
        self.SetInitialSize((300, 300))

        # Start the worker thread
        self.worker.start()

        # Event Handlers
        self.Bind(wx.EVT_CLOSE, self.OnClose)
        self.Bind(EVT_THREAD_UPDATE, self.OnThreadEvent)
```

```
def OnClose(self, event):
    # Stop the worker thread
    self.worker.Stop()
    event.Skip()
```

Here is the event handler that the `ThreadSafeFrame` bound to the `EVT_THREAD_UPDATE` event binder for the custom `ThreadUpdateEvent` class. This method will be called after the `CountingThread` posts a new update event to do the GUI updates on the main GUI thread:

```
def OnThreadEvent(self, event):
    if event.GetId() == self.threadId():
        # Handle event to update Displayed Count
        value = event.GetValue()
        self.panel.DisplayCount(value)
    else:
        event.Skip()

class ThreadSafePanel(wx.Panel):
    def __init__(self, parent):
        super(ThreadSafePanel, self).__init__(parent)

        # Attributes
        self.count = wx.StaticText(self, label="Count: ")

        # Setup
        self.__DoLayout()

    def __DoLayout(self):
        vsizer = wx.BoxSizer(wx.VERTICAL)
        hsizer = wx.BoxSizer(wx.HORIZONTAL)
        vsizer.AddStretchSpacer()
        hsizer.AddStretchSpacer()
        hsizer.Add(self.count)
        hsizer.AddStretchSpacer()
        vsizer.Add(hsizer, 0, wx.EXPAND)
        vsizer.AddStretchSpacer()
        self.SetSizer(vsizer)

    def DisplayCount(self, value):
        self.count.SetLabel("Count: %d" % value)

if __name__ == '__main__':
    app = ThreadSafetyApp(False)
    app.MainLoop()
```

How it works...

The point of this recipe was to show a generic pattern for updating the GUI from a background thread. To illustrate this, we created a simple `Frame` that has a `Panel` with a single `StaticTextCtrl` that will be updated by our `CountingThread` after each time that it has completed its arduous task of incrementing the count by one.

First, we created a new event type of `ThreadUpdateEvent`, and related event binder to use for transporting the data from the `CountingThread` to the main thread when it needs to tell the UI to update the displayed value. The `ThreadUpdateEvent` is used by the `CountingThread` in its `run` method by passing it to `PostEvent`, which is a thread-safe way to queue up some work for the main GUI thread.

`PostEvent` will place the event object into the `MainLoop`'s event queue so that after it has finished processing any current tasks, it will grab and dispatch this update event to the appropriate event handler in our `ThreadSafeFrame`. This is the key that makes it possible to safely update the GUI from a background thread.

If we had instead called the `Panel`'s `DisplayCount` method directly from within the context of the `CountingThread`, there is no guarantee that both threads would not be trying to access or modify the same data at the same time. For example, if the GUI thread was in the middle of processing an internal `PaintEvent` in order to redraw the `StaticTextCtrl`, the control's label value would be getting accessed. If, at the same time, in the `CountingThread`, it was trying to change that value, there would be potential memory corruption, which would cause the application to crash. By using an event, the update will be processed in the context of the main thread after it has finished any other pending tasks, eliminating the risk of collision since access to the variable would be controlled in a serialized manner by the main thread.

There's more...

The `CallAfter` function provided by wxPython can also be used to make calls to methods that affect a GUI object from a background thread. The `CallAfter` function encapsulates much of the event creation and processing internally, and can be more convenient and transparent for making simple changes to the GUI, as we did in this recipe. So let's take a little look at how `CallAfter` works and can be used:

```
wx.CallAfter(callable, *args, **kw)
```

`CallAfter` takes a function as its first argument. The `*args` and `**kw` are for specifying any positional or keyword arguments that should be passed the function specified by the first argument when it is called. So, for example, we could replace the three lines of code in our `CountingThread`'s `run` method that are creating and sending the custom event with the following:

```
wx.CallAfter(self.window.panel.DisplayCount,
             self.count)
```

Now, the `CallAfter` function will create and post an event that contains the function and its arguments to the App object on the main GUI thread. When the `MainLoop` gets to processing this event, it will get handled by an event handler belonging to the `App` object. This event handler will then just simply call the function with any of its specified arguments, so that it is called in the context of the main GUI thread.

It's important to understand that `CallAfter` means precisely that—the method will be called after the next iteration of the `MainLoop`. So you cannot expect to get a return value from the method that you pass to it since it will be called asynchronously to the scope of where you made the `CallAfter` call. So, just to be clear, `CallAfter` always returns `None`, meaning that you can't use it for code like the following:

```
value = wx.CallAfter(window.GetValue)
```

This is because `window.GetValue` isn't actually called until after the `CallAfter` function returns.

See also

▸ See the *Creating custom event classes* recipe in *Chapter 2, Responding to Events* for another example of creating custom events.

▸ See the *Threading tools* recipe in this chapter for some more examples and approaches to maintaining the thread safety of the GUI when working with background threads.

Threading tools

Maintaining thread safety can be cumbersome and difficult at times so in this recipe we will create three useful utilities that will make working with threads easier. We will create two decorator functions and a metaclass to help make applying thread safe rules to methods and functions as simple as adding a single line of code.

How to do it...

Here, will create a little utility module that can be used to help any wxPython application that needs to work with threads:

```
import wx
import threading
from types import FunctionType, MethodType

__all__ = ['callafter', 'synchfunct', 'ClassSynchronizer']
```

Starting here, we will create a simple decorator function that can be used to decorate any method in a GUI class, so that if a call to the decorated method is made from a background thread, it will automatically delegate the call to the `CallAfter` function:

```
def callafter(funct):
    """Decorator to automatically use CallAfter if
    a method is called from a different thread.
    """
    def callafterwrap(*args, **kwargs):
        if wx.Thread_IsMain():
            return funct(*args, **kwargs)
        else:
            wx.CallAfter(funct, *args, **kwargs)
    callafterwrap.__name__ = funct.__name__
    callafterwrap.__doc__ = funct.__doc__
    return callafterwrap
```

Next is the `Synchronizer` class, which is used as a helper class to synchronize an asynchronous call to the main GUI thread:

```
class Synchronizer(object):
    """Synchronize CallAfter calls"""
    def __init__(self, funct, args, kwargs):
        super(Synchronizer, self).__init__()

        # Attributes
        self.funct = funct
        self.args = args
        self.kwargs = kwargs
        self._synch = threading.Semaphore(0)
```

This method will be called by this class's `Run` method using `CallAfter` to execute it on the main GUI thread. It simply calls the function and releases the `Semaphore`:

```
    def _AsynchWrapper(self):
        """This part runs in main gui thread"""
        try:
            self.result = self.funct(*self.args,
                                      **self.kwargs)
        except Exception, msg:
            # Store exception to report back to
            # the calling thread.
            self.exception = msg
        # Release Semaphore to allow processing back
        # on other thread to resume.
        self._synch.release()
```

The `Run` method is called by the background thread, and uses `CallAfter` to delegate the function call to the main GUI thread. It then `acquires` the `Semaphore` so that the execution will pause at that line in the background thread until the `_AsyncWrapper` method calls `release`:

```
def Run(self):
    """Call from background thread"""
    # Make sure this is not called from main thread
    # as it will result in deadlock waiting on the
    # Semaphore.
    assert not wx.Thread_IsMain(), "Deadlock!"
    # Make the asynchronous call to the main thread
    # to run the function.
    wx.CallAfter(self._AsynchWrapper)
    # Block on Semaphore release until the function
    # has been processed in the main thread by the
    # UI's event loop.
    self._synch.acquire()
    # Return result to caller or raise error
    try:
        return self.result
    except AttributeError:
        raise self.exception
```

Next up is the `syncfunct` decorator which works the same way as the `CallAfter` decorator, except that it uses the `Synchronizer` to make the calls from the background thread synchronous:

```
def synchfunct(funct):
    """Decorator to synchronize a method call from a worker
    thread to the GUI thread.
    """
    def synchwrap(*args, **kwargs):
        if wx.Thread_IsMain():
            # called in context of main thread so
            # no need for special synchronization
            return self.funct(*args, **kwargs)
        else:
            synchobj = Synchronizer(funct, args, kwargs)
            return synchobj.Run()

    synchwrap.__name__ = funct.__name__
    synchwrap.__doc__ = funct.__doc__
    return synchwrap
```

The final utility that we will present in this module is the `ClassSynchronizer` metaclass, which can be used to automatically apply the `synchfunct` decorator to all of the methods in a class:

```
class ClassSynchronizer(type):
    """Metaclass to make all methods in a class threadsafe"""
    def __call__(mcs, *args, **kwargs):
        obj = type.__call__(mcs, *args, **kwargs)

        # Wrap all methods/functions in the class with
        # the synchfunct decorator.
        for attrname in dir(obj):
            attr = getattr(obj, attrname)
            if type(attr) in (MethodType, FunctionType):
                nfunct = synchfunct(attr)
                setattr(obj, attrname, nfunct)

        return obj
```

How it works...

Decorators and MetaClasses can be a little intimidating at first if you haven't used them before, so let's take a look at each of our three new utilities one by one and see how they work and how to use them in your code.

The first utility is the `callafter` decorator. This is a very simple decorator that will just wrap a function in `CallAfter` when called from a thread that is not the GUI thread. Since it uses `CallAfter`, this decorator should only be used for methods that don't expect a return value, such as setting a value or doing an update that you don't need feedback from on the background thread. The usage of this decorator is very simple. See the following example snippet:

```
class MyPanel(wx.Panel):
    @callafter
    def SetSomeGuiValues(self, values):
        self.ctrl1.SetValue(values[0])
        ...
        self.ctrlN.SetValue(values[N])
```

Now the `SetSomeGuiValues` method can be called from any thread in the application. A decorator function takes another function as an argument and returns a new function that usually wraps the existing function in some new behavior. So when our module is initialized by Python, it will see that the decorator arguments in the class will apply the decorator to the function and then rebind the function to the new one returned by the decorator. Our `callafter` decorator simply wraps the given function in a check to see if it is being called from the main thread, and if not, it uses `CallAfter` to run the function.

Next is the `synchfunct` decorator. This decorator uses our `Synchronizer` class to make it possible to synchronize inter-thread calls to functions. This method can be used when a background thread needs to make a call to retrieve a value from the GUI in a synchronous manner. The `synchfunct` decorator works pretty much the same as our `callafter` one, so let's look at how the `Synchronizer` makes it possibly to turn the asynchronous `CallAfter` function into a synchronous call.

The `Synchronizer` class, like the `CallAfter` function, takes a function and any of its arguments as parameters to initialize it. It also creates a `Semaphore` object from the `threading` module to use for synchronizing the actions. The `Synchronizer`'s `Run` method uses `CallAfter` to call the passed-in function. After calling `CallAfter`, the `Run` method will block on the `Semaphore`'s `acquire` call. This will halt execution of the rest of the code in the `Run` function and the background thread until the `_AsynchWrapper` method has called `release` on the `Semaphore` after it has finished running the passed-in function back on the main thread. When `release` has been called, the `Run` method will continue past its `acquire` call and will either return the result from the function that was run on the main thread or raise an exception if one was raised by calling that method.

Last, we have the `ClassSynchronizer` metaclass. This metaclass will use the `synchfunct` decorator to make every method in a class thread safe. First, let's take a quick look at the snippet below, in order to show how to use this metaclass, and then we will check out how it works:

```
class MyPanel(wx.Panel):
    __metaclass__ = ClassSynchronizer
    def __init__(self, parent, *args, **kwargs)
```

Can't get much easier than that, can it? When the Python interpreter initializes the class, it will see our `__metaclass__` declaration, which will result in our `ClassSynchronizer`'s `__call__` method getting called. In `__call__`, we use `dir` to enumerate all of the given class's items from its dictionary. Then, for each item in the class that is a `MethodType` or `FunctionType`, we apply the `synchfunct` decorator in order to get a newly-wrapped version of the method, and then use the wrapped version to replace it with.

There's more...

Included in the sample code that accompanies this topic is the full `threadtools` module shown above, plus a sample application that shows some additional usage examples of the `callafter` and `syncfunct` decorators, as well as the `ClassSynchronizer` metaclass in an application that fetches HTML from a given URL and displays it in a `TextCtrl`.

See also

▸ See the *Understanding thread safety* recipe in this chapter for more information about using threads with a GUI.

▸ See the *Using decorators* recipe in *Chapter 9, Design Approaches and Techniques* for another example of using decorator functions.

Using Timers

A `Timer` is an object that can be created to send out events on a regular periodic basis. Typically, a `Timer` is used to run short, atomic tasks, such as status checks and updates, but can also be leveraged to keep the UI active during a long-running task by performing tasks in incremental steps instead of one long blocking call. However, since a `Timer` will run in the context of the main GUI thread, it is necessary to be able to design the execution of the long-running task to be able to be carried out in several smaller incremental steps, otherwise the UI will still become locked up while processing the `TimerEvent`. This recipe creates a simple framework for processing long-running tasks by using a Timer.

How to do it...

First, we will create a base class that defines an interface for tasks to derive from:

```
class TimerTaskBase(object):
    """Defines interface for long running task
    state machine.
    """
    TASK_STATE_PENDING, \
    TASK_STATE_RUNNING, \
    TASK_STATE_COMPLETE = range(3)
    def __init__(self):
        super(TimerTaskBase, self).__init__()

        # Attributes
        self._state = TimerTaskBase.TASK_STATE_PENDING

    #---- Interface ----#

    def ProcessNext(self):
        """Do next iteration of task
        @note: must be implemented by subclass
        """
        raise NotImplementedError
```

```
        def InitTask(self):
            """Optional override called before task
            processing begins
            """
            self.SetState(TimerTaskBase.TASK_STATE_RUNNING)

        #---- Implementation ----#

        def GetState(self):
            return self._state

        def SetState(self, state):
            self._state = state
```

Next, the `TimerTaskMixin` class can be used to add the functionality for using a `Timer` to process `TimerTaskBase`-derived task objects to any window class:

```
    class TimerTaskMixin(object):
        """Mixin class for a wxWindow object to use timers
        for running long task. Must be used as a mixin with
        a wxWindow derived class!
        """
        def __init__(self):
            super(TimerTaskMixin, self).__init__()

            # Attributes
            self._task = None
            self._timer = wx.Timer(self)

            # Event Handlers
            self.Bind(wx.EVT_TIMER, self.OnTimer, self._timer)

        def __del__(self):
            # Make sure timer is stopped
            self.StopProcessing()
```

The `OnTimer` method will be called once every 100ms, when the `Timer` generates a new event. Each time, it will call the `TimerTask` object's `ProcessNext` method to allow it to perform the next step in its processing:

```
        def OnTimer(self, event):
            if self._task is not None:
                self._task.ProcessNext()
                state = self._task.GetState()
                if state == self._task.TASK_STATE_COMPLETE:
                    self._timer.Stop()
```

```
def StartTask(self, taskobj):
    assert not self._timer.IsRunning(), \
            "Task already busy!"
    assert isinstance(taskobj, TimerTaskBase)
    self._task = taskobj
    self._task.InitTask()
    self._timer.Start(100)

def StopProcessing(self):
    if self._timer.IsRunning():
        self._timer.Stop()
```

How it works...

First, let's take a look at our `TimerTaskBase` class, which defines the basic interface that our `TimerTaskMixin` class will use to execute the long running task. The `TimerTaskBase` class is very simple. It provides a `ProcessNext` method that must be overridden by a subclass in order to implement the processing of the next chunk of the task's work. This method will be called each time that the `TimerTaskMixin` class's Timer fires a `TimerEvent`. The other method, `InitTask`, is an optional override for a subclass to implement. It will be called immediately prior to the first `ProcessNext` call, and can be used to perform any set-up that the task may require prior to processing.

The `TimerTaskMixin` class is a mixin class that can be used with any `wx.Window`-derived class, such as a `Frame` or `Panel`. It adds the framework for managing a `TimerTask` object. This simple framework adds a `StartTask` method that can be used by the UI to start the processing of a `TimerTask`. `StartTask` takes the `TimerTask` object that needs to be processed, and then starts the `Timer`. The `Timer` will fire every 100ms in order to call the task's `ProcessNext` method, until the task reports that its state is in a completed state.

There's more...

In the full sample code that accompanies this topic, there is a simple example application that uses this framework for transcribing a string of DNA code to RNA, as an example of breaking up a bigger task into many smaller tasks that are to be processed during timer events.

See also

▶ See the *Handling events* recipe in *Chapter 2, Responding to Events* for more information on event handling.

▶ See the *Using mixin classes* recipe in *Chapter 9, Design Approaches and Techniques* for more information on and examples of working with mixin classes.

Capturing output

This recipe takes a number of the concepts put forth earlier in this chapter, to create an `OutputWindow` component that can be used to capture console output from a subprocess and redirect it to a text display in an application. It will use `Thread`s and `Timer`s to implement a high-performance solution to this task, so let's get started and take a look at the code.

 When run on Windows, this recipe makes use of the pywin32 extension module.(`http://sourceforge.net/projects/pywin32/`)

How to do it...

In this recipe, we will create two classes. The first will be a worker thread class that will run the `subprocess` and report its output to the GUI. The second will be the GUI component that makes use of the worker thread and displays its output:

```
import wx
import wx.stc as stc
import threading
import subprocess
```

The `ProcessThread` class will run a `subprocess` and read the process's output from its output pipe, and then pass the data back to the thread's `parent` object:

```
class ProcessThread(threading.Thread):
    """Helper Class for OutputWindow to run a subprocess in
    a separate thread and report its output back
    to the window.
    """
    def __init__(self, parent, command, readblock=4096):
        """
        @param parent: OutputWindow instance
        @param command: Command line command
        @param readblock: amount to read from stdout each read
        """
        assert hasattr(parent, 'AppendUpdate')
        assert readblock > 0
        super(ProcessThread, self).__init__()

        # Attributes
        self._proc = None
        self._parent = parent
        self._command = command
        self._readblock = readblock

        # Setup
        self.setDaemon(True)
```

Here, in the `ProcessThread`'s `run` method, we use the `subprocess` module from the Python standard library to start and run the process that we want to get output from:

```python
def run(self):
    # Suppress popping up a console window
    # when running on windows
    if subprocess.mswindows:
        suinfo = subprocess.STARTUPINFO()
        try:
            from win32process import STARTF_USESHOWWINDOW
            suinfo.dwFlags |= STARTF_USESHOWWINDOW
        except ImportError:
            # Give up and use hard coded value
            # from Windows.h
            suinfo.dwFlags |= 0x00000001
    else:
        suinfo = None

    try:
        # Start the subprocess
        outmode = subprocess.PIPE
        errmode = subprocess.STDOUT
        self._proc = subprocess.Popen(self._command,
                                      stdout=outmode,
                                      stderr=errmode,
                                      shell=True,
                                      startupinfo=suinfo)
    except OSError, msg:
        self._parent.AppendUpdate(unicode(msg))
        return
```

Here, we just loop as long as the process is running, reading its output and appending it to the `parent` object's update queue:

```python
        # Read from stdout while there is output from process
        while True:
            self._proc.poll()
            if self._proc.returncode is None:
                # Still running so check stdout
                txt = self._proc.stdout.read(self._readblock)
                if txt:
                    # Add to UI's update queue
                    self._parent.AppendUpdate(txt)
            else:
                break
```

Next, we have the GUI control for displaying a process's output. This class will use the `ProcessThread` to run a process and be the receiver for its data. It will maintain a list of threads so that there can be an arbitrary number of processes running at the same time.

```python
class OutputWindow(stc.StyledTextCtrl):
    def __init__(self, parent):
        super(OutputWindow, self).__init__(parent)

        # Attributes
        self._mutex = threading.Lock()
        self._updating = threading.Condition(self._mutex)
        self._updates = list()
        self._timer = wx.Timer(self)
        self._threads = list()

        # Setup
        self.SetReadOnly(True)

        # Event Handlers
        self.Bind(wx.EVT_TIMER, self.OnTimer)

    def __del__(self):
        if self._timer.IsRunning():
            self._timer.Stop()
```

The `AppendUpdate` method is used by the `ProcessThread` to pass data to this control. The updates are appended to a list that we guard with a lock to ensure that only one thread is accessing it at a time:

```python
    def AppendUpdate(self, value):
        """Thread safe method to add updates to UI"""
        self._updating.acquire()
        self._updates.append(value)
        self._updating.release()
```

Next, we have a `Timer` event handler to periodically check the update list and apply them to the GUI:

```python
    def OnTimer(self, event):
        """Check updates queue and apply to UI"""
        # Check Thread(s)
        tlist = list(self._threads)
        for idx, thread in enumerate(tlist):
            if not thread.isAlive():
                del self._threads[idx]
```

```
                # Apply pending updates to control
                ind = len(self._updates)
                if ind:
                    # Flush update buffer
                    self._updating.acquire()
                    self.SetReadOnly(False)
                    txt = ''.join(self._updates[:])
                    self.AppendText(txt)
                    self.GotoPos(self.GetLength())
                    self._updates = list()
                    self.SetReadOnly(True)
                    self._updating.release()


                if not len(self._threads):
                    self._timer.Stop()
```

Finally, the StartProcess method is what the application can use to tell the control to start a new process:

```
        def StartProcess(self, command, blocksize=4096):
            """Start command. Blocksize can be used to control
            how much text must be read from stdout before window
            will update.
            """
            procthread = ProcessThread(self, command, blocksize)
            procthread.start()
            self._threads.append(procthread)
            if not self._timer.IsRunning():
                self._timer.Start(250)
```

How it works...

First, let's jump in with a look at our ProcessThread class. This is the worker thread that the OutputWindow uses to start an external process and capture its output from. The constructor takes three arguments: a parent window, a command-line string, and an optional keyword parameter that can specify the amount of text to block on reading from the process's standard output on each iteration. Setting the readblock parameter to a small number will result in more responsive updates from the ProcessThread. However, setting it too low on a process that outputs lots of data can result in lots of small, inefficient updates. So it's generally best to try to select a value that is as large as is appropriate for the given process's output.

The `ProcessThread`'s `run` method is where it does all its work. First, we have to handle a special case for Windows, because `subprocess.POpen` can cause a command window to be opened when running shell commands. The use of the `startupflags` can be used to suppress this behavior since we want to show the output in our `OutputWindow` instead. Next, we use the `subprocess` module's `POpen` class to run the command specified in the constructor. Finally, the thread just enters a simple loop that checks to see if the process is still running, and if it is it then blocks the read of the specified amount of text from the processes output pipe. After the text has been read, it calls the `OutputWindow`'s `AppendUpdate` method to add the output to its update queue.

Now, let's see how the `OutputWindow` works to display the text that the `ProcessThread` captures. The `OutputWindow` derives from `StyledTextCtrl` because this can handle larger amounts of text with generally better performance than the standard `TextCtrl`, and has a more powerful API for working with the text in the buffer, should we decided to add some additional functionality at a later date. In the `OutputWindow`'s constructor, we did a few important things. First, we created a lock to use for guarding the update queue so that only one thread can modify it at a time. If a second thread tries to `acquire` the lock while another thread has it, it will cause the second thread to wait at the `acquire` call until the lock is released by the other thread. The second is the update queue, third is the `Timer` that will be used to poll the update queue periodically, and finally we have a list to keep references to the `ProcessThread`(s) that are started.

The remaining methods in the `OutputWindow` class are all used to manage the updates from the `ProcessThread`(s) that it owns. `StartProcess` creates and starts a new `ProcessThread`, as well as the `OutputWindow`'s update Timer if it hasn't been previously started. `AppendUpdate` is a thread-safe method for background threads to call and add updates to the `OutputWindow`. This method is safe to directly call from a background thread because the data object that it is modifying is guarded by a lock that will prevent more than one thread from modifying the object at the same time. This method was chosen over posting events from the worker threads because it can help to keep the UI more responsive during high-volume updates, because it allows the updates to the UI to be grouped into a smaller number of larger updates as opposed to many small updates which can lead to the UI becoming locked up while processing all the events. Last but not least is the `OnTimer` method, where the actual UI updates occur. `OnTimer` first checks and removes any threads that have finished running from the thread pool, and then it acquires the lock to make sure it has exclusive access to the update queue. After acquiring the lock, it proceeds to flush all the queued updates to the `OutputWindow`, and then empties the queue and releases the lock.

There's more...

See the sample code that accompanies this topic for a small, sample application that makes use of the OutputWindow to create a GUI display for running the ping command:

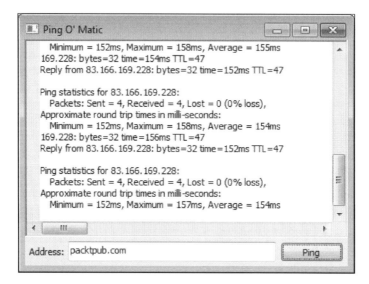

See also

▶   See the *Understanding thread safety* recipe in this chapter for a discussion of what thread safety is as it relates to the GUI.

▶   See the *Using Timers* recipe in this chapter for another example of using Timers.

12
Building and Managing Applications for Distribution

In this chapter, we will cover:

- ▸ Working with `StandardPaths`
- ▸ Persisting the state of the UI
- ▸ Using the `SingleInstanceChecker`
- ▸ Exception handling
- ▸ Optimizing for OS X
- ▸ Supporting internationalization
- ▸ Distributing an application

Introduction

An application's infrastructure provides the backbone for the application's inner workings, which are often things that are not directly apparent to the user but are critical to the application's functionality. This includes things such as storing configuration and external data files, error handling, and installation. Each of these areas provides important functionality and contributes to the usability and the end-user's overall perception of the application. In this chapter, we will take an in-depth tour of a number of these topics and more, in order to provide you with the appropriate tools to help build and distribute your application.

Working with StandardPaths

Nearly every non-trivial application is going to have the need to store data to use between usage of the program and to load resources such as images. The question is where to put this stuff? The appropriate locations where the operating system and users expect to find these files will vary from platform to platform. This recipe shows how to use `wx.StandardPaths` to manage an application's configuration and resource files.

How to do it...

Here, we will create a thin wrapper utility class to help manage an application's configuration files and data. The constructor will ensure that any predefined directories have been set up in the configuration storage location on the system.

```
class ConfigHelper(object):
    def __init__(self, userdirs=None):
        """@keyword userdirs: list of user config
                              subdirectories names
        """
        super(ConfigHelper, self).__init__()

        # Attributes
        self.userdirs = userdirs

        # Setup
        self.InitializeConfig()

    def InitializeConfig(self):
        """Setup config directories"""
        # Create main user config directory if it does
        # not exist.
        datap = wx.StandardPaths_Get().GetUserDataDir()
        if not os.path.exists(datap):
            os.mkdir(datap)
        # Make sure that any other application specific
        # config subdirectories have been created.
        if self.userdirs:
            for dname in userdirs:
                self.CreateUserCfgDir(dname)
```

Here, we add a helper function to create a directory in the current user's data directory:

```
    def CreateUserCfgDir(self, dirname):
        """Create a user config subdirectory"""
        path = wx.StandardPaths_Get().GetUserDataDir()
        path = os.path.join(path, dirname)
        if not os.path.exists(path):
            os.mkdir(path)
```

The next function can be used to get the absolute path to a file or directory in the user's data directory:

```
def GetUserConfigPath(self, relpath):
    """Get the path to a resource file
    in the users configuration directory.
    @param relpath: relative path (i.e config.cfg)
    @return: string
    """
    path = wx.StandardPaths_Get().GetUserDataDir()
    path = os.path.join(path, relpath)
    return path
```

Finally, the last method in this class can be used to check if a given configuration file has been created yet or not:

```
def HasConfigFile(self, relpath):
    """Does a given config file exist"""
    path = self.GetUserConfigPath(relpath)
    return os.path.exists(path)
```

How it works...

The `ConfigHelper` class just provides a thin simple wrapper around some of the `StandardPaths` methods, in order to make it a little easier to use. When the object is created, it will make sure that the user data directory and any of its application-specific subdirectories have been created. The `StandardPaths` singleton uses the application's name to determine the name of the user's data directory. Because of this, it is important to wait until the `App` object has been created and had its name set with `SetAppName`.

```
class SuperFoo(wx.App):
    def OnInit(self):
        self.SetAppName("SuperFoo")
        self.config = ConfigHelper()
        self.frame = SuperFooFrame(None, title="SuperFoo")
        self.frame.Show()
        return True

    def GetConfig(self):
        return self.config
```

The `CreateUserCfgDir` provides a convenient way to create a new directory inside the user's main configuration directory. `GetUserConfigPath` can be used to get the full path to a file or directory in the configuration directory or subdirectory, by using a path relative to the main directory. Finally, `HasConfigFile` is a simple way to check if a file exists in the user's configuration files.

There's more...

The `StandardPaths` singleton provides a number of other methods to get other system and installation-specific installation paths. The following table describes some of these additional methods:

Methods	Description
GetConfigDir()	Returns the system-level configuration directory
GetDataDir()	Returns the application's global (non user specific) data directory
GetDocumentsDir()	Returns the current user's documents directory
GetExecutablePath()	Returns the path to the currently-running executable
GetPluginsDir()	Returns the path to where the application's plug-ins should reside
GetTempDir()	Returns the path to the system's TEMP directory
GetUserConigDir()	Returns the path to the current user's configuration directory

See also

▶ See the *Creating Singletons* recipe in *Chapter 9, Design Approaches and Techniques* for a discussion about what singletons, such as the `StandardPaths` object, are.

▶ See the *Persisting the state of the UI* recipe in this chapter for more information on storing confirmation information.

Persisting the state of the UI

A common feature that many applications have is to be able to remember and restore their window size and position between launches of the program. This is not a built-in feature provided by the toolkit, so this recipe will create a simple `Frame` base class that will automatically save and restore its size and position on the desktop between uses of the application.

How to do it...

This example shows one approach to creating a `Frame` class that will automatically restore its position and size between runs of the program:

```
class PersistentFrame(wx.Frame):
    def __init__(self, *args, **kwargs):
        super(PersistentFrame, self).__init__(*args, **kwargs)
```

```
# Setup
wx.CallAfter(self.RestoreState)

# Event Handlers
self.Bind(wx.EVT_CLOSE, self._OnClose)
```

Here, we handle EVT_CLOSE for when the Frame is closing, in order to save its position and size to the Config object, which is the registry on Windows and a .ini file on other platforms:

```
def _OnClose(self, event):
    position = self.GetPosition()
    size = self.GetSize()
    cfg = wx.Config()
    cfg.Write('pos', repr(position.Get()))
    cfg.Write('size', repr(size.Get()))
    event.Skip()
```

The RestoreState method restores the currently-stored window state or the default state if nothing has been stored yet:

```
def RestoreState(self):
    """Restore the saved position and size"""
    cfg = wx.Config()
    name = self.GetName()
    position = cfg.Read(name + '.pos',
                        repr(wx.DefaultPosition))
    size = cfg.Read(name + '.size',
                    repr(wx.DefaultSize))
    # Turn strings back into tuples
    position = eval(position)
    size = eval(size)
    # Restore settings to Frame
    self.SetPosition(position)
    self.SetSize(size)
```

How it works...

The PersistentFrame should be used as a base class for any Frame in an application that should persist its size and position on exit. The way in which this class works is rather simple, so let's take a quick look at how it works.

First, in order to save its size and position, the Persisistent Frame binds an event handler to EVT_CLOSE. Its _OnClose method will then be called when the user closes the Frame. In this event handler, we simply get the current size and position of the Frame and save it to a wx.Config object, which will be the registry on Windows and a .ini file on other platforms.

Conversely, when the `PersistentFrame` is created, it tries to read the previously-saved size and position from the configuration. This happens in the `RestoreState` method, which is initiated with `CallAfter`. This was done to make sure that we don't restore the settings until after the `Frame` has been created, so that if a subclass sets up some default sizes they won't override the last state that the user left it in. In `RestoreState`, if there is stored information for the `Frame`, it will load the strings and convert them back to tuples using the `eval` function, and then will simply apply the settings.

There's more...

For simplicity, we just used `wx.Config` for storing the settings between running the application. We could have also used `StandardPaths` and written out our own configuration file to the user's configuration directory, like we did in the previous recipe in order to ensure that this information was kept where the user expects it to be.

See also

▸ See the *Working with StandardPaths* recipe in this chapter for information about another class that can help with storing and locating configuration information.

Using the SingleInstanceChecker

Sometimes it is desirable to only allow a single instance of an application to exist at any given time. The `SingleInstanceChecker` class provides a way to detect if any instances of the application are already running. This recipe creates an `App` class that uses the `SingleInstanceChecker` to maintain only a single running instance of the application on the computer at one time, and also uses a simple IPC mechanism to allow any subsequent instances of the application to send a message to the original instance to tell it to open a new window.

How to do it...

Here, we will create an `App` base class that ensures that only one instance of the process is running at a time, and supports a simple, socket-based inter-process communication mechanism to inform an already-running instance that a new one tried to start:

```
import wx
import threading
import socket
import select
```

```
class SingleInstApp(wx.App):
    """App baseclass that only allows a single instance to
    exist at a time.
    """
    def __init__(self, *args, **kwargs):
        super(SingleInstApp, self).__init__(*args, **kwargs)

        # Setup (note this will happen after subclass OnInit)
        instid = "%s-%s" % (self.GetAppName(), wx.GetUserId())
        self._checker = wx.SingleInstanceChecker(instid)
        if self.IsOnlyInstance():
            # First instance so start IPC server
            self._ipc = IpcServer(self, instid, 27115)
            self._ipc.start()
            # Open a window
            self.DoOpenNewWindow()
        else:
            # Another instance so just send a message to
            # the instance that is already running.
            cmd = "OpenWindow.%s" % instid
            if not SendMessage(cmd, port=27115):
                print "Failed to send message!"

    def __del__(self):
        self.Cleanup()
```

The `SingleInstanceChecker` needs to be explicitly deleted when the application exits to ensure that the file lock that it creates is released:

```
    def Cleanup(self):
        # Need to cleanup instance checker on exit
        if hasattr(self, '_checker'):
            del self._checker
        if hasattr(self, '_ipc'):
            self._ipc.Exit()

    def Destroy(self):
        self.Cleanup()
        super(SingleInstApp, self).Destroy()

    def IsOnlyInstance(self):
        return not self._checker.IsAnotherRunning()
```

```
def DoOpenNewWindow(self):
    """Interface for subclass to open new window
    on ipc notification.
    """
    pass
```

The `IpcServer` class implements the inter-process communication by opening a connection to a socket on the local loopback of the machine. This has been implemented as a background thread that loops, waiting for messages, until it is told to exit:

```
class IpcServer(threading.Thread):
    """Simple IPC Server"""
    def __init__(self, app, session, port):
        super(IpcServer, self).__init__()

        # Attributes
        self.keeprunning = True
        self.app = app
        self.session = session
        self.socket = socket.socket(socket.AF_INET,
                                    socket.SOCK_STREAM)

        # Setup TCP socket
        self.socket.bind(('127.0.0.1', port))
        self.socket.listen(5)
        self.setDaemon(True)
```

The `run` method runs the server thread's main loop of checking the socket for messages and using `CallAfter` to notify the `App` to call its `DoOpenNewWindow` method when the server has received an `'OpenWindow'` command:

```
def run(self):
    """Run the server loop"""
    while self.keeprunning:
        try:
            client, addr = self.socket.accept()

            # Read from the socket
            # blocking up to 2 seconds at a time
            ready = select.select([client,],[], [],2)
            if ready[0]:
                recieved = client.recv(4096)

                if not self.keeprunning:
                    break
```

```
                    # If message ends with correct session
                    # ID then process it.
                    if recieved.endswith(self.session):
                        if recieved.startswith('OpenWindow'):
                            wx.CallAfter(self.app.DoOpenNewWindow)
                        else:
                            # unknown command message
                            pass
                    recieved = ''
            except socket.error, msg:
                print "TCP error! %s" % msg
                break

        # Shutdown the socket
        try:
            self.socket.shutdown(socket.SHUT_RDWR)
        except:
            pass

        self.socket.close()

    def Exit(self):
        self.keeprunning = False
```

The `SendMessage` function is used to open a client connection to the `IpcServer`'s socket and send it the given message:

```
def SendMessage(message, port):
    """Send a message to another instance of the app"""
    try:
        # Setup the client socket
        client = socket.socket(socket.AF_INET,
                               socket.SOCK_STREAM)
        client.connect(('127.0.0.1', port))
        client.send(message)
        client.shutdown(socket.SHUT_RDWR)
        client.close()
    except Exception, msg:
        return False
    else:
        return True
```

Included with the code that accompanies this chapter is a complete running application showing how to use the above framework. To test it out, try starting multiple instances of the application on the same computer, and see that only the original process is running and that each subsequent launch results in a new window being opened in the original process.

How it works...

We packed a lot of stuff into a small amount of code in this recipe, so let's go through how each class works.

The `SingleInstApp` class creates a `SingleInstanceChecker` object to make it possible to detect if there is already another instance of the application running. As a part of the ID for the `SingleInstanceChecker`, we used the user's login ID to make sure that the instance checker is only checking for other instances that the same user has started.

In our `SingleInstanceApp` object's `__init__` method, it is important to realize the order of operations that will take place when a derived class is initialized. Calling the base `wx.App` class `__init__` will result in the derived class's virtual `OnInit` being called, and then after that the rest of the code in the `SingleInstApp`'s `__init__` will run. If it detects that this is the first instance of the application running, it will create and start our `IpcServer`. If not, it will simply create and send a simple string command to the other, already-running, `IpcServer` object to tell it to inform the other application instance to create a new window.

Before moving on to look at the `IpcServer` class, one very important thing to keep in mind when using the `SingleInstanceChecker` is that you need to explicitly delete it when you are done with it. If it is not deleted, the file lock that it uses for determining if another instance is active or not may never get released, which can cause problems on future launches of the program.

The `IpcServer` class is a simple class derived from `Thread` that uses a TCP socket for inter-process communication. As mentioned, the first `SingleInstanceApp` that is started will create an instance of this server. The server will run in its own thread, checking for messages at the socket. The `IpcServer` thread's `run` method just runs a loop, checking the socket for new data. If it is able to read a message, it checks that the last part of the message matches the key that was used to create the App's `SingleInstanceChecker`, to make sure that the command is coming from another instance of the application. We have only designed support for a single `'OpenWindow'` command in our simple IPC protocol right now, but it could be easily expanded to support more. Upon receiving an `OpenWindow` message, the `IpcServer` will use `CallAfter` to call the `SingleInstanceApp`'s interface method `DoOpenNewWindow` to inform the application to open a new instance of its main window.

The last part of this little framework is the `SendMessage` function, which is used as a client method to connect and send a message to the `IpcServer`.

See also

▶ See the *Understanding inheritance limitations* recipe in *Chapter 1, Getting Started with wxPython* for an explanation about overriding virtual methods in wxPython classes.

▶ See the *Understanding thread safety* recipe in *Chapter 11, Responsive Interfaces* for more information about working with threads in a wxPython GUI.

Exception handling

In even seemingly-simple applications, it can be difficult to account for all possible error conditions that could occur in the application. This recipe shows how to handle unhandled exceptions, and how to display a notification to the user to let them know that an unexpected error has happened, before the application exits.

How to do it...

For this recipe, we will show how to create a simple exception hook to handle and inform the user of any unexpected errors that occur while the program is running:

```python
import wx
import sys
import traceback

def ExceptionHook(exctype, value, trace):
    """Handler for all unhandled exceptions
    @param exctype: Exception Type
    @param value: Error Value
    @param trace: Trace back info
    """
    # Format the traceback
    exc = traceback.format_exception(exctype, value, trace)
    ftrace = "".join(exc)
    app = wx.GetApp()
    if app:
        msg = "An unexpected error has occurred: %s" % ftrace
        wx.MessageBox(msg, app.GetAppName(),
                      style=wx.ICON_ERROR|wx.OK)
        app.Exit()
    else:
        sys.stderr.write(ftrace)

class ExceptionHandlerApp(wx.App):
    def OnInit(self):
        sys.excepthook = ExceptionHook
        return True
```

How it works...

This recipe showed a very simple way to create an exception hook to catch unhandled exceptions in the application. During the start-up of the application, all that we needed to do was replace the default `excepthook` function with our own `ExceptionHook` function. The `ExceptionHook` function will then be called any time that an unhandled exception is raised in the application. In this function, all we do is pop up a `MessageBox` to show that an unexpected error has occurred, and then tell the `MainLoop` to exit.

There's more...

The purpose of this example was to show the process of how to handle these errors in a graceful manor. So we kept it pretty simple by just using a `MessageBox`. It would be easy to extend and customize this example to also log the error, or to allow the user to send a notification to the developer of the application so that the error can be debugged.

Optimizing for OS X

There are a number of things that can be done in a wxPython application in order to help it fit in better when running on a Macintosh OS X system. There are a number of things that users expect from an application on OS X, and this recipe shows some of the things to do in order to make sure your application runs and looks good on OS X as well as on other platforms. This will include the proper positioning of standard menus and menu items, main window behavior, and how to enable some Macintosh-specific functionality.

How to do it...

As an example of some of the things to take into consideration, we will create a simple application that shows how to make an application conform to Macintosh UI standards:

```python
import wx
import sys

class OSXApp(wx.App):
    def OnInit(self):
        # Enable native spell checking and right
        # click menu for Mac TextCtrl's
        if wx.Platform == '__WXMAC__':
            spellcheck = "mac.textcontrol-use-spell-checker"
            wx.SystemOptions.SetOptionInt(spellcheck, 1)
        self.frame = OSXFrame(None,
                        title="Optimize for OSX")
```

```python
        self.frame.Show()
        return True

    def MacReopenApp(self):
        self.GetTopWindow().Raise()


class OSXFrame(wx.Frame):
    """Main application window"""
    def __init__(self, *args, **kwargs):
        super(OSXFrame, self).__init__(*args, **kwargs)

        # Attributes
        self.textctrl = wx.TextCtrl(self,
                                    style=wx.TE_MULTILINE)

        # Setup Menus
        mb = wx.MenuBar()
        fmenu = wx.Menu()
        fmenu.Append(wx.ID_OPEN)
        fmenu.Append(wx.ID_EXIT)
        mb.Append(fmenu, "&File")
        emenu = wx.Menu()
        emenu.Append(wx.ID_COPY)
        emenu.Append(wx.ID_PREFERENCES)
        mb.Append(emenu, "&Edit")
        hmenu = wx.Menu()
        hmenu.Append(wx.NewId(), "&Online Help...")
        hmenu.Append(wx.ID_ABOUT, "&About...")
        mb.Append(hmenu, "&Help")

        if wx.Platform == '__WXMAC__':
            # Make sure we don't get duplicate
            # Help menu since we used non standard name
            app = wx.GetApp()
            app.SetMacHelpMenuTitleName("&Help")

        self.SetMenuBar(mb)
        self.SetInitialSize()


if __name__ == '__main__':
    app = OSXApp(False)
    app.MainLoop()
```

How it works...

This simple application creates a `Frame` with a `MenuBar` and a `TextCtrl` in it, and demonstrates a few things to take note of when preparing an application that will be deployed to Macintosh systems.

Starting in our `OSXApp` object's `OnInit` method, we used the `SystemOptions` singleton to enable the native context menu and spellchecking feature of the `TextCtrl` objects on OS X. This option is disabled by default; setting it to `1` enables it. Also in our `OSXApp` class, we overrode the `MacReopenApp` method, which is a callback for an `AppleEvent` that occurs when the application's dock icon is clicked on. We overrode it to make sure that this click will cause our application's main window to be brought to the front, as expected.

Next, in our `OSXFrame` class, it can be seen that there is some special handling needed for the `Menus`. All native OS X applications have some common elements in their menus. All applications have a Help menu, a Windows menu, and an Application menu. If your application needs to create a custom Help or Windows menu, then some additional steps are necessary to make sure that they will work as expected on OS X. In our previous example, we created a custom Help menu that included a mnemonic accelerator in its title for Windows/GTK to use with keyboard navigation. Since the menu title is not the same as the default, we needed to call `SetMacHelpMenuTitleName` on the `App` object so that it knows that our Help menu should be used. If we omit this step, our application will end up with two help menus shown in the `MenuBar` on OS X. The other important thing to note is to use stock IDs whenever possible for menu items. The About, Exit, and Preferences entries in particular will always be shown under the Application menu on OS X. By using the stock IDs for these items, wxPython will ensure that they end up in the proper locations on each platform.

There's more...

Included below are some additional Macintosh-specific methods and notes, for quick reference.

wx.App Macintosh specific methods

There are some other additional Macintosh-specific helper methods that belong to the `App` object that can be used to customize the handling for the three special menu items. These methods will be a no-op when the application is running on another platform.

Methods	Description
`SetMacAboutMenuItemId`	Change the ID used to identify the `About` menu item from `ID_ABOUT` to a custom value
`SetMacExitMenuItemId`	Change the ID used to identify the `Exit` menu item from `ID_EXIT` to a custom value

Methods	Description
SetMacPreferencesMenuItemId	Change the ID used to identify the Preferences menu item from ID_PREFERENCES to a custom value
SetMacSupportPCMenuShortcuts	Enable the use of menu mnemonics on OS X

wx.MenuBar

It is possible to disable the automatic creation of the Windows menu on OS X by using the `wx.MenuBar`'s static `SetAutoWindowMenu` method. Calling `SetAutoWindowMenu` with the value of `False` before creating a `MenuBar` will prevent the Windows menu from being created.

See also

- ▶ See the *Utilizing Stock IDs* recipe in *Chapter 1, Getting Started with wxPython* for a detailed discussion about using the built-in stock IDs.

- ▶ See the *Handling Apple events* recipe in *Chapter 2, Responding to Events* for an example of how handle AppleEvents in a wxPython application.

- ▶ See the *Distributing an application* recipe in this chapter for a discussion of how to distribute an application on OS X.

Supporting internationalization

In the interconnected world that we live in today, it is very important to take internationalization into account when developing an application's interface. There is very little to lose in designing an application that completely supports internationalization right from the beginning, but a whole lot to lose if you don't. This recipe will show how to set up an application to use wxPython's built-in support for interface translations.

How to do it...

Below, we will create a complete sample application that shows how to support localization in a wxPython application's user interface. The first thing to note is the alias for `wx.GetTranslation` that we use below to wrap all interface strings in the application:

```
import wx
import os

# Make a shorter alias
_ = wx.GetTranslation
```

Next, during the creation of our `App` object, we create and save a reference to a `Locale` object. We then tell the `Locale` object where we keep our translation files, so that it knows where to look up translations when the `GetTranslation` function is called:

```
class I18NApp(wx.App):
    def OnInit(self):
        self.SetAppName("I18NTestApp")
        # Get Language from last run if set
        config = wx.Config()
        language = config.Read('lang', 'LANGUAGE_DEFAULT')

        # Setup the Locale
        self.locale = wx.Locale(getattr(wx, language))
        path = os.path.abspath("./locale") + os.path.sep
        self.locale.AddCatalogLookupPathPrefix(path)
        self.locale.AddCatalog(self.GetAppName())

        # Local is not setup so we can create things that
        # may need it to retrieve translations.
        self.frame = TestFrame(None,
                               title=_("Sample App"))
        self.frame.Show()
        return True
```

Then, in the rest, we create a simple user interface that will allow the application to switch the language between English and Japanese:

```
class TestFrame(wx.Frame):
    """Main application window"""
    def __init__(self, *args, **kwargs):
        super(TestFrame, self).__init__(*args, **kwargs)

        # Attributes
        self.panel = TestPanel(self)

        # Layout
        sizer = wx.BoxSizer(wx.VERTICAL)
        sizer.Add(self.panel, 1, wx.EXPAND)
        self.SetSizer(sizer)
        self.SetInitialSize((300, 300))

class TestPanel(wx.Panel):
    def __init__(self, parent):
        super(TestPanel, self).__init__(parent)

        # Attributes
        self.closebtn = wx.Button(self, wx.ID_CLOSE)
```

```
        self.langch = wx.Choice(self,
                                choices=[_("English"),
                                         _("Japanese")])

        # Layout
        self.__DoLayout()

        # Event Handler
        self.Bind(wx.EVT_CHOICE, self.OnChoice)
        self.Bind(wx.EVT_BUTTON,
                  lambda event: self.GetParent().Close())

    def __DoLayout(self):
        vsizer = wx.BoxSizer(wx.VERTICAL)
        hsizer = wx.BoxSizer(wx.HORIZONTAL)

        label = wx.StaticText(self, label=_("Hello"))
        hsizer.AddStretchSpacer()
        hsizer.Add(label, 0, wx.ALIGN_CENTER)
        hsizer.AddStretchSpacer()

        langsz = wx.BoxSizer(wx.HORIZONTAL)
        langlbl = wx.StaticText(self, label=_("Language"))
        langsz.AddStretchSpacer()
        langsz.Add(langlbl, 0, wx.ALIGN_CENTER_VERTICAL)
        langsz.Add(self.langch, 0, wx.ALL, 5)
        langsz.AddStretchSpacer()

        vsizer.AddStretchSpacer()
        vsizer.Add(hsizer, 0, wx.EXPAND)
        vsizer.Add(langsz, 0, wx.EXPAND|wx.ALL, 5)
        vsizer.Add(self.closebtn, 0, wx.ALIGN_CENTER)
        vsizer.AddStretchSpacer()

        self.SetSizer(vsizer)

    def OnChoice(self, event):
        sel = self.langch.GetSelection()
        config = wx.Config()
        if sel == 0:
            val = 'LANGUAGE_ENGLISH'
        else:
            val = 'LANGUAGE_JAPANESE'
        config.Write('lang', val)

if __name__ == '__main__':
    app = I18NApp(False)
    app.MainLoop()
```

How it works...

The little sample application above shows how to make use of the support for translations in a wxPython application. Changing the selected language in the `Choice` control and restarting the application will change the interface strings between English and Japanese. Making use of translations is pretty easy, so let's just take a look at the important parts that make it work.

First, we created an alias of _ for the function `wx.GetTranslation`, so that it is shorter to type and easier to read. This function should be wrapped around any string in the application that will be shown to the user in the interface.

Next, in our Application's `OnInit` method, we did a few things to set up the proper locale information for loading the configured translations. First, we created a `Locale` object. It is necessary to keep a reference to this object so that it does not get garbage collected. Hence, we saved it to `self.locale`. Next, we set up the `Locale` object to let it know where our translation resource files are located, by first calling `AddCatalogLookupPathPrefix` with the directory where we keep our translation files. Then we tell it the name of the resource files for our application by calling `AddCatalog` with the name of our application object. In order for the translations to be loaded, the following directory structure is required for each language under the catalog lookup path prefix directory:

    Lang_Canonical_Name/LC_MESSAGES/CatalogName.mo

So, for example, for our application's Japanese translation, we have the following directory layout under our locale directory.

    ja_JP/LC_MESSAGES/I18NTestApp.mo

After the `Locale` object has been created, any calls to `GetTranslation` will use the locale to load the appropriate string from the `gettext` catalog file.

There's more...

wxPython uses `gettext`-formatted files for loading string resources from. There are two files for each translation. The `.po` file (Portable Object) is the file that is edited to create the mapping of the default string to the translated version. The other file is the `.mo` file (Machine Object) which is the compiled version of the `.po` file. To compile a `.po` file to a `.mo` file, you need to use the `msgfmt` tool. This is part of `gettext` on any Linux platform. It can also be installed on OS X through `fink`, and on Windows through `Cygwin`. The following command line statement will generate the `.mo` file from the given input `.po` file.

```
msgfmt ja_JP.po
```

Distributing an application

Once the application that you have been working on is complete, it is time to put together a way to distribute the application to its users. wxPython applications can be distributed like any other Python application or script, by creating a `setup.py` script and using the `distutils` module's `setup` function. However, this recipe will focus on how to create standalone executables for Windows and OS X by creating a build script that uses `py2exe` and `py2app` respectively for the two target platforms. Creating a standalone application makes it much easier for the user to install the application on their system, which means that more people are likely to use it.

Getting ready

To build standalone binaries, some extension modules are needed in addition to wxPython. So if you haven't already done so, you will need to install `py2exe` (Windows) or `py2app` (OS X).

How to do it...

Here, we will create a simple `setup.py` template that, with a few simple customizations, can be used to build Windows and OS X binaries for most wxPython applications. The **Application Information** section here at the top can be modified to specify the application's name and other specific information.

```python
import wx
import sys

#---- Application Information ----#
APP = "FileEditor.py"
NAME = "File Editor"
VERSION = "1.0"
AUTHOR = "Author Name"
AUTHOR_EMAIL = "authorname@someplace.com"
URL = "http://fileeditor_webpage.foo"
LICENSE = "wxWidgets"
YEAR = "2010"

#---- End Application Information ----#
```

Here, we will define a method that uses `py2exe` to build a Windows executable from the Python script specified in the `APP` variable in the Application Information section:

```
RT_MANIFEST = 24

def BuildPy2Exe():
    """Generate the Py2exe files"""
    from distutils.core import setup
    try:
        import py2exe
    except ImportError:
        print "\n!! You dont have py2exe installed. !!\n"
        exit()
```

Windows binaries have a manifest embedded in them that specifies dependencies and other settings. The sample code that accompanies this chapter includes the following two XML files that will ensure that the GUI has the proper themed controls when running on Windows XP and greater:

```
pyver = sys.version_info[:2]
if pyver == (2, 6):
    fname = "py26manifest.xml"
elif pyver == (2, 5):
    fname = "py25manifest.xml"
else:
    vstr = ".".join(pyver)
    assert False, "Unsupported Python Version %s" % vstr
with open(fname, 'rb') as handle:
    manifest = handle.read()
    manifest = manifest % dict(prog=NAME)
```

The `OPTS` dictionary specifies the `py2exe` options. These are some standard settings that should be good for most applications, but they can be tweaked further if necessary for specific use cases:

```
OPTS = {"py2exe" : {"compressed" : 1,
                    "optimize" : 1,
                    "bundle_files" : 2,
                    "excludes" : ["Tkinter",],
                    "dll_excludes": ["MSVCP90.dll"]}}
```

The `windows` keyword to the `setup` function is used to specify that we are creating a GUI application and is used to specify what the application icon and manifest are to embed in the binary:

```
setup(
    name = NAME,
    version = VERSION,
```

```
            options = OPTS,
            windows = [{"script": APP,
                            "icon_resources": [(1, "Icon.ico")],
                            "other_resources" : [(RT_MANIFEST, 1,
                                                        manifest)],
                       }],
            description = NAME,
            author = AUTHOR,
            author_email = AUTHOR_EMAIL,
            license = LICENSE,
            url = URL,
            )
```

Next we have our OS X build method that uses py2app to build the binary applet bundle:

```
def BuildOSXApp():
    """Build the OSX Applet"""
    from setuptools import setup
```

Here, we define a PLIST, which is very similar in purpose to the manifest used by Windows binaries. It is used to define some information about the application that the OS uses to know what roles the application fills.

```
    # py2app uses this to generate the plist xml for
    # the applet.
    copyright = "Copyright %s %s" % (AUTHOR, YEAR)
    appid = "com.%s.%s" % (NAME, NAME)
    PLIST = dict(CFBundleName = NAME,
            CFBundleIconFile = 'Icon.icns',
            CFBundleShortVersionString = VERSION,
            CFBundleGetInfoString = NAME + " " + VERSION,
            CFBundleExecutable = NAME,
            CFBundleIdentifier = appid,
            CFBundleTypeMIMETypes = ['text/plain',],
            CFBundleDevelopmentRegion = 'English',
            NSHumanReadableCopyright = copyright
            )
```

The following dictionary specifies the py2app options that setup() will use when building the application:

```
    PY2APP_OPTS = dict(iconfile = "Icon.icns",
                    argv_emulation = True,
                    optimize = True,
                    plist = PLIST)
```

```
setup(
    app = [APP,],
    version = VERSION,
    options = dict( py2app = PY2APP_OPTS),
    description = NAME,
    author = AUTHOR,
    author_email = AUTHOR_EMAIL,
    license = LICENSE,
    url = URL,
    setup_requires = ['py2app'],
    )


if __name__ == '__main__':
    if wx.Platform == '__WXMSW__':
        # Windows
        BuildPy2Exe()
    elif wx.Platform == '__WXMAC__':
        # OSX
        BuildOSXApp()
    else:
        print "Unsupported platform: %s" % wx.Platform
```

How it works...

With the previous set-up script, we can build standalone binaries on both Windows and OS X for our `FileEditor` script. So let's take a look at each of the two functions, `BuildPy2exe` and `BuildOSXApp`, to see how each of them works.

`BuildPy2exe` performs the necessary preparations in order to run `setup` for building a standalone binary on Windows machines by using `py2exe`. There are three important parts to take note of in this function. First is the section where we create the manifest. Between versions 2.5 and 2.6, the Windows runtime libraries that were used to build the Python interpreter binaries changed. Due to this, we need to specify different dependencies in our binary's manifest in order for it to be able to load the correct runtimes and give our GUI application the correct themed appearance. The two possible manifests for either Python 2.5 or 2.6 are included with this topic's sample source code.

Second is the `py2exe` options dictionary. This dictionary contains the `py2exe` specific options to use when bundling the script. We used five options: `compressed`, `optimize`, `bundle_files`, `excludes`, and `dll_excludes`. The `compressed` option states that we want to compress the resulting `.exe` file. The `optimize` says to optimize the Python byte code. We can specify 0, 1, or 2 here, for different levels of optimizations. The `bundle_files` option specifies the level at which to bundle dependencies into the `library.zip` file. The lower the number (1-3), the greater the number of files that will be bundled into the ZIP file, reducing the overall number of individual files that need to be distributed. Using 1 can often cause problems with wxPython applications, so using 2 or 3 is suggested. Next, the `excludes` option is a list of modules to exclude from the resulting bundle. We specified `Tkinter` here just to ensure that none of its dependencies accidentally get drawn in making our binary larger. Finally, the `dll_excludes` option was used to work around an issue when using `py2exe` with Python 2.6.

Third and finally is the `windows` parameter in the `setup` command. This is used to specify that we are building a GUI application, and is where we specify the application's icon to embed into the `.exe` as well as the manifest that we spoke of earlier.

Running `setup` with `py2exe` is as simple as the following command line statement:

```
python setup.py py2exe
```

Now let's look at how `py2app` works. It is very similar to `py2exe` and actually even a little easier to use since there is no need to worry about runtime dependencies like there is on Windows. The main difference is the `PLIST`, which is somewhat similar to a manifest on Windows, but is used to define some application behavior and to store information about the application for use by the operating system. `Py2app` will use the specified dictionary to generate the `Plist` XML file in the resulting application. To learn about the available `Plist` options, see the properly listed documentation available at `http://developer.apple.com`. The `PLIST` dictionary is passed to `py2app` through the setup function's `options` parameter, along with the other `py2app` options that we specified, such as the application's icon. Also, very similar to `py2exe`, running `py2app` just requires the following command line statement:

```
python setup.py py2app
```

There's more...

Included below is some additional information about some specific distribution dependency issues for Windows applications, as well as some references for creating installers for applications on Windows and OS X.

Py2Exe dependencies

After running the `py2exe` setup command, make sure that you review the list of dependencies that were not included, and that are listed at the end of the output. There are a couple of additional files that you may need to manually include in your application's `dist` folder for it to run properly when deployed on a different computer. For Python 2.5, the `msvcr71.dll` and `gdiplus.dll` files are typically needed. For Python 2.6, the `msvcr90.dll` and `gdiplus.dll` files are needed. The `msvcr.dll` files are copyrighted by Microsoft, so you should review the licensing terms to make sure you have the rights to redistribute them. If not, users may be required to install them separately using the freely-availably redistributable runtime package that can be downloaded from Microsoft's website.

Installers

After building your application with either `py2exe` or `py2app`, you will need a way to help the application's users to properly install the files onto their systems. For Windows, there are a number of options available for building installers: NSIS (`http://nsis.sourceforge.net`) and Inno Setup (`http://www.jrsoftware.org/isinfo.php`) are two popular free options. On OS X, the necessary tools are already installed. Simply use the Disk Utility application to make a disk image (`.dmg`) file and then copy the built applet into it.

Index

Symbols

.mo file 272
.po file 272
_AsyncWrapper method 243

A

AboutBox
  setting up, in application 116, 117
AboutDialogInfo object
  methods 118
AboutDialogInfo object, fields
  SetArtists(list_of_strings) 118
  SetDevelopers(list_of_strings) 118
  SetDocWriters(list_of_strings) 118
  SetIcon(icon) 118
  SetLicense(license_string) 118
  SetTranslators(list_of_strings) 118
  SetWebSite(url_string) 118
AboutDialogInfo object, methods
  SetCopyright 118
  SetDescription 118
  SetName 118
  SetVersion 118
AddChild method 28
AddCheckLabelTool method 68
AddControl method 68
AddEasyTool method 67
AddFoldPanelWindow method 98
AddMany method 147
AddRadioLabelTool method 68
AddRoot method 80
AddSeparator method 68
AddSpacer method 147
AddTool method 216
Append method 63

AppendItems method 63
alignment flags
  about 151
  wx.ALIGN_BOTTOM 151
  wx.ALIGN_CENTER_HORIZONTAL 151
  wx.ALIGN_CENTER_VERTICAL 151
  wx.ALIGN_CENTRE_HORIZONTAL 151
  wx.ALIGN_CENTRE_VERTICAL 151
  wx.ALIGN_LEFT 151
  wx.ALIGN_RIGHT 151
  wx.ALIGN_TOP 151
App.GetTopWindow mehod 14
App class
  creating 260
AppendMenu function 65
AppendUpdate method   251
AppEventHandlerMixin class 43
AppleEvents
  about 48
  handling 48
  working 49
application infrastructure
  about 255
  managing, wx.StandardPaths used 256, 257
application window
  creating 122, 123
ApplyStyles method 106
App objects
  about 8
  working 9
AquaButton 57
arbitrary shapes
  drawing 171-173
ArtProvider
  about 210
  customizing 210, 211
  working 211

AUI_MGR_ALLOW_ACTIVE_PANE flag 166
AUI_MGR_ALLOW_FLOATING flag 166
AUI_MGR_DEFAULT flag 166
AUI_MGR_HINT_FADE flag 166
AUI_MGR_LIVE_RESIZE flag 166
AUI_MGR_NO_VENETIAN_BLINDS_FADE flag 166
AUI_MGR_RECTANGLE_HINT flag 166
AUI_MGR_TRANSPARENT_DRAG flag 166
AUI_MGR_TRANSPARENT_HINT flag 166
AUI_MGR_VENETIAN_BLINDS_HINT flag 166
AuiFrameManager 163
AuiManager object
   about 165
   methods 165
AuiManager object, flags
   about 166
   AUI_MGR_ALLOW_ACTIVE_PANE 166
   AUI_MGR_ALLOW_FLOATING 166
   AUI_MGR_DEFAULT 166
   AUI_MGR_HINT_FADE 166
   AUI_MGR_LIVE_RESIZE 166
   AUI_MGR_NO_VENETIAN_BLINDS_FADE 166
   AUI_MGR_RECTANGLE_HINT 166
   AUI_MGR_TRANSPARENT_DRAG 166
   AUI_MGR_TRANSPARENT_HINT 166
   AUI_MGR_VENETIAN_BLINDS_HINT 166

B

back attribute 87
BalloonTip class
   methods 109
BalloonTip class, methods
   SetBalloonColour(colour) 109
   SetMessageColour(colour) 109
   SetTitleColour(colour) 109
   SetTitleFont(font) 109
BalloonTip constructor
   keyword arguments 108
BalloonTip constructor, keyword arguments
   message 108
   shape 108
   tipstyle 108
   topicon 108
   toptitle 108

BalloonTip
   about 107
   displaying 108
BaseDialogStrategy class 195
behavior flags
   about 151
   wx.EXPAND 151
   wx.FIXED_MINSIZE 151
   wx.RESERVE_SPACE_EVEN_IF_HIDDEN 151
   wx.SHAPED 151
Bind method
   parameters 31
Bitmap
   about 15
   image file, displaying 15
   image file, loading 15
   image file formats 16
   working 16
BitmapButton 56
BitmapPrinter class
   about 139
   working 140
BlockingPanel
   OnButton method 235
bold modifier 87
border flags
   about 151
   wx.ALL 151
   wx.BOTTOM 151
   wx.LEFT 151
   wx.RIGHT 151
   wx.TOP 151
BoxSizer
   about 144
   panel size, managing 144, 145
   working 146
BoxSizer, methods
   about 146
   AddSpacer 146, 147
BoxSizerPanel class
   _DoLayout method 146
   about 144
BuildPy2exe 276
bundle_files option 276
Button class 53
   AquaButton 57
   BitmapButton 56

examples 54, 55
GenericButtons 57
GradientButton 56
PlateButton 56
ToggleButton 56
working 56

C

callafter decorator
working 244
CallAfter function 236, 240
threading tools 241
CaptionBox class 176
CheckBoxes
about 57
Get3StateValue method, using 58
options, offering 57, 58
Set3StateValue, using 58
working 58
CheckListCtrlMixin class 205 221
Choice control
about 62
AppendItems method 63
append method 63
choices, providing 62
Insert method 63
SetItems method 63
working 62, 63
ClassSynchronizer metaclass
working 245
clearSigInt argument, 9
Clipboard
about 20
data types 21
text, obtaining 20
working 21
CodeEditorBase class 85
ColumnSorterMixin class 205, 222
compressed option 276
ConfigHelper class 257
Configuration class 191
context menus. *See* **pop-up menus**
CONTROL_CHECKABLE flag 183
CONTROL_CHECKED flag 183
CONTROL_CURRENT flag 183

CONTROL_DISABLED flag 183
CONTROL_EXPANDED flag 183
CONTROL_FOCUSED flag 183
CONTROL_ISDEFAULT flag 183
CONTROL_PRESSED flag 184
CONTROL_SELECTED flag 184
CONTROL_UNDETERMINED flag 184
control flags
CONTROL_CHECKABLE 183
CONTROL_CHECKED 183
CONTROL_CURRENT 183
CONTROL_DISABLED 183
CONTROL_EXPANDED 183
CONTROL_FOCUSED 183
CONTROL_ISDEFAULT 183
CONTROL_PRESSED 184
CONTROL_SELECTED 184
CONTROL_UNDETERMINED 184
controls
adding, to StatusBar 212-215
CountingThread class 237
CreateBitmap method 210
CreateButtonSizer method, flags
wx.CANCEL 156
wx.HELP 157
wx.NO 157
wx.NO_DEFAULT 157
wx.OK 156
wx.YES 156
CreateContextMenu method 70
CreateUserCfgDir 257
custom button class
creating, RendererNative class used 180-182
custom control
creating 226-229
custom event class
about 41
creating 41
working 42
custom lexer
using 223, 225
writing 223, 225
custom MessageBox clone
creating 156
custom resource handler
preparing 160, 162

CustomTreeCtrl
about 77
EnableSelectionGradient() function 81
EnableSelectionVista() function 81
files, browsing 77-79
SetBackgroundColour ()function 81
SetBackgroundImage () function 81
SetButtonsImageList() function 81
SetConnectionPen() function 81
working 80

D

data types, Clipboard
wx.BitmapDataObject 21
wx.CustomDataObject 21
wx.DataObjectComposite 21
wx.FileDataObject 21
wx.URLDataObject 21
decorator class 207
decorator method
creating 207
decorators 206
delegate method 207
Device Context (DC) 167
Dialog class 59
dialogs 121
dialogs, types
about 121
modal 121
modeless 121
dir() call 28
dll_excludes option 277
DoGetBestSize method 168, 170, 175
DoOpen method 124, 125
DoSaveAs method 124, 125
drag and drop
about 22
custom drop target class, defining 22, 23
using 22, 23
working 24
DragAndDrop class 206
DrawArc(x1,y1,x2,y2,xcenter,ycenter) function 173
DrawArc method 172, 173
DrawBitmap(bmp,x,y,useMask=False) function 173

DrawCheckBox method 183
DrawCheckMark(x,y,width,height) function 173
DrawChoice method 183
DrawCircle(x,y,radius) function 173
DrawCircle method 173
DrawComboBoxDropButton method 183
DrawComboBox method 183
DrawDropArrow method 183
DrawEllipse(x,y,width,height) function 174
DrawEllipticArc(x,y,w,h,start,end) function 174
DrawHeaderButton method 183
DrawIcon(icon, x, y) function 174
DrawImageLabel(lbl,bmp,rect,align) function 174
drawing routines
flicker, reducing in 184, 185
DrawItemSelectionRect method 183
DrawLabel(text,rect,align) function 174
DrawLine(x1,y1,x2,y2) function 174
DrawPoint(x,y) function 174
DrawPolygon(points,x,y) function 174
DrawPushButton method 183
DrawRadioButton method 183
DrawRectangle(x,y,w,h) function 174
DrawRectangle method 172
DrawRotatedText(text,x,y,angle) function 174
DrawRoundedRectangle(x,y,w,h,angle) function 174
DrawSpline(points) function 174
DrawSplitterBorder method 183
DrawSplitterSash method 183
DrawText(text,x,y) function 174
DrawTextCtrl method 183
DrawTreeItemButton method 183

E

EasyToolBar class 67
EnableLineNumbers method 87
eol modifier 87
events, Notebook class
EVT_NOTEBOOK_PAGE_CHANGED 92
EVT_NOTEBOOK_PAGE_CHANGING 92
event handlers
managing, EventStack used 43, 44

event handling, wxPython
  steps 30
  working 31
EventMgrApp class 45
event propagation, wxPython
  about 32
  steps 32, 33
  working 34
events
  about 29
  AppleEvents, handling 48
  custom event classes 41
  EventStack, using 43
  handling 30
  KeyEvents, handling 34
  propagating 30, 31
  UpdateUI Events 37
events, TaskBarIcon class
  EVT_TASKBAR_CLICK 90
  EVT_TASKBAR_LEFT_DCLICK 90
  EVT_TASKBAR_LEFT_DOWN 90
  EVT_TASKBAR_LEFT_UP 90
  EVT_TASKBAR_MOVE 90
  EVT_TASKBAR_RIGHT_DCLICK 90
  EVT_TASKBAR_RIGHT_DOWN 90
  EVT_TASKBAR_RIGHT_UP 90
EventStack
  about 43
  event handlers, managing 43, 44
  working 45
EVT_NOTEBOOK_PAGE_CHANGED event 92
EVT_NOTEBOOK_PAGE_CHANGING event 92
EVT_TASKBAR_CLICK event 90
EVT_TASKBAR_LEFT_DCLICK event 90
EVT_TASKBAR_LEFT_DOWN event 90
EVT_TASKBAR_LEFT_UP event 90
EVT_TASKBAR_MOVE event 90
EVT_TASKBAR_RIGHT_DCLICK event 90
EVT_TASKBAR_RIGHT_DOWN event 90
EVT_TASKBAR_RIGHT_UP event 90
excepthook function 266
exception
  handling 265, 266
exception handling 265
exception hook
  creating 265

ExceptionHook function 266
excludes option 277
ExpansionState class 206
expose decorator 208

F

face attribute 87
FibonacciController class 200
FibonacciModel class 199
FileDialog
  about 122
  files, selecting 122-126
  modes 125
  parameters 126
  style flags 126
  using 125, 126
FileDialog, parameters
  defaultDir 126
  defaultFile 126
FileDialog, style flags
  wx.FD_CHANGE_DIR 126
  wx.FD_DEFAULT_STYLE 126
  wx.FD_FILE_MUST_EXIST 126
  wx.FD_MULTIPLE 126
  wx.FD_OPEN 126
  wx.FD_OVERWRITE_PROMPT 126
  wx.FD_PREVIEW 126
  wx.FD_SAVE 126
files
  selecting, with FileDialog 122-126
FindReplaceData
  flags 132
FindReplaceData, flags
  about 132
  wx.FR_MATCHCASE 132
  wx.FR_WHOLEWORD 132
FindReplaceDialog
  about 127
  style flags 132
  text, searching 127-131
FindReplaceDialog, style flags
  wx.FR_NOMATCHCASE 132
  wx.FR_NOUPDOWN 132
  wx.FR_NOWHOLEWORD 132
  wx.FR_REPLACEDIALOG 132
FindWindowById method 14

FindWindowByLabel(label) method 15
FindWindowByName(name) method 15
flags, AuiManager object
about 166
AUI_MGR_ALLOW_ACTIVE_PANE 166
AUI_MGR_ALLOW_FLOATING 166
AUI_MGR_DEFAULT 166
AUI_MGR_HINT_FADE 166
AUI_MGR_LIVE_RESIZE 166
AUI_MGR_NO_VENETIAN_BLINDS_FADE 166
AUI_MGR_RECTANGLE_HINT 166
AUI_MGR_TRANSPARENT_DRAG 166
AUI_MGR_TRANSPARENT_HINT 166
AUI_MGR_VENETIAN_BLINDS_HINT 166
flags, CreateButtonSizer method
wx.CANCEL 156
wx.HELP 157
wx.NO 157
wx.NO_DEFAULT 157
wx.OK 156
wx.YES 156
flags, FindReplaceData
about 132
wx.FR_MATCHCASE 132
wx.FR_WHOLEWORD 132
FlatNotebook class
about 93
style flags 95
using 93
working 94
FlexGridSizer 152
flicker
about 184
reducing, in drawing routines 184, 185
FNB_ALLOW_FOREIGN_DND style flag 95
FNB_BACKGROUND_GRADIENT style flag 95
FNB_BOTTOM style flag 95
FNB_COLORFUL_TABS style flag 95
FNB_DCLICK_CLOSES_TABS style flag 95
FNB_DEFAULT_STYLE style flag 95
FNB_FANCY_TABS style flag 95
FNB_HIDE_ON_SINGLE_TAB style flag 95
FNB_MOUSE_MIDDLE_CLOSES_TABS style flag 95
FNB_NO_NAV_BUTTONS style flag 95
FNB_NO_X_BUTTON style flag 95
FNB_NODRAG style flag 95

FNB_TABS_BORDER_SIMPLE style flag 95
FNB_VC71 style flag 95
FNB_VC8 style flag 95
FoldPanelBar
about 97
AddFoldPanel method 98
CaptionBar 98
simplifying 97, 98
working 98
fore attribute 87
Frame
about 9
subclassing 10
working 10, 11
frame base class
creating 163, 164
Frame class
creating 258, 259

G

GCDC 179
GenericButtons 57
GetChildren method 14
GetConfigDir() method 258
GetDataDir() method 258
GetDocumentsDir() method 258
GetExecutablePath() method 258
GetParent method 14
GetPluginsDir() method 258
GetSelection method 38
GetTempDir() method 258
gettext formatted files
using 272
GetTopLevelParent() method 15
GetUserConfigPath 257
GetUserConigDir() method 258
GradientButton 56
GradientButton class 53
GraphicsContext
about 177
custom control, creating 178, 179
GridBagSizer class
about 152
layout, controlling with 152
working 153
GridSizer 152

H

HasConfigFile 257

I

icons, adding to Windows
  steps 17
  working 18
ImageCanvas widget 168, 170
ImageDialog
  about 132
  images, acquiring 132-135
images
  acquiring, with ImageDialog 132-135
inheritance limitations
  demonstrating 26, 27
  working 28
Inno Setup 278
Insert method 63
InsertColumn method 76
installers
  about 278
  Inno Setup 278
  NSIS 278
internationalization 269
IpcServer class
  about 262
  working 264
IsSelected method 83
italic modifier 87

K

KeyEvents
  about 34
  handling 34, 35
  working 36
keyword arguments, BalloonTip constructor
  message 108
  shape 108
  tipstyle 108
  topicon 108
  toptitle 108
keyword arguments, wx.App class
  clearSigInt 9
  filename 9

  redirect 9
  useBestVisual 9

L

lambda function 31
layout
  controlling, with GridBagSizer 152, 153
layout behavior
  SizerItems borders, modifying 148-150
  SizerItems flags, modifying 148-150
  SizerItems proportions, modifying 148-150
LC_EDIT_LABELS style flag 76
LC_HRULE style flag 76
LC_ICON style flag 76
LC_LIST style flag 76
LC_NO_HEADER style flag 76
LC_REPORT style flag 76
LC_SINGLE_SEL style flag 77
LC_SMALL_ICON style flag 76
LC_SORT_ASCENDING style flag 76
LC_SORT_DESCENDING style flag 76
LC_VIRTUAL style flag 77
LC_VRULE style flag 76
lines
  drawing 171-173
ListCtrl
  about 74
  data, listing 74, 75
  style flags 76
  virtual mode 77
  working 76
ListCtrlAutoWidthMixin class 205
ListCtrl mixins
  about 220
  CheckListCtrlMixin 205, 220
  ColumnSorterMixin 205
  ListCtrlAutoWidthMixin 205, 220
  ListRowHighlighter 205, 220
  TextEditMixin 205
  working with 221
ListRowHighlighter class 205
LoadBitmap(name) method 159
LoadDialog(parent, name) method 159
LoadFrame(parent, name) method 159
LoadIcon(name) method 159
LoadMenu(name) method 159

LoadMenuBar(parent, name) method 159
LoadPanel(parent, name) method 159
LoadToolBar(parent, name) method 159
localization
    supporting, in wxPython applications 269-272
LoggerMixin class
    creating 203
    using 204
logging functionality
    adding, to classes 203, 204
Log method 203

M

Machine Object file. *See* .mo file
MacOpenFile method 49
MacReopenApp method 49
MenuBar
    working 65
Menus
    about 63
    adding , to Frame 63, 65
    MenuBar 63
    MenuItems 63
    MenuItems, customizing 66
    submenus 65
    working 65
MessageBox
    about 100
    displaying 100, 101
    style flags 102
MessageBox, style flags
    wx.CANCEL 102
    wx.ICON_ERROR 102
    wx.ICON_INFORMATION 102
    wx.ICON_QUESTION 102
    wx.ICON_WARNING 102
    wx.NO 102
    wx.NO_DEFAULT 102
    wx.OK 102
    wx.YES 102
    wx.YES_DEFAULT 102
    wx.YES_NO 102
message keyword argument 108
metaclass 188

mixin classes
    about 203
    working 205
modal dialog 121
modeless dialog 121
Model View Controller. *See* MVC
MouseEvents
    about 39
    using, in program 39, 40
    working 40, 41
    wx.EVT_LEFT_DCLICK 40
    wx.EVT_MIDDLE_DCLICK 41
    wx.EVT_MIDDLE_DOWN 41
    wx.EVT_MIDDLE_UP 41
    wx.EVT_MOUSE_EVENTS 41
    wx.EVT_MOUSEWHEEL 40
    wx.EVT_RIGHT_DCLICK 41
    wx.EVT_RIGHT_DOWN 40
    wx.EVT_RIGHT_UP 41
MVC
    about 197, 198
    application framework, designing 202
MyFrame class 10
MyPanel class 76
MyTimeEvent class 42

N

NB_BOTTOM style flag 92
NB_FIXEDWIDTH style flag 92
NB_LEFT style flag 92
NB_MULTILINE style flag 92
NB_NOPAGETHEME style flag 92
NB_RIGHT style flag 92
NB_TOP style flag 92
non-blocking GUI
    about 232
    illustrating 232
    working 235, 236
Notebook class
    about 90
    events 92
    styles, adding 92
    tabs, adding 91
    working 91

Notebook class, events
EVT_NOTEBOOK_PAGE_CHANGED 92
EVT_NOTEBOOK_PAGE_CHANGING 92
Notebook class, styles
NB_BOTTOM 92
NB_FIXEDWIDTH 92
NB_LEFT 92
NB_MULTILINE 92
NB_NOPAGETHEME 92
NB_RIGHT 92
NB_TOP 92
NSIS 278
Nth Fibonacci number
calculating 232-234

O

observer pattern
about 190
implementing 190-194
OnBeginDocument(start, end) method 140
OnBeginPrinting() method 140
OnButton handler 217
OnButton method 235
OnChar method 47
OnData(x, y, drag_result) method 24
OnDragOver(x, y, drag_result) method 24
OnDrawItemBackground method 83
OnDrop(x, y) method 24
OnEndDocument() method 140
OnEndPrinting() method 140
OnEnter(x, y, drag_result) method 24
OnGetItemText method 77
OnInit method 9
OnLeave() method 24
OnPaint handler 169, 170
OnPreparePrinting() method 140
OPEN mode, FileDialog 124
optimize option 276
output, capturing
about 249
ProcessThread class, working 252, 253
steps 249-252
OutputWindow class 253

P

PaintDC
functions 173, 174
PaintDC, functions
DrawArc(x1,y1,x2,y2,xcenter,ycenter) 173
DrawBitmap(bmp,x,y,useMask=False) 173
DrawCheckMark(x,y,width,height) 173
DrawCircle(x,y,radius) 173
DrawEllipse(x,y,width,height) 174
DrawEllipticArc(x,y,w,h,start,end) 174
DrawIcon(icon, x, y) 174
DrawImageLabel(lbl,bmp,rect,align) 174
DrawLabel(text,rect,align) 174
DrawLine(x1,y1,x2,y2) 174
DrawPoint(x,y) 174
DrawPolygon(points,x,y) 174
DrawRectangle(x,y,w,h) 174
DrawRotatedText(text,x,y,angle) 174
DrawRoundedRectangle(x,y,w,h,angle) 174
DrawSpline(points) 174
DrawText(text,x,y) 174
Panel class 36
PlateButton 56
pop-up menus
about 69
using, ways 69
working 70
PopulateList method 76
PopupMenuMixin class 70
Portable Object file. *See* **.po file**
PostEvent function
about 42, 236
custom event type, creating 237
Print dialogs
about 135
using 137, 138
ProcessEvent method 42
ProcessNext method 248
ProcessThread class 249
programming 187
ProgressDialog
about 111, 113
style flags 115
working 114, 115

ProgressDialog, style flags
  wx.PD_APP_MODAL 115
  wx.PD_AUTO_HIDE 115
  wx.PD_CAN_ABORT 115
  wx.PD_CAN_SKIP 115
  wx.PD_ELAPSED_TIME 115
  wx.PD_ESTIMATED_TIME 115
  wx.PD_REMAININT_TIME 115
  wx.PD_SMOOTH 115
ProgressStatusBar class
  about 215
  creating 212
pubsub messages 193
pubsub module 190, 193
Py2Exe dependencies 277
py2exe options dictionary 276
PyDropTarget class 24
PyEventBinder class 42
PythonCodeEditor class 88
PyValidator class 47

R

rect argument 185
references control
  about 13
  FindWindowByLabel() 15
  FindWindowByName() 15
  GetTopLevelParent () 15
  steps 13, 14
  working 14
Refresh method 185
RegisterMenuHandle method 45
RegisterUpdateUIHandler method 45
RendererNative class
  about 180
  control flags 183, 184
  custom button class, creating 180-182
  methods 182, 183
RendererNative methods
  DrawCheckBox 183
  DrawChoice 183
  DrawComboBox 183
  DrawComboBoxDropButton 183
  DrawDropArrow 183
  DrawHeaderButton 183
  DrawItemSelectionRect 183

  DrawPushButton 183
  DrawRadioButton 183
  DrawSplitterBorder 183
  DrawSplitterSash 183
  DrawTextCtrl 183
  DrawTreeItemButton 183
resources files
  managing, wx.StandardPaths used 256, 257
RestoreState method 259
reusable Dialog class, creating
  strategy pattern, used 195, 197
Run method 243

S

SAVE mode, FileDialog 124
screen drawing
  about 168
  slideshow widget, creating 168-171
ScrolledPanel
  about 96
  scrolling with 96
  working 96
SearchBar control
  creating 218, 219
SendMessage function 263
SetArtists(list_of_strings) field 118
SetAutoWindowMenu method 269
SetBalloonColour(colour) method 109
SetBitmapDisabled method 56
SetBitmapFocus method 56
SetBitmapHover method 56
SetBitmapLabel method 56
SetBitmapSelected method 56
**SetBottomGradientColour(colour) method
    106**
SetCopyright method 118
SetDescription method 118
SetDevelopers(list_of_strings) field 118
SetDocWriters(list_of_strings) field 118
SetDrawFooterLine(bool) method 106
SetDrawHeaderLine(bool) method 106
SetDropShadow(bool) method 106
SetDropTarget method 24
SetEndDelay(int) method 106
SetIcon(icon) field 118
SetInitialSize method 147

SetItems method 62
SetLicense(license_string) field 118
SetMacAboutMenuItemId method 268
SetMacExitMenuItemId method 268
SetMacPreferencesMenuItemId method 269
SetMacSupportPCMenuShortcuts method
    269
SetMessageColour(colour) method 109
SetMessageFont(font) method 109
SetMiddleGradientColour(colour) method 106
SetName method 118
SetSomeGuiValues method 244
SetTitleColour(colour) method 109
SetTitleFont(font) method 109
SetToolBar method 67
SetToolTipString method 104
SetTopGradientColour(colour) method 106
SetTopWindow method 11
SetTranslators(list_of_strings) field 118
SetupScrolling method 97
SetUseFade(bool) method 106
SetVersion method 118
SetWebSite(url_string) field 118
shape keyword argument 108
shapes
  drawing 171-173
simple number generator application
  creating 198-201
simple smiley face control
  defining 171-173
SingleInstanceChecker class
  about 260
  using 261-264
SingleInstApp class 264
SingletonDialog class 190
singleton objects
  about 188
  ArtProvider 188
  ColourDatabase 188
  SystemSettings 188
singleton pattern
  about 188
  creating 188
  implementing, in Python 189, 190
size attribute 87
Sizer classes 144
Skip() method 34

slideshow widget
  creating 168-171
SlowFib function 236
SplashScreen class
  creating 109
  working 110
StandardPaths singleton
  about 257
  methods 258
StandardPaths singleton, methods
  about 258
  GetConfigDIr() 258
  GetDataDir() 258
  GetDocumentsDir() 258
  GetExecutablePath() 258
  GetPluginsDir() 258
  GetTempDir() 258
  GetUserConigDir() 258
StartProcess method 252
StaticBox
  about 71
  controls, adding 71
  working 71
StatusBar
  about 212
  controls, adding to 212-215
StdDialogButtonSizer
  about 154
  using 156
stock button
  about 52
  creating 52
  stock IDs, viewing 53
  working 52, 53
Stock IDs
  about 18
  using 19
  working 19
StrategyDialog 197
strategy pattern
  about 194
  implementing 195, 197
StyledTextCtrl
  about 84, 88, 222, 225
  lexers, using 225
  working 87, 88

style flags, FindReplaceDialog
wx.FR_NOMATCHCASE 132
wx.FR_NOUPDOWN 132
wx.FR_NOWHOLEWORD 132
wx.FR_REPLACEDIALOG 132

style flags, FlatNotebook class
FNB_ALLOW_FOREIGN_DND 95
FNB_BACKGROUND_GRADIENT 95
FNB_BOTTOM 95
FNB_COLORFUL_TABS 95
FNB_DCLICK_CLOSES_TABS 95
FNB_DEFAULT_STYLE 95
FNB_FANCY_TABS 95
FNB_HIDE_ON_SINGLE_TAB 95
FNB_MOUSE_MIDDLE_CLOSES_TABS 95
FNB_NO_NAV_BUTTONS 95
FNB_NO_X_BUTTON 95
FNB_NODRAG 95
FNB_TABS_BORDER_SIMPLE 95
FNB_VC71 95
FNB_VC8 95

style flags, FileDialog
wx.FD_CHANGE_DIR 126
wx.FD_DEFAULT_STYLE 126
wx.FD_FILE_MUST_EXIST 126
wx.FD_MULTIPLE 126
wx.FD_OPEN 126
wx.FD_OVERWRITE_PROMPT 126
wx.FD_PREVIEW 126
wx.FD_SAVE 126

style flags, Frame
wx.CLIP_CHILDREN 11
wx.DEFAULT_FRAME_STYLE 11
wx.MAXIMIZE_BOX 11
wx.MINIMIZE_BOX 11
wx.RESIZE_BORDER 11
wx.SYSTEM_MENU 11

style flags, ListCtrl
LC_EDIT_LABELS 76
LC_HRULE 76
LC_ICON 76
LC_LIST 76
LC_NO_HEADER 76
LC_REPORT 76
LC_SINGLE_SEL 77
LC_SMALL_ICON 76
LC_SORT_ASCENDING 76
LC_SORT_DESCENDING 76
LC_VIRTUAL 77
LC_VRULE 76

style flags, MessageBox
wx.CANCEL 102
wx.ICON_ERROR 102
wx.ICON_INFORMATION 102
wx.ICON_QUESTION 102
wx.ICON_WARNING 102
wx.NO 102
wx.NO_DEFAULT 102
wx.OK 102
wx.YES 102
wx.YES_DEFAULT 102
wx.YES_NO 102

style flags, ProgressDialog
wx.PD_APP_MODAL 115
wx.PD_AUTO_HIDE 115
wx.PD_CAN_ABORT 115
wx.PD_CAN_SKIP 115
wx.PD_ELAPSED_TIME 115
wx.PD_ESTIMATED_TIME 115
wx.PD_REMAININT_TIME 115
wx.PD_SMOOTH 115

style flags, TextCtrl
wx.TE_CENTER 61
wx.TE_LEFT 61
wx.TE_MULTILINE 61
wx.TE_PROCESS_ENTER 61
wx.TE_PROCESS_TAB 61
wx.TE_READONLY 61
wx.TE_RICH2 61
wx.TE_RIGHT 61

style flags, ToolBars
wx.TB_BOTTOM 68
wx.TB_DOCKABLE 68
wx.TB_FLAT 68
wx.TB_HORIZONTAL 68
wx.TB_NO_TOOLTIPS 68
wx.TB_TEXT 68
wx.TB_VERTICAL 68

styles, Notebook class
NB_BOTTOM 92
NB_FIXEDWIDTH 92
NB_LEFT 92
NB_MULTILINE 92
NB_NOPAGETHEME 92

NB_RIGHT 92
NB_TOP 92
supertooltip.GetStyleKeys() method 106
SuperToolTip class
about 104
methods 106
working 105
SuperToolTip class, methods
SetBottomGradientColour(colour) 106
SetDrawFooterLine(bool) 106
SetDrawHeaderLine(bool) 106
SetDropShadow(bool) 106
SetEndDelay(int) 106
SetMiddleGradientColour(colour) 106
SetTopGradientColour(colour) 106
SetUseFade(bool) 106
synchfunct decorator
working 245
SystemSettings object
about 174
PyPanel custom control, creating 175, 176

T

TaskBarIcon class 90
TaskBarIcon class, events
EVT_TASKBAR_CLICK 90
EVT_TASKBAR_LEFT_DCLICK 90
EVT_TASKBAR_LEFT_DOWN 90
EVT_TASKBAR_LEFT_UP 90
EVT_TASKBAR_MOVE 90
EVT_TASKBAR_RIGHT_DCLICK 90
EVT_TASKBAR_RIGHT_DOWN 90
EVT_TASKBAR_RIGHT_UP 90
text
searching, with FindReplaceDialog 127-131
text-editor application
creating 122
TextCtrl
about 59, 61
style flags 61
using 59, 60
working 60
TextCtrl, style flags
wx.TE_CENTER 61
wx.TE_LEFT 61
wx.TE_MULTILINE 61

wx.TE_PROCESS_ENTER 61
wx.TE_PROCESS_TAB 61
wx.TE_READONLY 61
wx.TE_RICH2 61
wx.TE_RIGHT 61
TextEditMixin class 205, 222
TextEditPanel class 162
TextFrame class 38
ThreadSafeFrame class 238
thread safety
CallAfter function 240
ClassSynchronizer metaclass, using 244
maintaining 236-239
syncfunct decorator, working 243
utility module, creating 241, 242
working 240
ThreadUpdateEvent class 239
Timer
about 246
framework for long running tasks, creating 246, 247
working 248
TimerTaskBase class 248
tipstyle keyword argument 108
ToggleButton 56
ToolBar
AddCheckLabelTool method 68
AddControl method 68
AddRadioLabelTool method 68
AddSeparator method 68
events 68
methods 68
ToolBars, style flags
wx.TB_BOTTOM 68
wx.TB_DOCKABLE 68
wx.TB_FLAT 68
wx.TB_HORIZONTAL 68
wx.TB_NO_TOOLTIPS 68
wx.TB_TEXT 68
wx.TB_VERTICAL 68
ToolBarFrame class 67
ToolBars
about 66
defining 66
style flags 68
working 67

ToolTips
about 102
working 104
ToolWindow class
creating 215, 216
working 217
topicon keyword argument 108
toptitle keyword argument 108
TransferToWindow method 48
tray icons
about 89
working 90
working with 89
TreeCtrl 77
TreeCtrl mixins
DragAndDrop 206
ExpansionState 206
VirtualTree 206
two-stage widget creation
about 24
steps 25
working 25

U

UpdateUIEvent method 38
UpdateUI Events
about 37
using 37, 38
working 38
working, modes 39
underline modifier 87
user interface
state, persisting 258-260

V

Validate method 47
Validator
about 45
creating 45, 46
working 47
VirtualTree class 206
VListBox
about 81
creating 81, 82
IsSelected method 83

OnDrawItemBackground method 83
working 83

W

window hierarchy
about 12
working 12
Windows
icons, adding to 17
windows keyword 274
wx.ALIGN_BOTTOM flag 151
wx.ALIGN_CENTER_HORIZONTAL flag 151
wx.ALIGN_CENTER_VERTICAL flag 151
wx.ALIGN_CENTRE_HORIZONTAL flag 151
wx.ALIGN_CENTRE_VERTICAL flag 151
wx.ALIGN_LEFT flag 151
wx.ALIGN_RIGHT flag 151
wx.ALIGN_TOP flag 151
wx.ALL flag 151
wx.App class 9
wx.App class, keyword arguments
clearSigInt 9
filename 9
redirect 9
useBestVisual 9
wx.App Macintosh specific methods
about 268
SetMacAboutMenuItemId 268
SetMacExitMenuItemId 268
SetMacPreferencesMenuItemId 269
SetMacSupportPCMenuShortcuts 269
wx.BOTTOM flag 151
wx.CANCEL flag 102, 156
wx.Control class 168
wx.EVT_PAINT 168
wx.EXPAND flag 151
wx.FD_CHANGE_DIR flag 126
wx.FD_DEFAULT_STYLE flag 126
wx.FD_FILE_MUST_EXIST flag 126
wx.FD_MULTIPLE flag 126
wx.FD_OPEN flag 126
wx.FD_OVERWRITE_PROMPT flag 126
wx.FD_PREVIEW flag 126
wx.FD_SAVE flag 126
wx.FIXED_MINSIZE flag 151
wx.FR_DOWN flag 132

wx.FR_MATCHCASE flag 132
wx.FR_NOMATCHCASE flag 132
wx.FR_NOUPDOWN flag 132
wx.FR_NOWHOLEWORD flag 132
wx.FR_REPLACEDIALOG flag 132
wx.FR_WHOLEWORD flag 132
wx.GetApp method 14
wx.GetTranslation 269
wx.HELP flag 157
wx.ICON_ERROR flag 102
wx.ICON_INFORMATION flag 102
wx.ICON_QUESTION flag 102
wx.ICON_WARNING flag 102
wx.LEFT flag 151
wx.lib.agw.supertooltip module 104
wx.lib.agw package 105
wx.lib.imagebrowser module 132
wx.lib.mixins.listctrl module 205 222
wx.lib.mixins.treectrl module 206
wx.lib package 190
wx.MenuBar
  about 269
  SetAutoWindowMenu method 269
wx.MessageBox function 101
wx.NO_DEFAULT flag 102, 157
wx.NO flag 102, 157
wx.OK flag 102, 156
wx.Panel class 168
wx.PD_APP_MODAL flag 115
wx.PD_AUTO_HIDE flag 115
wx.PD_CAN_ABORT flag 115
wx.PD_CAN_SKIP flag 115
wx.PD_ELAPSED_TIME flag 115
wx.PD_ESTIMATED_TIME flag 115
wx.PD_REMAININT_TIME flag 115
wx.PD_SMOOTH flag 115
wx.RESERVE_SPACE_EVEN_IF_HIDDEN flag
    151
wx.RIGHT flag 151
wx.SHAPED flag 151
wx.SPLASH_CENTRE_ON_PARENT flag 111
wx.SPLASH_CENTRE_ON_SCREEN flag 111
wx.SPLASH_NO_CENTRE flag 111
wx.SPLASH_NO_TIMEOUT flag 111

wx.SPLASH_TIMEOUT flag 111
wx.StandardPaths
  about 256
  application configuration, managing 256, 257
  resources files, managing 256, 257
wx.TOP flag 151
wx.Window class 168
wx.YES_DEFAULT flag 102
wx.YES_NO flag 102
wx.YES flag 102, 156
wxPython
  about 7, 25, 121
  buttons 53
  events 29
  gettext formatted files, using 272
  utilities 51
  window hierarchy 12
wxPython2.8
  GraphicsContext object 177, 179
wxPython applications
  distributing 273-277
  localization, supporting 269-272
  optimizing, for OS X 266, 268
  basic patterns, building from 8

X

XmlResource object
  about 159
  methods 159
  using 159
XmlResource object, methods
  LoadBitmap(name) 159
  LoadDialog(parent, name) 159
  LoadFrame(parent, name) 159
  LoadIcon(name) 159
  LoadMenu(name) 159
  LoadMenuBar(parent, name) 159
  LoadPanel(parent, name) 159
  LoadToolBar(parent, name) 159
XML resources
  using 157, 159
XRC 157
XrcTestFrame class 163

Thank you for buying
wxPython 2.8 Application Development Cookbook

About Packt Publishing

Packt, pronounced 'packed', published its first book "*Mastering phpMyAdmin for Effective MySQL Management*" in April 2004 and subsequently continued to specialize in publishing highly focused books on specific technologies and solutions.

Our books and publications share the experiences of your fellow IT professionals in adapting and customizing today's systems, applications, and frameworks. Our solution based books give you the knowledge and power to customize the software and technologies you're using to get the job done. Packt books are more specific and less general than the IT books you have seen in the past. Our unique business model allows us to bring you more focused information, giving you more of what you need to know, and less of what you don't.

Packt is a modern, yet unique publishing company, which focuses on producing quality, cutting-edge books for communities of developers, administrators, and newbies alike. For more information, please visit our website: www.packtpub.com.

About Packt Open Source

In 2010, Packt launched two new brands, Packt Open Source and Packt Enterprise, in order to continue its focus on specialization. This book is part of the Packt Open Source brand, home to books published on software built around Open Source licences, and offering information to anybody from advanced developers to budding web designers. The Open Source brand also runs Packt's Open Source Royalty Scheme, by which Packt gives a royalty to each Open Source project about whose software a book is sold.

Writing for Packt

We welcome all inquiries from people who are interested in authoring. Book proposals should be sent to author@packtpub.com. If your book idea is still at an early stage and you would like to discuss it first before writing a formal book proposal, contact us; one of our commissioning editors will get in touch with you.

We're not just looking for published authors; if you have strong technical skills but no writing experience, our experienced editors can help you develop a writing career, or simply get some additional reward for your expertise.

CherryPy Essentials: Rapid Python Web Application Development

ISBN: 978-1-904811-84-8   Paperback: 272 pages

Design, develop, test, and deploy your Python web applications easily

1. Walks through building a complete Python web application using CherryPy 3

2. The CherryPy HTTP:Python interface

3. Use CherryPy with other Python libraries

4. Design, security, testing, and deployment

Python 2.6 Graphics Cookbook

ISBN: 978-1-849513-84-5   Paperback: 330 pages

Over 100 great recipes for creating and animating graphics using Python

1. Create captivating graphics with ease and bring them to life using Python

2. Apply effects to your graphics using powerful Python methods

3. Develop vector as well as raster graphics and combine them to create wonders in the animation world

4. Create interactive GUIs to make your creation of graphics simpler

5. Part of Packt's Cookbook series: Each recipe is a carefully organized sequence of instructions to accomplish the task of creation and animation of graphics as efficiently as possible

Please check **www.PacktPub.com** for information on our titles

2235524R00164

Printed in Great Britain
by Amazon.co.uk, Ltd.,
Marston Gate.